The Literary Relationship of
Lord Byron & Thomas Moore

THE LITERARY RELATIONSHIP OF

Lord Byron &
Thomas Moore

JEFFERY W. VAIL

THE JOHNS HOPKINS UNIVERSITY PRESS
BALTIMORE AND LONDON

The Johns Hopkins University Press
2715 North Charles Street
Baltimore, Maryland 21218-4363
www.press.jhu.edu

Library of Congress Cataloging-in-Publication Data
Vail, Jeffery W.
The literary relationship of Lord Byron and Thomas Moore /
Jeffery W. Vail.
p.   cm.
Includes bibliographical references (p.   ) and index.
ISBN 0-8018-6500-X (alk. paper)
1. Byron, George Gordon Byron, Baron, 1788–1824—Criti-
cism and interpretation. 2. Byron, George Gordon Byron,
Baron, 1788–1824—Friends and associates. 3. Byron, George
Gordon Byron, Baron, 1788–1824—Influence. 4. Moore,
Thomas, 1779–1852—Criticism and interpretation. 5. Eng-
lish poetry—19th century—History and criticism. 6. Moore,
Thomas, 1779–1852—Friends and associates. 7. Moore,
Thomas, 1779–1852—Influence. 8. Authorship—
Collaboration. I. Title.
PR4388.V35 2001
821'.709—dc21   00–028201

A catalog record for this book is available
from the British Library.

For my parents, William and Carole Vail

AND FOR

Claire

The fountain-light of all my day,
The master-light of all my seeing.

CONTENTS

A C K N O W L E D G M E N T S

Many friends and colleagues helped and supported me during my work on Byron and Moore over the last few years. First and foremost I offer my gratitude to Charles E. Robinson for his unfailing generosity and invaluable assistance. He has been an inspiration and a friend, and I could never thank him enough. I also enjoyed the honor and privilege of working with Donald H. Reiman, whose unmatched knowledge of the English Romantics as well as his many kind attentions were indispensable to me. Carl Dawson's and Philip Flynn's supportive words and criticisms of my dissertation were among the most gratifying results of my labors. I wish also to thank John Clubbe, whose generous spirit has cheered me on my way since the beginning.

I must also thank the Pierpont Morgan Library, the John J. Burns Library at Boston College, the Boston Public Library, the Carl H. Pforzheimer Collection at the New York Public Library, the Mariam Canaday Library at Bryn Mawr College, and the Bodleian Library at Oxford University for kind permission to use portions of previously unpublished letters of Thomas Moore. In particular I wish to thank Doucet Devin Fischer and Stephen Wagner of the Pforzheimer Collection, and Steven Tomlinson of the Bodleian Library.

My sincere thanks also to Geoffrey Bond and Haidee Jackson of the British Byron Society, who took me on a tour of Newstead Abbey and favored me with many kindnesses; and the Right Honorable Michael Foot, Peter Cochran, Steven Jones, Thorlac Turville-Petre, and Joy Linsley, for showing a kind interest in my work.

A portion of chapter 5 was published in the *Byron Journal* and is used here with permission.

Finally, I thank my parents, Carole and William Vail, for supporting my academic pursuits and for always believing in me.

BCP   *Lord Byron: The Complete Poetical Works.* Ed. Jerome J.
McGann. 7 vols. Oxford: Clarendon Press, 1980–93.

BLJ   *Byron's Letters and Journals.* Ed. Leslie A. Marchand. 12 vols.
Cambridge: Harvard UP, 1973–82.

MCP   *The Poetical Works of Thomas Moore. Collected by Himself.* 10 vols.
London: Longmans, 1840–41.

MJ   *The Journal of Thomas Moore.* Ed. Wilfred S. Dowden. 6 vols.
Newark: U of Delaware P, 1983–91.

ML   *The Letters of Thomas Moore.* Ed. Wilfred S. Dowden. 2 vols.
Oxford: Oxford UP, 1964.

MLB   *Letters and Journals of Lord Byron, with Notices of His Life.* Ed.
Thomas Moore. 2 vols. London: John Murray, 1830–31.

Introduction

In 1821 Lord Byron began a satire called *The Blues, a Literary Eclogue* in which the two primary characters are thinly disguised versions of himself and Thomas Moore. In this poem Byron attempted to re-create imaginatively the lost world of his youthful fame in Regency London in the years 1811–15. It is a world in which Byron (as Tracy) and Moore (as Inkel),[1] popular as they are as writers, stand uncomfortably on the periphery of a culture of humbugging authors and bluestockings. The poem begins with Byron and Moore symbolically situated outside the closed door of a lecture hall in which much of the literary and fashionable world has gathered to hear Scamp's (Coleridge's) "vile nonsense" (l. 45).[2] Inkel calls Scamp a fool, and Tracy responds: "And the crowd of to-day shows that one fool makes many. / But we two will be wise" (ll. 57–58). The two poets withdraw, not wishing to join the fatuous rituals of the London literati any more than they have to.

Tracy's statement "but we two will be wise" is one of the most succinct and revealing of Byron's many comments upon his personal and literary relationship with Thomas Moore. To Byron, Moore was the one man he could always run to, literally or imaginatively, when the cant of the world became intolerable. Moore was, like Byron, a literary lion of the Regency, but also like Byron he always felt somewhat out of place in the houses of the London great; Moore, after all, was an Irish Catholic and the son of a Dublin grocer, and Byron was (secretly) a bisexual and came from an impoverished family without a lord's typical complement of connections and relatives. As Byron explained to Murray: "Now Moore and I—the one by circumstances & the other by birth—happened to be free of the corporation—& to have entered into its pulses and passions 'quarum partes fuimus.' Both of us have learnt by this much which nothing else could have taught us" (*BLJ* 8:207). Both men liked nothing better than to flee a party and dine quietly together in a club, where they could relax and laugh freely at the "Bores and Blues" of the London season. As early as 1812 and as late as 1821 they discussed starting their own newspaper together, in which, as Moore put it, they would "write Epistles to each other—in all measures and all styles upon all possible subjects— laugh at the world—weep for ourselves—quiz the humbugs—scarify the scoundrels—in short do every thing that the mixture of fun & philosophy there is in both of us can inspire" (*ML* 1:176). Moore's phrasing—laughing at the world and weeping for ourselves—suggests both the ironic distance and the tragic isolation that both Byron and Moore felt characterized their dealings with the society in which they moved. Like Tracy, Moore suggests that "we two will be wise": Byron and Moore have declared an alliance with each other and independence from a society marked by insincerity and cant.

The close friendship between Byron and Moore was founded in some measure upon this worldly, cynical perspective that they shared, both having had the experience of feeling themselves at the center and at the periphery of fashionable life at the same time. They also had very similar temperaments. Both men were skeptics and wits, "men of the world" as Byron put it, whose democratic sentiments were tempered by aristocratic prejudices. Both admired Napoleon and despised the Prince Regent. They were well-traveled and experienced writers who viewed politics as a more serious and important profession than "scribbling." When the two friends were subjected to repeated newspaper attacks in 1814, Byron told Moore, "I believe that most of our hates and likings have been hitherto nearly the same; but from henceforth, they must, of necessity, be one and indivisible" (*BLJ* 4:62).

The depth of Byron's affection for Moore is best revealed in his letters, which abound with flattering references to the Irish poet. Moreover, Byron abandoned pretense in his letters to Moore; as he explained to Lady Melbourne in 1813, "I have to write—first—a soothing letter to C[aroline Lamb] a sentimental one to X Y Z.—a sincere one to T. Moore—" (*BLJ* 3:98). Trusting "no one more" than Moore (*BLJ* 9:123), Byron chose him to edit his memoirs and to be his defender in the event of his death. In a letter to Mary

Shelley, Byron wrote that the only two people in the world for whom he felt anything like friendship were Lord Clare and Moore (*BLJ* 10:34), and Lady Blessington recorded that Byron numbered only John Cam Hobhouse, Clare, and Moore among his friends.[3] Byron evidently told Moore about his relationship with Augusta Leigh,[4] and may even have entrusted him with the secret of his bisexuality.[5]

Samuel Rogers first introduced Byron to Moore on 4 November 1811, at a dinner at Rogers's home that was held for the express purpose of making peace between the two poets. Their quarrel had originated in 1810, when Moore learned that Byron had avowed his authorship of the 1809 *English Bards and Scotch Reviewers* on the title page of the poem's second edition. In that poem, Byron had attacked Moore, assailing his poems for their supposed immorality and ridiculing him personally. Moore was nine years older than Byron, and when they met Byron was a virtual unknown whereas Moore had been a famous poet for a decade. Despite this difference, Byron and Moore took to each other from the moment they met. Moore wrote in his biography of Byron: "From the time of our first meeting, there seldom elapsed a day that Lord Byron and I did not see each other; and our acquaintance ripened into intimacy and friendship with a rapidity of which I have seldom known an example" (*MLB* 1:322). Byron's letters to others in these weeks glow with enthusiasm for his new friend: he calls Moore "the Epitome of all that is exquisite in poetical or personal accomplishments" and proudly writes: "Moore and I are on the best of terms. . . . Moore [is] an Epitome of all that's delightful" (*BLJ* 2:129); he also calls Moore's company "delectable" and considers Rogers and Moore to be the "men most alive to true taste" in England (*BLJ* 2:146). For about five months, between 4 November 1811 and early May 1812, Byron and Moore were constant companions in the nightly round of balls, parties, and theatergoing that occupied the fashionable world of London. During these months they dined together as often as they could (Moore's dinner engagements were often booked up weeks in advance) at St. Alban's Tavern or Stevens's; years later Byron said: "My tete-a-tete suppers with Moore are among the most agreeable impressions I retain of the hours I passed in London: they are the redeeming lights in the gloomy picture."[6] Byron met Moore's wife, and in March 1812 Moore helped avert a duel between Byron and Colonel Harry Greville, whom Byron had disparaged in *Childe Harold's*

Pilgrimage. Moore was present when Byron met Caroline Lamb and later helped convince Byron to end the affair. Moore was also with Byron the first time he met the future Lady Byron.[7]

Moore's personal charm was almost legendary, but Byron and he developed a special bond. Byron delighted in Moore's wicked sense of humor, his love of pleasure, his philosophical skepticism, and his lack of literary pretension—this last being a quality Byron often remarked upon as separating Moore from the other authors he met. Unlike the more earnest Shelley or Hunt, Moore refused to take himself or Byron too seriously, and, after being deified by everyone else around him, Byron was delighted when Moore would tease him about his melancholy pose. Their "harmony of mind" (as Hoover H. Jordan expresses it) was such that in January or February 1812, just *before* Byron's great success with *Childe Harold,* Moore suggested publishing their poetry jointly, an idea Byron would eagerly pursue as late as 1821.

The two poets shared the adulation of London society during 1812, Byron for *Childe Harold* (published on 10 March) and Moore both for his popular "Parody of a Celebrated Letter" (which appeared in March) and for his new *Irish Melodies.* Moore's impassioned performances of these songs were the highlights of every party he attended. Both poets were besieged by invitations and admirers and were the darlings of London generally and the Whig luminaries in particular. Moore returned to his home in the country by April, and he and Byron began a lively and affectionate correspondence which would last the rest of their lives. In 1813 Moore wrote: "The only very faithful and voluminous correspondent I have is Lord Byron, which is exceedingly delightful to me, as he is just as gay a companion and correspondent as he is a sombre and horrific poet" (*ML* 1:282). Byron told Thomas Medwin, "I correspond with no one so regularly as with Moore,"[8] and he told James Hamilton Browne that Moore was "the most humorous and witty of all his correspondents."[9]

The next time Byron and Moore encountered each other in person was a year later, in early May 1813. Once again they plunged together into the London season for about four months, until they parted in August or September 1813. By then, Byron was celebrated for *The Giaour* and Moore for his songs and his enormously successful *Intercepted Letters; or, The Twopenny Post-Bag,* a collection of political satires on the Regent and others. Byron loved the *Post-Bag* and offered to review it for Murray's *Quarterly Review,* but Murray declined. Moore and Byron spent time with Rogers and the dramatist Richard Brinsley Sheridan, and in May and June the two poets visited Leigh Hunt in jail to express their solidarity with his opposition to the government. Hunt recalled: "It was very pleasant to see Lord Byron and Moore together. They harmonized admirably."[10]

On 1 February 1814 Byron's *The Corsair* was published, containing a glowing and politically charged dedication to Moore. In the following weeks both Byron and Moore were violently and repeatedly abused by several newspapers because of Byron's poem "Lines to a Lady Weeping," which was included in the volume. Moore and Byron reunited in London for about a month in May 1814, during the national celebration Byron called the "Summer of the Sovereigns." They were together almost daily, going to the theater many times, especially to see repeated performances of Edmund Kean in *Othello*. They ate at Watier's and other clubs in the evenings and usually stayed up all night talking, not parting until it was "broad daylight" (*MLB* 1:558). On 14 August 1814 Byron became the godfather of Moore's newborn daughter, Olivia Byron Moore.

The two poets were next together in London for three or four weeks in December of the same year. They saw each other frequently, and dined together several times at Douglas Kinnaird's house, where, Moore writes, "music,—followed by its accustomed sequel of supper, brandy and water, and not a little laughter,—kept us together, usually, till rather a late hour" (*MLB* 1:597). On 7 December Byron wrote Annabella Milbanke: "Moore is in town—I was so glad to see him again—that I am afraid I was rather too 'exquisite in my drinking' at dinner yesterday" (*BLJ* 4:240). The two friends set aside 15 December for a visit to Hunt in prison, but Byron apparently canceled the engagement.[11] In one of his letters to Byron during these weeks, Moore wrote: "I feel Bessy [Moore's wife] was right in her jealousy of you—if I were to see so much of you as lately, you would be a dangerous rival to her—." As a joke, Byron and Moore even began wearing identical coats (*ML* 1:343).

Although they could not suspect it at the time, that December would be the second to last time the two friends would ever see each other. Moore was absent from London during all of 1815, and Byron had his hands full with his marriage, bailiffs, and his work for Drury Lane. On 25 April 1816 Byron left England forever, around this time starting his farewell poem to Moore beginning "My boat is on the shore." Moore attempted to defend Byron during the aftermath of his separation from his wife by writing a mocking review of Lady Caroline Lamb's *Glenarvon* for the *Edinburgh Review,* which Jeffrey unfortunately decided not to publish.[12] It was not until 7 October 1819 that Moore was able to visit Byron in Venice. Moore was at that time in temporary exile himself due to the criminal acts of a deputy he had appointed to replace him years earlier as admiralty registrar in Bermuda. After they met again in Venice in 1819, Moore stayed at Byron's Palazzo Mocenigo for five days; he asked his friend to join him on his trip, but Byron was unable to leave, and so Moore continued on to Rome. Byron told Lady Blessington that Moore's visit had an "intoxicating" effect on him, and, according to Emma Fagnani, "[Teresa Guiccioli] said she so longed to understand English when she was witness to the boyish, wordy frolics Byron and Moore enjoyed together."[13] Moore updated Byron on the stories being told about him in England, and Byron, wanting to help his friend out of his financial difficulties, gave Moore his memoirs in order that he might sell their publication rights to John Murray. Byron told Medwin, "I know no man I would go further to serve than Moore."[14] Murray advanced Moore two thousand guineas for the rights to the memoirs with the stipulation that Moore would edit them. Since 1813 Byron had been determined that Moore should write his life and/or posthumously edit his works in the event of his early death (*BLJ* 3:75). After Byron died in 1824, Moore undertook years of painstaking research and overcame many obstacles in order to produce a massive two-volume biography of Byron after being forced by Murray, Hobhouse, and others to acquiesce to the destruction of Byron's memoirs. Moore's *Letters and Journals of Lord Byron, with Notices of His Life* appeared in 1830 and 1831 and remained the standard well into the twentieth century.

II

To their contemporaries, it was only natural to view the artistic achievements of Byron and Moore in relation to each other. In the first place, it was well known that the two poets were the closest of friends and it was universally recognized that their poetry often shared common themes, attitudes, and styles. Furthermore, to a large extent they were performing for the same audience, a fact that the *Edinburgh Review* noted in 1823, when it observed that the two poets "[divided] the Poetical Public between them" and that they were read by "the same extended circle of taste and fashion."[15] Byron and Moore were very successful at discerning and satisfying the tastes of this upper-class readership, a readership entirely different from that of Wordsworth, Hunt, or Keats—or even Shelley. The two poets were both acutely aware of their shared audience and frequently consulted each other upon what their readers currently wanted, whether it was the right time to publish a particular work, or what the future of the literary marketplace would look like. This sensitivity and responsiveness to their readers' desires often led Byron and Moore to produce poems in a similar genre or style within a year or two or even within mere months of each other's productions. Their very presence together on the same stage, their conversations about their audience, and their willingness to write for the taste of the times help account for some of the similarities between their literary outputs, especially in the period between 1812 and 1817.

Byron and Moore were always considered highly individual poets in their own rights, and in some respects of course were starkly different as artists. However, their works feature similarities both particular and general that were much more apparent to the poets' contemporaries than they are to modern scholarship, which has almost completely lost sight of Moore's writings and their significance. Both poets wrote satires, oriental poems, and "national" melodies, sometimes writing upon the same subjects at the same time. Both used their poetry to comment directly upon the public events of their age. Both were persistent and outspoken champions of classical Whig liberalism and foes of governmental oppression, and their satires assailed the same public figures and the same aspects of English society. Both employed the exotic as well as the erotic, both were often religiously and philosophically skeptical in their poetry, and both were routinely accused of indecency and impiety.

This network of similarities between the ways Byron and Moore employed genre, sexuality, religion, politics, and social criticism led many critics and readers to see the two poets as the leading lights of their own "school" of poetry, a school often thought to threaten the morals of young people and of Britain as a whole. The *Weekly Entertainer* in 1816 endorsed this view, portraying them as "Caled" and "Waled," two Persian poets notable for the warmth of their verses.[16] In 1817 the *British Review* condemned Byron and Moore as the two principal practitioners of the "new Oriental school" that was ruining the morality of English youth.[17] A two-part article appearing on 1 November 1819 and 1 January 1820 in the *New Monthly Magazine* savagely attacked the "poetical creed" of Byron and Moore on moral and religious grounds.[18] When Robert Southey excoriated what he called the Satanic School of poetry in the dedication to his *A Vision of Judgment,* the two Satanic poets he had in mind were not Byron and Shelley, as is commonly thought, but Byron and Moore.[19] Though he mentioned neither by name, it is clear that he expected his readers to know to whom he was referring. Byron wrote: "in [Southey's] preface to his 'Vision'—he actually called upon the legislature to fall upon Moore[,] me—& others" (*BLJ* 9:62). In an 1824 article in the *London Magazine* entitled "The Characteristic of the Present Age of Poetry," George Darley identified Byron and Moore as leading representatives of the "modern school" of "Sensuality."[20] A letter from Lady Louisa Stuart to a friend in 1831 sums up the way in which Moore and Byron were often regarded: "They have been fatal people," founding a "very bad school" and encouraging others to write verse as "disgusting" and "unnatural" as their own.[21]

Critics and writers who did not charge Byron and Moore with the creation of a school still tended to see their poetry, their personalities, and their careers as closely related. In the 1815 edition of Leigh Hunt's *Feast of the Poets* Byron and Moore approach Apollo together and then withdraw chatting with each other (149–51). In 1820 *Blackwood's* featured a fanciful, panoramic view of modern poetry called "Shufflebotham's Dream," in which Wordsworth, Southey, and many other contemporary poets earnestly perform songs on peculiar instruments while "L——d B——n and little M——re [laugh], behind, as if they would split."[22] In Shelley's *Adonais* Byron and Moore are the "mountain shepherds" who come together, "midst others of less note," to pay tribute to Keats. To Shelley, Byron is "the Pilgrim of Eternity," and Ireland has sent Moore from her wilds, "the sweetest lyrist of her saddest wrong" (399). Shelley thus associates Byron with *Childe Harold* and Moore with his political *Irish Melodies,* associations that stress each poet's most "serious" and melancholy productions and that position them as fitting representatives of poetry in an "age of despair." Late in his life, the author Henry Taylor recalled: "When I was young Byron and Moore had filled the souls of old and young with their forms of passion. . . . [They had] the most thrilling power, over the largest audience, for the time being, that any poets of this country had ever exercised."[23] Taylor also wrote that Moore's "genius, though of course with much diversity, was yet too much akin to Byron's" for either poet to avoid comparison with the other.[24] In 1851 D. M. Moir wrote that Moore "in the externals of poetry. . . seemed to bear a stronger affinity [to Byron] than to any other author."[25] The American *Byron and Moore Gallery,* a collection of lavish illustrations of the poets' works published in 1871, presented another conventional view of their similarities: "Of all the poets of modern times, Byron and Moore have proved themselves the most eminently qualified to illustrate the charms of female grace and beauty: their poems, melodies and songs, teem with all that is most rare, impassioned and refined; forming a beau-ideal, wherein, 'the angel yet the woman too,' fills up the measure of the soul's content."[26]

Twentieth-century scholars have made a few tentative attempts to rediscover the interconnectedness of the poetry of Byron and Moore, but most of these studies are biographical accounts of the poets' friendship and only glance at their mutual artistic influence.[27] Many scholars have recognized the fact of the influence without analyzing it in detail; for instance, Carl Woodring in his *Politics in English Romantic Poetry* notes that Moore "exerted influences of subject and literary device on every stage of Byron's career as a poet."[28] Hoover Jordan's article "Byron and Moore" comes the closest to being a true influence study, sketching many similarities between their works and attributing them to the poets' "interchange of ideas" and "harmony of mind."[29] Jordan's study is too brief, however, to achieve anything more than this general conclusion. In his classic study of Byron, *Fiery Dust,* Jerome J. McGann closely examines Moore's 1801 *Poetical Works of the Late Thomas Little, Esq.* as the primary inspiration for Byron's *Hours of Idleness.*[30] Aside from Jordan and McGann, modern scholars have neglected to treat this subject in any detail, most likely because of the notorious difficulty of accurately distinguishing the influence of a particular artistic voice or vision from the general climate of themes and styles present in a given moment in literary history. However, although no such study can approach conclusiveness, evidence of the instances and nature of Byron's and Moore's intertextual relationship abound, and careful analysis of this evidence has the potential to add significantly to our understanding not only of Byron and Moore but of the literary and public discourses of the society for which they wrote.

III

The kind of influence that Byron and Moore exerted upon each other as artists was almost the opposite of that which characterized the relationship between Byron and Shelley. Byron and Shelley exerted a primarily negative influence upon each other's works, each stimulating the other to refute his notions of epistemology and the nature and destiny of mankind.[31] Between Byron and Moore the influence was positive, and far less rooted in matters of philosophy. Moore wrote that Shelley's "strange, mystic speculations" would turn Byron's mind "away from worldly associations and topics into more abstract and untrodden ways of thought" (*MLB* 2:24). In contrast Moore's conversations with Byron, in person and in their letters to each other, turned almost wholly upon "worldly associations and topics," such as the public figures and events of the day. This down-to-earth, practical mind-set informed Moore's ideas about poetry. Like Byron, Moore had little sympathy with Shelleyan abstraction or Wordsworthian "metaquizzical" poetry, and together they saw their poetical roles as those of close observers and commentators upon the particular mores, sins, and follies of the society around them. Moore would have agreed with the spirit, if not the tone, of Byron's angry comments to James Hogg about the "despicable impostors" of modern poetry such as Robert Southey: "They know nothing of the world; and what is poetry, but the reflection of the world? What sympathy have this people with the spirit of this stirring age?" (*BLJ* 4:85).

Byron's desire to connect his poetry to "the world" was fostered and intensified by his friendship with Moore during his years of English fame. Although Moore was a prolific author, his primary interests were politics and the fate of Ireland. Moore's first consideration when writing was how best to use his skills to benefit the political causes he believed in. His writings were therefore intimately bound up in "the world" and in his "stirring age." As Byron's "father confessor" and guide through London high life, Moore had a great influence on the course of Byron's early politics and poetry up until 1815. Neither man was content to be a Shelleyan "unacknowledged legislator of the world"; both yearned to have a more immediate and practical effect upon the politics of England, and they lamented that they could not achieve a position of direct political power. To make up for this relative powerlessness,

Byron and Moore encouraged each other to use their writings as a medium of public address, to oppose the conservative policies of the British government, and to support liberal causes like Catholic emancipation, parliamentary reform, and the rights of the oppressed in Ireland and abroad.

It is partly in the political dimension of their writing that Byron and Moore had the greatest impact upon each other's work. Each saw the other as his primary political ally in the realm of literature, and each was delighted most by the other's overtly political poems and statements. During the early months of 1812, for instance, Byron followed Moore's example of using the *Morning Chronicle* as a medium for his anonymous poems attacking the government, and Moore's "Parody of a Celebrated Letter" stimulated Byron to try his hand at a similar style of satire. Although Moore denied that he was exclusively attached to any one party, at that time he was actually the chief literary spokesman for the Whigs and the liberal causes with which they were associated, and he and Lord Holland, the Whig leader, saw a potentially powerful ally in Byron. Moore encouraged Byron directly and by example to write against the government and vigorously to pursue his parliamentary career. It was probably Moore's success with his barrage of lighthearted political attacks in 1812–13 that persuaded Byron to abandon his attempts at formal neoclassical satire and to try his hand at lighter sociopolitical satires such as "Waltz" and "The Devil's Drive." Both poets were eager to proclaim their political and poetical alliance: they made plans for their projected joint newspaper; Moore solicited poems from Byron to include in his *Intercepted Letters; or, The Twopenny Post-Bag;* and Byron announced his solidarity with Moore in no uncertain terms in his dedication to *The Corsair.* Later in Byron's career Moore's direct influence upon the politics of his poetry lessened but remained significant, as in the case of "The Irish Avatar," which was directly inspired by Moore's "Lines on the Entry of the Austrians into Naples, 1821." Moore kept the idea of a political alliance with Byron alive even when Byron's popularity had waned, dedicating his satire *Fables for the Holy Alliance* to Byron in 1823.

Separate from but often related to this strain of political influence was the formal influence of each writer's work upon the other's, such as that of Moore's *Irish Melodies* upon Byron's *Hebrew Melodies,* or that of Byron's Turkish tales upon Moore's *Lalla Rookh.* This "amicable sort of mutual plagiarism between them," as the *Monthly Review* called it in 1818, originated partly in their love for each other's works and partly in their sensitivity to the desires of the poetry-buying public.[32] They never lost sight of the "extended circle of taste and fashion" that constituted the majority of their audience. The reviewer for the *Monthly* compared Byron and Moore to two country squires pursuing game onto each other's property "by the laws of fair and gentlemanly sporting," a simile that emphasizes not only the friendliness of the poets' interaction but additionally the special air of gentility that their works possessed partly by virtue of the class of their readers. These readers wanted elegant songs to sing and splendid quartos of exotic, materialistic orientalism, and Byron and Moore gave them what they wanted. This is not to say that they viewed their melodies and oriental poetry cynically, however; they created some of their most emotionally powerful and politically trenchant verse in the process of satisfying this taste for exoticism and spectacle.

The last and perhaps most important locus of influence in the relationship between Byron and Moore can be found in Byron's body of lyric poetry, and the underlying attitude of ironic detachment informing it. The *Monthly Review* perceptively wrote that "in the comparatively few lyric productions of Lord Byron he is often the *alter idem* of Mr. Moore," and with good reason.[33] Byron's enthusiasm for writing lyric poems was inspired at an early age by Moore's second volume of poetry, the 1801 *Poetical Works of the Late Thomas Little, Esq.*, a playful book of love lyrics that were alternately sentimental and cynical as well as nakedly "insincere" by conventional "Romantic" standards. Moore was always skeptical of the extravagant claims made for the sincerity of Romantic poetry by Wordsworth and others, and by writing such "insincere" poetry in the persona of the fictitious Thomas Little, a sensitive, spontaneous youth who tragically died at the age of twenty-one, Moore was able to exploit and explode this and other conventions of the Romantic lyric. Byron memorized *Little's Poems*, as the book was commonly called, and their stylistic influence on Byron's early lyrics is obvious, but Moore's uniquely skeptical treatment of Romantic self-expression had an even more lasting effect on Byron's lyric poetry in that it impelled Byron toward the development of what McGann calls Byron's "lyrical dandyism": his radical rejection of the criterion of Wordsworthian sincerity and his understanding of the lyric poem as a mask or a pose.[34] When Byron writes in *Don Juan* "And feeling, in a poet, is the source / Of other's feeling; but they are such liars, / And take all colours / like the hands of dyers" (III, ll. 790–92), he is in agreement with Moore's ideas about the essential falseness and feebleness of poetry as a form of truthful utterance. The self-conscious and deliberately artificial qualities of many of Moore's lyric poems exercised a lasting influence upon Byron's own innovative subversions of the conventional Romantic lyric.

The irony of the literary relationship between Byron and Moore is that to some degree the two poets switched places in the years 1817–18. In 1817 Moore's long-awaited magnum opus *Lalla Rookh* appeared, and, although the public reaction was overwhelmingly favorable, nearly all the critics considered the work an imitation of Byron, which to a great degree it was. In 1818 Byron's *Beppo* appeared, a work in which Byron finally perfected his own version of the lighthearted style of satire Moore had mastered as early as 1812. Francis Jeffrey wrote of the style of *Beppo:* "The nearest approach to it is to be found . . . in several passages of Mr. Moore, and the author of the facetious miscellany, entitled, the Twopenny Post Bag [also Moore]."[35] *Lalla Rookh* and *Beppo* mark critical turning points in Moore's and Byron's poetic careers. Moore had found a form and style that allowed him to indulge his imagination more fully than any of his works had before, while Byron had managed to achieve a type of carefree, irreverent, and flexible satire that had always previously eluded him. The story of the literary relationship between Byron and Moore up to that point is the story of how each writer stimulated the other to discover and explore aspects of his talent that might otherwise have remained undiscovered.

"In short a '*young Moore*'"

Early Lyrics

Sometime in early 1809, Ireland's most famous poet, Thomas Moore, learned of the publication of an anonymous satire that impugned both his poetry and his personal honor. The unknown author of *English Bards and Scotch Reviewers* (published in March 1809) had called Moore a "melodious advocate of lust" and accused his poetry of being "immoral" (l. 290). Moore was used to such charges; what angered him much more about the new satire was that it cast aspersions upon Moore's conduct during his participation in a duel with Francis Jeffrey three years earlier. This duel had been interrupted by police, who reportedly discovered that the combatants' pistols were not loaded, a fact generally interpreted as proof that Moore and Jeffrey were both cowards and their combat a sham. The widely circulated stories about this farcical duel had so humiliated Moore in 1806 that he had been forced to write a letter to the newspapers denying the allegation, and since then he had hoped that the public would have forgotten the whole episode. The popular new satire ensured that the public would not.

Moore soon learned that *English Bards* was the work of a young neophyte named Lord Byron. However, since it was published anonymously, Moore did not choose to answer formally or acknowledge the insult. Anonymous attacks were generally considered too cowardly and scurrilous for a gentleman to notice, and Moore tried to live according to the gentleman's code. The situation changed when the second edition of the satire appeared later in 1809 bearing Byron's name on the title page. On New Year's Day 1810 Moore sent a direct challenge to Byron, accusing him of "giving the lie" to the statement of denial Moore had sent to the newspapers in 1806. Moore now made preparations for a duel with Byron, not realizing that Byron would not receive the letter because he was out of the country. Byron would not even hear of the existence of Moore's letter until 6 June 1810, when he was in Constantinople.

By the time Byron finally returned to England, nearly two years had passed, and Moore's letter still lay unopened in the possession of Byron's friend Francis Hodgson. During that period Moore had married and his anger had cooled considerably. He and Byron then exchanged several awkward letters, in the course of which Byron, without actually apologizing, did explain that he had not known about Moore's statement about the duel and had not meant to contradict it. This satisfied Moore, and the two poets agreed to call a truce and meet on friendly terms for dinner at the house of Moore's friend, the poet Samuel Rogers, on 4 November 1811. Rogers also invited Thomas Campbell. Byron, a newcomer to the literary world, was understandably excited and honored to be so suddenly admitted into the fellowship of three of the most celebrated poets of his time. In fact, all three, including Moore, were poets whom Byron greatly admired and whom he would, throughout his career, consistently rank higher in ability than such poets as Wordsworth, Keats, or Coleridge. During Rogers's dinner Byron and Moore charmed and amused each other and found they shared many interests and beliefs. Their meeting instantly transformed the two potential combatants into close friends.

I

By the time Byron satirized Moore in *English Bards,* he had in fact been a lover of Moore's poetry for many years. Byron's first known exposure to his writing occurred in 1803, eight years before Samuel Rogers brought the two men together for the first time. In that year, the fifteen-year-old Byron eagerly pored over Moore's *The Poetical Works of the Late Thomas Little, Esq.,* which had been published in the summer of 1801. These lyrical poems are characterized by a playfully mischievous attitude toward love, sex, and romantic self-expression. Several of the poems were considered daringly erotic and all pretended to be the products of the author's actual passionate feelings. Byron responded to these qualities and emulated them in his early poetry; as Susan J. Wolfson and Peter J. Manning observe, "Moore's erotic manner leaves traces throughout Byron's early verse."[1] *Little's Poems* was almost certainly Byron's most important inspiration for *Hours of Idleness* and for the three other volumes of his lyric poetry he assembled between 1806 and 1808.

Little's Poems was Moore's attempt to duplicate the astonishing success of his first book, *Odes of Anacreon*, which had been published in 1800. The twenty-year-old Moore had sailed to England in March 1799, the poor Catholic son of a Dublin grocer, halfheartedly intending to study law at the Middle Temple. A little over a year later his *Odes* boasted a subscription list including dukes, earls, viscounts, and the Prince of Wales himself, and upon the success of the volume Moore was enthusiastically welcomed into the highest social circles of London. On 3 August 1800, Moore was personally presented to the Prince, who told Moore he felt honored to patronize such an impressive work.[2] In his journal in 1839 Moore would look back and marvel "that I should so immediately on my coming to London have got into that upper region where I have remained ever since" (*MJ* 5:2062). Moore's success was due partly to his *Odes*, which sold nine costly editions by 1815, and partly to his great personal charm. Moore's social and literary skills complemented each other at the start of his career as they would continue to do throughout his life; his charm and wit, as well as his willingness to exercise his musical talents for the entertainment of his hosts, not only secured him access to the drawing rooms of the great but also won over readers and purchasers of his works.

The *Odes of Anacreon* had an elegant eroticism, a lush and voluptuous style, and an erudite scholarship that all bespoke the arrival of a new and unique literary talent. The poems earned Moore his first nickname, "Anacreon Moore," and they remained popular decades after they were written. The *Odes* are mostly in praise of wine and love, and their profusions of gushing grapes, snowy necks, and flowery breezes, combined with the melodious versification for which Moore would always be known, succeed in evoking a sensation of sensual intoxication. Both this intoxicating quality, as well as the poems' colorful, hedonistic Hellenism, mark Moore as an important stylistic precursor of Keats.[3] The poems' dramatic situations take place in a hazy, idealized pagan world, far removed from contemporary events and concerns, a characteristic that doubtless contributed to their contemporary popularity. Moore was a man deeply concerned with British and Irish politics from his youth at college to his old age, but he knew that with the failed Irish rebellion of 1798 and the Act of Union still fresh in the minds of his English readers, the last thing they wanted from him was anything smacking of Irish nationalism. An imaginative escape from events such as the Irish troubles, the harsh repression of domestic dissent, and the war with Napoleon was what upper-class English consumers of poetry wanted, and it was what Moore chose to provide.

Whereas the *Odes* were both a popular and a critical success, the reputation of Moore's next book was to become an albatross around his neck that he spent at least the next twenty years trying to shake off. *The Poetical Works of the Late Thomas Little, Esq.* was another collection of mostly amorous verse, but unlike the *Odes, Little's Poems* situated its sighing young lovers in England and in the present day and employed a much more colloquial style. There were other differences as well that caused the same critics who praised the *Odes* to condemn *Little's Poems.* The *Odes* were an expensive quarto of elegant classical verse approved by the future king and filled with learned notes and commentary, with a scholarly preface that affected to disapprove of Anacreon's moral laxity. The book cost a guinea and was therefore guaranteed an upper-class readership. *Little's Poems,* on the other hand, cost a third less, being at seven shillings a small pseudonymous octavo filled with what the critics considered pretty rhymes about sex and the joys of infidelity, written in a style that a reader of any age could easily understand. The *Poetical Register* rose to defend the modesty of young women against Moore's seductiveness: "The volume contains so large a proportion of libertinism, that it ought never to be opened by any female who has any pretensions to delicacy."[4] Though Moore's name did not appear in the first edition, by 1802 he was generally known to be the author, and early in that year Robert Southey's notice of the volume in the *Critical Review* set the tone for many reviewers to follow:

> The extracts that we have given abundantly prove the genius of the author. Why will he degrade himself by thus miserably applying it? The age in which we live has imposed upon him the necessity of employing decent language; but few ages have ever been disgraced by a volume more corrupt in its whole spirit and tendency. We have not been avaricious in its praise; but this book is mischievous in proportion to its merit. The Monk had its spots;—this is leprous all over.[5]

In the same year Coleridge also associated the "wanton" poems of Little with Matthew Lewis's *The Monk:* "My head turns giddy, my heart sickens, at the very thought of seeing such books in the hands of a child of mine. . . . [Lewis and Little] have sold provocatives to vulgar Debauchees, & vicious school-boys."[6]

Little's Poems certainly provoked at least one vicious schoolboy. In 1820 Byron wrote to Moore: "I have just been turning over Little, which I knew by heart in 1803, being then in my fifteenth summer. Heigho! I believe all the mischief I have ever done, or sung, has been owing to that confounded book of yours" (*BLJ* 7:117). Earlier, in 1813, Byron told Moore: I remember, when about fifteen, reading your poems [at Newstead Abbey],—which I can repeat almost now,—and asking all kinds of questions about the author, when I heard that he was not dead according to the preface; wondering if I should ever see him—and though, at that time, without the smallest poetical pro-pensity myself, very much taken, as you may imagine, with that volume (*BLJ* 3:96). Byron's remarks emphasize the two features of *Little's Poems* that at-tracted him the most: its "mischievous" eroticism and its focus on the per-sonality of "Thomas Little."[7] Both the eroticism and the feigned personalism of Moore's book would exert a powerful influence on Byron's early poems, as they would on those of many other budding poets at the time. Moore's poems were widely read, with an eleventh edition in 1813 and a fifteenth in 1822,[8] and a writer for *Bentley's Miscellany* in 1853 recalled that when they first appeared they "produced a sort of revolution. . . . They sounded every depth and shallow of the passion, and supplied a medium of expression for every lover under the sun."[9] It is this "revolution" that provoked John Wilson Croker's rebuke in 1804: "I could wish [Little's] sentiments were but half as correct as his versification; but the only Venus he worships, is she whom the Scholiast on Aristophanes calls 'Γεννετυλλι,' and what is worse, he makes all the young people in the Empire, worship her too."[10] Byron's comment that before reading Little he was "without the smallest poetical propensity" him-self is significant; in 1818 Byron also recalled that "when a boy, I could never bear to read any poetry whatever without disgust and reluctance."[11] Moore may well deserve the credit for awakening Byron's interest in poetry.

The preface that Byron referred to in his letter to Moore was supposedly written by a friend of Thomas Little, "the Editor." According to this friend, Little had recently died at the age of twenty-one, leaving behind a mass of poems never intended for publication. Nonetheless, Little's friend had de-cided to publish them as a memorial, and he affected to be diffident about their literary merit:

> The Poems which I take the liberty of publishing were never intended by the Author to pass beyond the circle of his friends. He thought, with some justice, that what are called Occasional Poems must always be insipid and uninteresting to the greater part of their readers. The particular situations in which they were written, the character of the author and of his associates, all these peculiarities must be known and felt before we can enter into the spirit of such compositions. This consideration would have always, I believe, prevented Mr. LITTLE from submitting these trifles of the moment to the eye of dispassionate criticism. (iii–iv)

Despite the modesty of the editor's tone, he clearly claimed a certain merit for these "trifles." The preface implied that because these poems were inspired by genuine feeling and not the desire to please the public, they possessed a peculiar artlessness and sincerity. The editor favorably contrasted Little's models, "the early poets of our own language," with the classical writers of amorous poetry, whose works were either too insincere or too crude. The editor explained: "If [Little] ever expected to find in the ancients that delicacy of sentiment and variety of fancy which are so necessary to refine and animate the poetry of love, he was much disappointed" (v). Little's "fondest ambition" was to attain the "simplicity" of the early English poets (xi).

The editor also suggested that the poems' sincerity of feeling and expression resulted from the author's youth and that the "warm coloring" and "luxuriance" of his young imagination made his poems slightly deficient in strict virtue. He begged the indulgence of the reader on account of the poet's youth (a tactic Byron would later employ in his preface to *Hours of Idleness*). The editor explained that

> most of these Poems were written at so early a period, that their errors may claim some indulgence from the critic: their author, as unambitious as indolent, scarce ever looked beyond the moment of composition; he wrote as he pleased, careless whether he pleased as he wrote. It may likewise be remembered, that they were all the productions of an age when the passions very often give a colouring too warm to the imagination; and this may palliate, if it cannot excuse, that air of levity which pervades so many of them. The "aurea legge, s'ei piace ei lice,"[12] he too much pursued, and too much inculcates. (iv–v)

The preface conjured up the mythic figure of the artistic youth, tragically cut down, like Chatterton, in the full bloom of his unappreciated talent. Little too came from humble origins: "His life was one of those humble streams which have scarcely a name on the map of life, and the traveller may pass it by without inquiring its source or direction" (xii).

Little's editor made a number of critical observations: the personal poems were meant to be read as vehicles of real sentiments directed toward real people; because of the poet's youth and lack of ambition, the poems had the fault of imperfect technique but also the advantage of genuine feeling; the "early poets of our own language" were better models than the "insincere" classical poets; and the poems' metrical and linguistic "simplicity" were virtues and not faults. The editor criticized "ostentatious displays" of "erudition" in classical poets dealing with "a subject so simple as love," calling them "vague and puerile . . . pedantic," and went on to say, "I believe the defects which a common reader condemns have been looked on rather as beauties by those erudite men, the commentators, who find a field for their ingenuity and research in . . . Grecian learning and quaint obscurities" (vi). The editor praised poets who possessed "genuine feeling," "a native sensibility," "fine and natural feeling" that "reaches the heart immediately" (vi–viii). The editor's emphasis on the personal, emotional, primitive, and colloquial echoes (albeit in an entirely less serious and polemical way) the ideas in Wordsworth's preface to the second edition of *Lyrical Ballads,* which appeared in 1800, the year before *Little's Poems.* Wordsworth's preface argued in favor of a poetry inspired by genuine feeling, free from the "gaudiness and inane phraseology" of the eighteenth-century neoclassical poets and their imitators, and written in simple language eschewing "artificial distinctions of style."[13]

The irony underlying Little's supposedly sincere poems and the claims of their Romantic editor is that Little himself is an invented character. The remarks of Little's editor suggest that his friend's poems are true examples of romantic self-expression—"overheard" poems, in John Stuart Mill's phrase—but in actuality Little himself is a fiction created by Moore. The occasions to which Little's "occasional" poems allude and the people to whom his poems are addressed are all inventions as well. The editor himself is also a fiction, a believer in critical notions to which Moore himself was largely unsympathetic. Moore made few explicit critical observations during his long career as a poet, but it is clear that he always doubted whether poetry that claimed to be both sincere and personal was ever as genuine as it claimed to be. Moore considered the writing of poetry primarily a process of labor and artifice, a "matter-of-fact thing" (*MJ* 4:1464), and he objected to the concept of poetry as the fruit of a "spontaneous overflow of powerful feelings"; in a typical letter of 1805 Moore called the writing of poetry the "drudgery of fancy—this slavery of imagination I am bound to" (*ML* 1:90). Years later Moore would articulate his beliefs most clearly in his biography of Byron:

> It is, indeed, only in those emotions and passions, of which imagination[14] forms a predominant ingredient,—such as love, in its first dreams, before reality has come to imbody or dispel them, or sorrow, in its wane, when beginning to pass away from the heart into the fancy,—that poetry ought ever to be employed as an interpreter of feeling. For the expression of all those immediate affections and disquietudes that have their root in the actual realities of life, the art of the poet, from the very circumstance of its being an art, as well as from the colored form in which it is accustomed to transmit impressions, cannot be otherwise than a medium as false as it is feeble. (*MLB* 1:664–65)

When Moore was asked in 1836 to write something upon the death of the young son of his friend Lord Lansdowne, he wrote in his diary: "It is strange how few people feel the sacredness of such subjects. The ornaments of Poetry and oratory are all very well on the ordinary topics of life—but there are feelings and sorrows which it is desecration to apply them to" (*MJ* 5:1819). Such a conception of art—as a way of ornamenting experience rather than revealing or illuminating it—is in direct opposition to the idea of Romantic lyricism that is represented by the poetry of Wordsworth and Shelley.[15]

Thomas Little the character is a product of Moore's skepticism about the authenticity of romantic self-expression. Little's lyric poems—based as they are on "the particular situations in which they were written, the character of the author and of his associates"—reveal him to be a silver-tongued seducer, alternately sentimental and unsentimental in his lovemaking and his poetry. They are apparently insincere by "Little's" own intention, because in many of them Little is attempting to deceive or cajole his lovers. Supposedly heartfelt declarations of love apparently made to respectable women alternate with short, lascivious poems like "To Phillis":

> Phillis, you little rosy rake,
>   That heart of yours I long to rifle;
> Come, give it me, and do not make
>   So much ado about *a trifle!*   (ll. 1–4)

"Epigram" is another typical lyric:

> Your mother says, my little Venus,
> There's *something not correct* between us,
>   And you're in fault as much as I:—
> Now, on my soul, my little Venus,
> I think 't would not be right, between us,
>   To let your mother tell a lie!   (ll. 1–6)

In several poems Little even cynically attempts to cajole young women out of their religious reservations. In "To Julia" his lover fears damnation after a sexual encounter:

> Then wipe away that timid tear,
> Sweet truant! you have naught to fear,
>   Though you were whelm'd in sin;
> Stand but at heaven's gate awhile,
> And you *so like an angel* smile,
>   They can't but *let you in.*   (ll. 13–18)

In another "Song" he asks a different woman:

> "Oh! Why should Platonic control, love,
>   Enchain an emotion so free?. . .
> Be an angel, my love, in the morning,
>   But oh! *be a woman to-night!*"   (ll. 25–26, 31–32)

His lack of regard for religion is more blatant in "Piety" (about "Sue, the pretty nun") and in "Morality, a Familiar Epistle" (in which Little declares himself a pleasure-loving skeptic who, after studying religion and philosophy, "only learn'd *to doubt* at last" [l. 14]). The latter poem is long and prominently positioned as the volume's penultimate lyric, partially explaining the motivations for Little's carefree life of seduction.

The constant alternation of apparently genuine love poems and romantic lyrics with cavalier sexual propositions to young women reveals Little, as a poet and as a man, to be a striker of poses and a wearer of masks. The editor himself hinted at this, mentioning in his preface that there were certain "seductive graces by which gallantry almost teaches [the dissipation of the heart] to be amiable" (x). In addition to exposing the truth behind Little's poetic self-expression, the volume also indicates Little's (and Moore's) ironic relationship to other elements of *Lyrical Ballads*-style Romanticism, as in "Nonsense," in which the Coleridgeian "supernatural" lyrical ballad undergoes a sudden deflation in the last line, a comic technique much like that which Byron would later apply in so many stanzas of *Don Juan*. "Nonsense" plays with the supernatural romantic lyric in order to undermine its legitimacy, just as the volume as a whole presents itself as a collection of occasional poems in order to discredit the idea of poetic sincerity. Little's pseudomedieval ballads "Reuben and Rose. A Tale of Romance" and "The Ring" and his natural reverie "A Reflection at Sea" seem to be no more than whims or casual experiments when placed in context with Little's other poetry.[16]

Thomas Little's poems essentially show him to be a hedonist who uses lyric poetry to flatter, charm, and seduce. He views each poem he writes as a masquerade or a performance, rather than a revelation or exploration of his own consciousness. Moore does not seem to want his readers to condemn Little; rather, he intends that Little's poems be appreciated for their mischievous humor and vivacity. Like Byron, Moore was no believer in poetic manifestoes or "systems," and Moore doubtless viewed the subject with too much equanimity to want to launch any kind of serious attack on Wordsworth's or anyone else's ideas. But Moore's volume does implicitly engage the subject of romantic self-expression and does demonstrate how "personal" lyric poetry may be counterfeited in order to achieve particular rhetorical effects. This is an idea that fascinated Byron throughout his life, and it is highly significant that it was Little's counterfeit lyrical romanticism that captured Byron's imagination immediately prior to his first serious attempts at writing poetry.[17]

II

Byron's first volume, *Fugitive Pieces*, privately printed in the autumn of 1806, features a dedication and a preface that echo the preface of *Little's Poems*, as well as containing poems that are very similar in their style and subject matter to those in that volume. The dedication reads, "To those friends, at whose request they were printed, for whose amusement or approbation they are solely intended; These trifles are respectfully dedicated, by the author."[18] Like Little's poems, these are "trifles," intended only to amuse those people to or for whom they were written. The first poem in the collection, "On Leaving N——st——d," announces the personal nature of those that follow. Like Little's editor, Byron craves indulgence for these "private" poems written by a young poet: "As these POEMS were never intended to meet the public eye, no apology is necessary for the form in which they now appear. They are printed merely for the perusal of a few friends to whom they are dedicated; who will look upon them with indulgence; and as most of them were composed between the age of 15 and 17, their defects will be pardoned or forgotten, in the youth and inexperience of the WRITER" (*BCP* 1:363). Although it is true that *Fugitive Pieces* was a trial run for Byron and therefore not intended for the public, many of its poems were soon publicly printed in *Hours of Idleness*. At this point, however, Byron could still disclaim any desire for fame, just as Little's editor did on behalf of his late friend.

The character of Thomas Little became a model upon which Byron based the character he created for himself in his poems. The Little poems, read together, have the total effect of fleshing out Little's personality, which is that of "Passion's warmest child." Byron was attracted to the personality portrayed in these poems, and this attraction led him to use his own poems to fashion the same sort of character for himself. In his poem "To the Sighing Strephon," Byron cavalierly claims: "'Tis true I am given to range, / If I rightly remember, / I've kiss'd a good number, / But there's pleasure, at least, in a change" (ll. 27–30).[19] This pose of carefree rakishness recalls Little's in such poems as "To ——": "'Tis not that I expect to find / A more devoted, fond, and true one, / With rosier cheek or sweeter mind— / Enough for me that she's a new one" (ll. 9–12). The overwhelming majority of Thomas Little's poems either address or regard a number of his seemingly countless lovers. Similarly, Byron's volume is filled with verses such as "To Caroline," "To A. ——," "To Miss E. P.," "To Mary," "To Maria ——," "To a Beautiful Quaker," and "To a Lady, who Presented the Author with a Lock of Hair, Braided with his Own, and Appointed a Night in December, to Meet him in the Garden." Both volumes feature poems to "Julia." Nearly all of the poems in *Fugitive Pieces* are about love in the abstract or claim to regard the author's loves in particular. Many are clearly intended to imply the wide scope of their author's sexual experience.

Marchand judges "many" of these poems to be "close imitations" of Little's poems, observing that in them Byron "imitat[ed] well some of the lilting anapestic lyrics of Moore, and sometimes improved on them. His facility in some of the lyric measures he learned from Moore was one of the chief merits of his occasional verse and was to bear fruit in *Hebrew Melodies* and in some of his early verses that sprang from genuine emotions, like 'Hills of Annesley! bleak and barren.'"[20] Specific parallels and verbal echoes between the

two volumes are numerous. Each features a poem called "The Tear," about a
lover weeping over a grave, and both have imitations of Catullus. "Little" has
a poem called "Fragments of College Exercises"; Byron has "Fragments of
School Exercises." Both poets celebrate "marriages" over which no priests
preside.[21] On the whole, Byron's erotic lyrics in this volume recall Little's
style, but the tone is more bitter, less jovial. There are certainly bitter and sorrowful lyrics in Little, but the majority of Byron's love poems are joyless and
deal with love lost or betrayed. The most important and pervasive influences
of Little's poems upon *Fugitive Pieces,* however, are their eroticism, their preoccupation with describing their own author, and, perhaps most important,
their exploitation and subversion of the ideal of poetic sincerity.

McGann has argued that the most characteristic feature of Byron's lyric
poetry is its "lyrical dandyism."[22] In McGann's formulation, Byron's technique
is to subvert romantic self-expression from within, by exploiting the conventions of the Wordsworthian lyric poem in order to assume a self-conscious
pose. Byron's lyric poetry, which claims to be confessional, in fact leaves its
author "anonymous" by virtue of its radical theatricality. The great importance of Byron's exposure to *Little's Poems* is that it was Byron's first known
encounter with poetry that struck this kind of factitious, playful pose of personalism and sincerity. In 1852 a writer for *Bentley's Miscellany* shrewdly noted
the "lyrical dandyism" of both poets: "There is evident insincerity in the
immorality of Moore, and still more of Byron."[23] Byron was not disturbed to
find that "Thomas Little" was an invented person; if anything, this discovery
seems to have made him even more intrigued. It was when Byron heard that
the author of the book "was not dead according to the preface" that Byron
"ask[ed] all kinds of questions about the author" and "wonder[ed] if [he]
should ever see him."

In *Fugitive Pieces* Byron fashioned his own persona: the amorous, haughty,
skeptical young lord. It was an idealized version of himself, a way of dramat-
ically presenting himself to the world while eliding his real insecurities and
confusions. This character would evolve in time into Childe Harold and other
Byronic heroes. As early as *Fugitive Pieces* Byron was inviting his readers to
believe that he was speaking in his own voice about his own life, but having
read *Little's Poems,* Byron must have been at least partially conscious that he
was performing, not confessing. With so many secrets and confusions in his
private life, even from a very early age (consider his abuse by May Gray, his

experience with Lord Grey de Ruthyn, and his love for John Edlestone), Byron must have quickly come to understand more than most poets the necessity of masks, as well as the inevitable evasions and selections involved in any public self-expression.

When Byron distributed the privately printed copies of *Fugitive Pieces* to his circle of friends and acquaintances, the books provoked a small scandal among the respectable inhabitants of Southwell. Byron was taken by surprise when his adviser and friend, the Reverend John Thomas Becher, protested to him about his poem "To Mary," which featured a warmth of imagery that no one even moderately acquainted with modern poetry in 1806 would have failed to trace back to Thomas Moore:

> [We] smile to think how oft we've done,
>> What prudes declare a sin to act is,
>> And never but in darkness practice.
>
> . . . .
>
> Now, by my soul, 'tis most delight
>> To view each other panting, dying,
>> In love's *extatic posture* lying,
>> Grateful to *feeling*, as to *sight*."   (ll. 37–39; 45–48)

It should not have been a surprise to Byron that such verses would cause an uproar among the families of Southwell, especially since these poems implied that Byron made love to the actual young Southwell daughters, whose reputations could ill afford to be damaged by such dubious notoriety. Byron's immediate reaction to the Reverend Becher's objections was to protest, but on 26 November, the same day he received Becher's letter of admonition, he called back all the distributed copies of *Fugitive Pieces* and destroyed those he recovered.

Around this time, Byron wrote his poem "To Those Ladies Who Have So Kindly Defended the Author from the Attacks of Unprovoked Malignity," which features several echoes of Moore's "To Julia. In Allusion to Some Illiberal Criticisms," the first poem in *Little's Poems*. In Moore's poem "the tear from Beauty's eye" and "the votive sigh" (ll. 21–22) arm Little against "the fume of vacant pride, / Which mantles o'er the pedant fool, / Like vapour on a stagnant pool!" (ll. 2–4). In Byron's, "Beauty's Sigh" and "the Beams of Beauty's Eye" chase the critics' "Clouds of hate away" (ll. 1–4). Little claims that he will disregard his critics as long as his female reader languishes over "my simple theme"; Byron's poem also thanks the female reader: "Oh I forgive the lying Throng, / From you alone I claim the Bays, / Since you approve my simple Song, / Their censure is my warmest praise" (ll. 9–12).

Before long Byron revised and republished his poems in a larger and less provocative collection called *Poems on Various Occasions,* which appeared sometime between 23 December 1806 and 13 January 1807. Byron sent a copy of the new volume to his friend John Pigot, along with a letter scornfully referring to the row over *Fugitive Pieces:* "That *unlucky* poem to my poor Mary, has been the cause of some Animadversion from *Ladies in years.* I have not printed it in this Collection in Consequence of my being pronounced, a *most profligate sinner,* in short a *'young Moore'* by Mrs. S—— your Oxon friend" (*BLJ* 1:103–4). It is evident from the letter's exultant tone that to have acquired the reputation of a "young Moore" was a great delight for Byron. It meant more than merely being an imitator of Moore's lyrics. By 1806 critics were routinely accusing Moore of trying to corrupt the youth of England with his poems, often applying such terms as "seducer," "pimp," or "pander." Moore's delight in posing as a fashionable ladies' man exacerbated the general identification of him with his fictitious Little. Before long the promising young poet of 1800 had become generally denounced not merely as a writer of erotic poems but as a debauched person himself. The truth about Moore was an entirely different matter, but the fact remained that to be called a "young Moore" in 1806 not only meant that one had written morally dangerous verses, but also implied that one was a creature of loose sexual habits.

Though Byron was unwilling to pursue this kind of reputation to the point of social ostracism (he did burn *Fugitive Pieces*), it is unquestionable that he was always pleased to be "held up as the votary of Licentiousness" (*BLJ* 1:146). His letter to Pigot, with its disdain for his moralizing detractors coupled with its self-aggrandizing tales of scandalous romance, foreshadows the more sophisticated sexual braggadocio of his letters to John Murray written during his exile years later. In his biography of Byron, Moore himself commented upon this feature of Byron's juvenile letters, calling it "that sort of display and boast of rakishness which is but too common a folly at this period of life, when the young aspirant to manhood persuades himself that to be profligate is to be manly" (*MLB* 1:120). It is not surprising, perhaps, that a shy, fatherless, lame, chubby youth, uncomfortable with his position in society and alienated from his mother, should want to court such a reputation for sexual attractiveness and prowess. Moore's "Little" poems taught Byron about the power of the poet to create a character, and Byron eagerly set about the task of creating one for himself that would compensate for his insecurities.

III

By the time Byron's "miraculously *chaste*" second volume appeared, Moore's fall from critical grace, which had begun with *Little's Poems,* had been accelerated by the publication of his third collection, *Epistles, Odes and Other Poems,* which appeared during the first half of 1806. It had been five years since the appearance of *Little's Poems,* during which time Moore had traveled to Bermuda, across America, and through Canada and had written scores of poems. *Epistles, Odes and Other Poems* sold well, but Moore, despite receiving the personal compliments of the Prince of Wales, remembered the harsh treatment he had received from the critics over *Little's Poems* and feared what the reviews might say.

In July 1806, Moore received the most devastating review of his career from Francis Jeffrey of the *Edinburgh Review.* In his preface to *Odes of Anacreon,* Moore had called Anacreon an "elegant voluptuary, diffusing the seductive charm of sentiment over passions and propensities at which rigid morality must frown" (*MCP* 1:25). Now Jeffrey accused Moore not only of engaging in the same kind of "seduction" but also with having the most sinister of motives. Jeffrey's assault on *Epistles, Odes and Other Poems* was immediate and merciless:

> [Moore] may boast . . . of being the most licentious of modern versifiers, and the most poetical of those who, in our times, have devoted themselves to the propagation of immorality. We regard this book, indeed, as a public nuisance. . . . There is nothing, it will be allowed, more indefensible than a cold blooded attempt to corrupt the purity of an innocent heart, and we can scarcely conceive any being more truly despicable, than he who . . . sits down to ransack the impure places of his memory for inflammatory images and expressions, and commits them laboriously to writing, for the purpose of insinuating pollution into the minds of unknown and unsuspecting readers.

Jeffrey considered the "coarse indecencies" of French writers and such English poets as Dryden and Rochester, saying in their favor that they at least did not attempt to trick their readers into reading their pornography by disguising it as something else. Moore's elegant style rendered him all the more dangerous:

> The immorality of Mr. Moore is infinitely more insidious and malignant. It seems to be his aim to impose corruption upon his readers, by concealing it under the mask of refinement; to reconcile them imperceptibly to the most vile and vulgar sensuality, by blending its language with that of exalted feeling and tender emotion; and to steal impurity into their hearts, by gently perverting the most simple and generous of their affections. In the execution of this unworthy task, he labours with a perseverance at once ludicrous and detestable.

According to Jeffrey, the chief "mischief" that Moore's poems were "calculated" to achieve is the corruption of "the purity of the female character." Jeffrey's review evinced a "fear of fiction" of the type commonly associated with the eighteenth-century novel; after describing the fundamentally irrational nature of women, he observed "how dangerous it must be for such beings to hang over the pages of a book, in which supernatural raptures, and transcendent passion, are counterfeited on every page."[24] Jeffrey's imagery, of Moore's volume being smuggled into the bedchambers of innocent virgins under the pretense of being respectable poetry, deliberately characterized Moore as a sort of rapist, a modern Lovelace intent on ruining a whole nation of Clarissas.

Jeffrey not only attacked Moore as a poet but also slandered him as a man. Jeffrey did not choose to consider the narrator of these love poems to be anyone other than Moore himself, and, accordingly, on the evidence of the poems, he accused Moore of promiscuity and his lovers of whoredom:

> He is at pains to let the world know that he is still fonder of roving, than of loving; and that all the Caras and the Fannys, with whom he holds dalliance in these pages, have had each a long series of preceding lovers, as highly favored as their present poetical paramour; that they meet without any purpose of constancy, and do not think it necessary to grace their connexion with any professions of esteem or permanent attachment.[25]

Moore at first tried to laugh off Jeffrey's ferocious attack, writing to a friend: "I hope I shall always be lucky enough to have such dull, prosing antagonists" (*ML* 1:102). In the days following the writing of this letter, however, Moore's outrage grew to such an extent that he decided to call Jeffrey out. This led to the farcical duel Byron later satirized in *English Bards*.

The poetry of *Epistles, Odes and Other Poems* is more varied than that found in Moore's two previous volumes. It includes odes on classical themes, ballads, experiments in irregular verse, amatory poems in the style of Little, descriptions of natural scenery, and Moore's first significant attempts at satire. The collection is unified by the inclusion of a series of nine verse epistles, addressed to friends in England and Ireland, which had been written at various stages during his journey through Bermuda, America, and Canada, and eventually back home to England. The frontispiece of the volume depicts the ship on which Moore traveled sailing near the Azores. The epistles are evenly spaced throughout the volume, giving the reader a sense of Moore's progress on his journey. This unifying technique, focusing the reader's attention upon the author himself instead of upon a fictional character like Thomas Little, made it almost inevitable that all the love poems would be read as genuine tributes of the actual writer to the actual women he met on his travels. Moore would be identified with the speaker(s) of his love poems in *Epistles, Odes and Other Poems* in the same way Byron would be identified with another traveling poet, Childe Harold, and for the same reason.

For all the assaults upon the volume by Jeffrey and others, it sold steadily and well for many years, reaching a fifteenth edition in 1817.[26] Two songs from the volume, "The Woodpecker" and the "Canadian Boat-song," were immensely popular and were often reproduced and sung.[27] Many of the shorter, more sentimental love poems were obviously designed to be copied into young ladies' albums and scrapbooks, a factor that helps account for Jeffrey's alarm. The "Odes to Nea" were very popular; Mary Shelley told Moore in 1839 that Percy Shelley had been a great admirer of his works, and she singled out his "unspeakably beautiful poems to Nea" as special favorites (*MJ* 5:2041).

In Byron's Ravenna Journal of 1821, he recalled himself and Edward Noel Long "buying, with vast alacrity, Moore's new quarto (in 1806), and reading it together in the evenings" (*BLJ* 8:24). Byron had therefore almost certainly read *Epistles, Odes and Other Poems* by the time *Fugitive Pieces* appeared, although judging from Byron's later comments to Moore it was *Little's Poems* that impressed him the most and that continued to influence his early poetry. Byron had toned down his poems' eroticism in *Poems on Various Occasions*, balancing the book more evenly between amatory poems and classical imitations and translations, but the "'*poesies Erotiques*'" of that volume, as Byron called them, were still found to be exceptionable (1:111). Accordingly, Byron's third collection, *Hours of Idleness,* published during the last week of June 1807, was tamer still.

In *Hours of Idleness* Byron attempted to flesh out a character, and in that respect the influence of *Little's Poems* is still apparent, but the more obviously recognizable traces of Little's eroticism are somewhat less in evidence. In the months before *Hours of Idleness* appeared, Byron assured his correspondents that the new volume would be more innocuous. To William Bankes, who had disapproved of the eroticism of *Poems on Various Occasions,* Byron explained, "My amatory pieces will be expunged, & others substituted, in their place" (*BLJ* 1:112). Byron told John Hanson that although his "amatory effusions" were "not to be wondered at from the *dissipated Life* I have lead," they would nevertheless be "cut out" (1:113). When the volume appeared, he wrote to Elizabeth Pigot that the ladies who bought it must be disappointed that there was "nothing *indecent* in the present publication," and then wrote, but crossed out, "sorry for it" (1:125). Byron's continued self-portraiture in his letters as an abandoned sybarite suggests that if he had had no fear of critical condemnation he would have been happy to leave the amatory pieces in. However, after witnessing the assaults upon Moore the previous year, Byron was undoubtedly wise to take this approach. The traces of Moore are still strong enough for Byron's new preface to caution: "I have not aimed at exclusive originality. . . . In the original pieces, there may appear a casual coincidence with authors, whose works I have been accustomed to read, but I have not been guilty of intentional plagiarism" (*BCP* 1:32–34).

The diffident and apologetic tone of this new preface recalls the preface of *Little's Poems*. Like Little's editor, Byron asked his audience for a special indulgence both because of his youth and because of his lack of ambition for poetic fame. The poems are "trifles," "the fruits of the lighter hours of a young man, who has barely completed his nineteenth year," written merely to "divert the dull moments of indisposition, or the monotony of a vacant hour" (*BCP* 1:32–34). Byron was sheepish about even having written his poems, doubted he would ever publish again, and insisted that poetry "is not my primary vocation." Henry Brougham's contempt for the false modesty of Byron's preface would be one of the aspects of his review that injured Byron the most.

Thomas Little spent most of his time making love, but harbored few illusions about love's permanence. Vows of constancy, marriage, and the sanctity of virginity were treated humorously by Little, with a worldly cynicism that showed that, however much a woman might turn his head, he never forgot that the passion that is love's principal charm does not last long. The poems of *Hours of Idleness* move beyond merely echoing Little's skeptical attitude and begin to reject the worth of even casual dalliance. McGann observes that Byron wanted to fashion a portrait of a young man who was grounded in reality and therefore capable of performing noble and heroic deeds, and that he therefore made "the ironic or satiric exposure of falsehood in all its forms" one of the major themes of the volume.[28] Accordingly, the amatory poems, such as "To M——," "To Woman," and "To ——" are about the pains and deceptions, rather than the joys, of love. Byron grouped the majority of the amatory poems together in the first half of the volume, framed by the buoyant "The First Kiss of Love" and the elegiac "Love's Last Adieu!" at their beginning and end, respectively. Each of these two poems is written in anapests, like many of Moore's best verses, and each begins with a quotation from Anacreon. The effect of this grouping is to suggest that the young lord is making a positive progression, from the ecstatic lovemaking of naive youth to a maturer knowledge of love's impermanence and illusions. It is as if the reader witnesses him traveling beyond being a roving Little and beginning to turn his gaze toward the responsibilities of being a sober-minded peer.

Michael G. Cooke claims that the poems of *Hours of Idleness* show Byron to be a "romantic lyrist" in the specifically Wordsworthian sense, "more spontaneously and more richly concerned with the problems of time, memory, knowledge, and nature than he is usually given credit for." Yet Cooke also measures the aesthetic success or failure of these poems according to the yardstick of Wordsworthian sincerity, calling, for instance, the "certain arch self-consciousness" in some of the poems a "disability."[29] Throughout his career, Byron would problematize the very notion of sincerity, not because he was an inferior poet but because he wrote from a more philosophically skeptical viewpoint than Wordsworth. It may be that the most important reason that the young Byron as well as the young Moore could not produce a lyric poetry of Wordsworthian sincerity was that their subject matter was primarily amorous love, as opposed to an abstracted and spiritualized love of nature. It is doubtless easier to appear perfectly sincere when such things as jealousy, sexuality, rejection, and competition do not enter into the picture at all.

Hours of Idleness contains coincidences with Moore's works: the two translations from Anacreon are of poems that Moore himself translated in the *Odes;* and Catullus is imitated, as he is in *Little's Poems.* But *Hours of Idleness* places its emphasis primarily upon the young lord's education and growing maturity, and only secondarily upon his pursuit of the "aurea legge." As the volume progresses, the poems' observations about love become more detached and critical. In "To Romance," the penultimate of the poems that deal with erotic love, the seductive illusions of love are resolutely sworn off without irony. The young lord abandons the search for love in favor of the search for "Truth":

> With shame, I own, I've felt [Fancy's] sway,
>   Repentant, now thy reign is o'er,
> No more thy precepts I obey,
>   No more on fancied pinions soar;
> Fond fool! to love a sparkling eye,
>   And think, that eye to Truth was dear,
> To trust a passing wanton's sigh,
>   And melt beneath a wanton's tear   (ll. 25–32)

The last poem but one in the volume is "To E.N.L. Esq.," which restates the young lord's renunciation of love (and the writing of love poetry) in a more wistful tone:

> Full often has my infant Muse,
>   Attun'd to love, her languid lyre,
> But, now, without a theme to chuse,
>   The strains in stolen sighs expire:
> My youthful nymphs, alas! are flown,
>   E—— is a wife, and C—— a mother,
> And Carolina sighs alone,
>   And Mary's given to another;
> And Cora's eye, which roll'd on me,
>   Can now no more my love recal,
>
> . . . .
>
> Thus has it been with Passion's fires,
>   As many a boy, and girl, remembers,
> While all the force of love expires,
>   Extinguish'd with the dying embers.   (ll. 59–68; 83–86)

The poem concludes by finding compensation for the "expiring strains" of love in the convivial comradeship of his male friends; passion, a thing "boys and girls" feel, is replaced by the more adult "sacred intellectual shower" of the company of men (l. 106). Indeed, women increasingly recede into the background in *Hours of Idleness;* of the last four poems in the volume, two are addressed to male friends, "The Episode of Nisus and Euryalus" deals with male friendship, and "Childish Recollections" affectionately enumerates several of the poet's male schoolfellows. The self-conscious resolution to "put away childish things" that Byron exhibits in "To Romance" and "To E.N.L. Esq." is a marked change from the enthusiastic proclamation of his love of dalliance in *Fugitive Pieces,* and even from that found in the Little-inspired love poems that occur prior to these two poems in *Hours of Idleness.*

Despite the greater length and prominence of the poems dealing with Byron's education and heritage and despite his deliberate efforts to "expunge and substitute," several reviewers of this volume still characterized the poems as predominantly amatory.[30] Byron's experience with his first two volumes had taught him not to carry his emulation of Moore too far, but a few of Byron's critics still remarked upon the resemblances to Moore in his roles as both Thomas Little and the British Anacreon. According to the *Universal Magazine,* "The prevailing cast of the poems before us is amatory, in these his lordship seems to have taken Mr. Moore for his model. They have not however his polish, his elegance, or his immorality." This reviewer also noted that Byron's translations of Anacreon, "though far above mediocrity, are yet below the elegant and spirited version of Mr. Moore."[31] The *Beau Monde,* while labeling Byron's translations "tame and prosaic," conceded that "it was a bold attempt to translate . . . Anacreon after Moore" and that it would be unreasonable to expect from a young man "those glowing sentiments which have recommended the works of Anacreon Moore . . . so strongly to the public favor."[32]

One of the two harshest attacks on *Hours of Idleness* (along with Brougham's) is also the review that draws the parallel between Moore and Byron the most explicitly. Hewson Clarke, whom Byron would later punish in *English Bards and Scotch Reviewers* and *Hints from Horace,* wrote in the *Satirist* that Moore was bad, but Byron was worse:

Mr. Anacreon Moore, a gentleman of great mind and small dimensions, has certainly a peculiar knack of writing little sonnets and epistles, that is to say, although his compositions are all gross nonsense, yet they are pleasant in their way; and if a man likes to be tickled with straws, he may find some amusement in reading them; but here *George Gordon Lord Byron, a minor,* presents us with a frightful ghost, an apparition of Moore, all his "soul-breathing glances," "blest inspirations," and "dearest remembrances," are breathed out of an inanimate spiritless string of stanzas, which all the brilliancy of the one is not able to enliven, nor all the *hard labour* of the other's *idleness* capable of making common sense.[33]

At this point, emulating Moore must have seemed to Byron a singularly unprofitable pursuit. He was condemned for his similarity to Moore on the one hand and for his inferiority to Moore on the other.

Doubtless frustrated by these comparisons and by the critical displeasure that his "poesies erotiques" continued to provoke, Byron omitted several of the remaining amatory poems in his second edition of *Hours of Idleness,* which appeared in March 1808 and was entitled *Poems, Original and Translated.* Of the seven poems dropped from the edition, four were after the style of Little: "The First Kiss of Love," "To a Beautiful Quaker," "Love's Last Adieu!" and "To a Lady, who Presented the Author with a Lock of Hair." Byron also omitted "Answer to Some Elegant Verses, Sent by a Friend to the Author, complaining that one of his descriptions was rather too warmly drawn," which had been written in response to Reverend Becher's criticism of *Fugitive Pieces.* Of the two other omissions, "Childish Recollections" was dropped for a special reason: Byron had reconciled with Dr. George Butler, whom he had satirized as "Pomposus" in that poem.

Although it is clear that the chief aim of Byron's omissions was once again to reduce the number of amatory poems, Byron did add one poem defiantly proclaiming that his admiration for Moore's love poetry was still strong. According to Byron, "To the Earl of [Clare]" was composed "soon after the appearance of a severe critique in a Northern review, on a new publication of the British Anacreon," meaning that of Jeffrey upon *Epistles, Odes and Other Poems* (*BCP* 1:372). In this poem Byron closely associates his own amorous writing with that of Little, but also reveals his somewhat ambivalent attitude toward Moore's influence:

7.

'Tis mine to waste on love my time,

Or vent my reveries in rhyme,

Without the aid of Reason;

> For Sense and Reason, (Critics know it,)
> Have quitted every amorous Poet,
>   Nor left a thought to seize on.
>
>   8.
> Poor LITTLE! sweet, melodious bard!
> Of late esteem'd it monstrous hard,
>   That he, who sang before all;
> He who the lore of love expanded,
> By dire Reviewers should be branded,
>   As void of wit and moral.
>
>   9.
> And yet, while Beauty's praise is thine,
> Harmonious favourite of the nine!
>   Repine not at thy lot;
> Thy soothing lays may still be read,
> When Persecution's arm is dead,
>   And Critics are forgot.   (ll. 37–54)

These verses praise Moore's talent and chastise his critics, but not before declaring Byron's generally negative opinion of the worth of amorous poetry. Although "Critics" know that amorous poets are bereft of "Sense and Reason" and although critics are explicitly mocked in the poem, still the irony of stanza seven is undercut when in stanza ten Byron writes, "Still, I must yield those worthies merit, / Who chasten with unsparing spirit, / Bad rhymes, and those who write them," and makes it clear that the "bad rhymes" these "worthies" censure are immoral ones (ll. 55–66).

By the time Byron's fourth volume appeared, the name of Thomas Moore (or Little) had become unavoidably associated with indecent and immoral poetry. Moore had been humiliated in the *Edinburgh Review,* in his duel with Jeffrey, and in the daily newspapers. He had fled the ridicule to which he felt exposed in London and gone back to Ireland to consider his next move. Although Moore's disasters had already occurred when Byron printed *Fugitive Pieces,* Moore's poetry had influenced Byron's so strongly that there was no hiding it, nor did Byron want to. However, beginning with the scandalized reactions of Rev. Becher and the rest of Southwell, Byron became increasingly aware of the dangers of being compared to Moore and being labeled an immoral poet. These dangers, along with Byron's natural desire to create his own distinctive poetic voice, apparently led him to attempt to refine the traces of Moore out of his collected poems. Yet there is no evidence that Byron's personal admiration for Moore's works had actually lessened by 1808, and his addition of "To the Earl of [Clare]" to *Poems, Original and Translated* in that year strongly suggests that it had not.

Byron was still apparently drawing comparisons between his own poems and Little's while compiling his new volume, however much he felt the necessity of removing the remaining amatory verses. Byron wrote to his publisher John Ridge on 11 November 1807 of that year to discuss the printing of *Poems, Original and Translated,* and, having been told by booksellers that his new volume ought to be smaller, Byron significantly requested that "the next Edition shall be printed & *bound* in the same manner, & in the same coloured Boards as Little" (*BLJ* 1:137). Byron seems to have had some difficulty deciding whether to invite or discourage comparisons of himself with a poet whom he loved but with whom he had become wary of being associated.

IV

The conventional wisdom of critics about the pernicious tendency of Moore's work fit in too well with Byron's general critique of modern literature for Byron to spare the "sweet, melodious bard" in *English Bards and Scotch Reviewers,* published in March 1809. Whatever his personal feelings, the inclusion of the notorious Little in his sweeping censure of England's degraded standards of taste was presumably too tempting a prospect. *Little's Poems* had become a byword for lowbrow poetry, and if Byron had avoided mentioning the still-popular and reprinted volume it would have seemed a strange omission. At any rate Byron was determined to ridicule Jeffrey for his abortive duel, and it would have been impossible to leave out Moore's embarrassing involvement in that affair.

An even more important factor influencing his satire of Moore was Byron's apparent determination in the face of ridicule to decisively abandon the sentimental, feminine, Little-esque style for its opposite, the intellectual, masculine, Popeian voice. Moore asserted in his biography that Byron deliberately set out to cultivate this new style: "Among the preparatives by which he disciplined his mind to the task was a deep study of the writings of Pope; and I have no doubt that from this period may be dated the enthusiastic admiration which he ever after cherished for this great poet" (*MLB* 1:157). Moore's close friendship with Byron lends the perfect confidence of this assertion a particular authority, as is the case with many of Moore's judgments regarding Byron. Examining Byron's youthful poetry (and his image of himself as poet) as an ultimately productive struggle between the extremes of Moore and Pope is a critical tactic that has never been adequately pursued.

Thomas Little is first mentioned in *English Bards* when Byron's satiric speaker complains of the volume of books flooding from the presses: "No dearth of Bards can be complained of now. . . . While SOUTHEY's Epics cram the creaking shelves, / And LITTLE's Lyrics shine in hot-pressed twelves" (ll. 124; 127–28). The sound of the couplet suggests the contrast between the massive size of Southey's epics and the small duodecimos of Little, but the coupling of Little with Southey also suggests their similar degree of worthlessness. On the whole, though, Byron treats Moore with comparative gentleness, and in truth Byron's occasional approving comments about Southey in subsequent years demonstrate that a considerable measure of insincerity pervades the whole poem. After contemptuously upbraiding Scott, Southey, Wordsworth, Coleridge, and M. G. Lewis, Byron comes to Moore:

> Who in soft guise, surrounded by a choir
> Of virgins melting, not to Vesta's fire,
> With sparkling eyes, and cheek by passion flush'd,
> Strikes his wild Lyre, whilst listening dames are hush'd?
> 'Tis LITTLE! young Catullus of his day,
> As sweet, but as immoral in his lay!
> Griev'd to condemn, the Muse must still be just,
> Nor spare melodious advocates of lust.
> Pure is the flame which o'er her altar burns;
> From grosser incense with disgust she turns:
> Yet, kind to youth, this expiation o'er,
> She bids thee, "mend thy line, and sin no more."   (ll. 283–94)

According to the canceled "Argument" that Byron originally intended to precede the poem, "the Poet" "revileth" Scott, "complaineth" about Southey, "inveigheth" against Wordsworth, "vituperate[s]" Lewis, but "gently rebuketh Thomas Little (the late)" (*BCP* 1:401).

Byron calls Little's verses as sweet as Catullus's, and as for Byron's rebuke to Little's "immorality," Byron later confessed to Moore in a letter of 29 January 1812: "Why do you say I dislike your poetry? I have expressed no such opinion, either in *print* or elsewhere. In scribbling myself, it was necessary to find fault, and I fixed on the trite charge of immorality, because I could discover no other" (*BLJ* 2:160). By Byron's own admission, his "motives" for writing *English Bards* were merely that "I was angry—& determined to be witty—& fighting in a crowd dealt my blows against all alike without distinction or discernment" (4:320). Byron's determination to be witty made him willing to feign deliberately a resentment he did not really feel. Byron's speaker is "griev'd to condemn" Little; he is not openly hostile as he is to most of the other poets he excoriates. The description of his performance in lines 283–86 could have been far more judgmental; instead of portraying merely an erotic atmosphere, Byron could have followed other critics of Moore and painted the scene as a bordello or seraglio.

Later in the poem Byron's speaker chides Lord Strangford for copying Moore and imagines adolescent girls abandoning William Lisle Bowles's "whining" love poetry "for LITTLE'S purer strain" (ll. 347–48). The description of the duel between Jeffrey and Moore is sixty-three lines long, but Moore is mentioned in only two lines, and Byron's object in writing the section is clearly to ridicule Jeffrey, whom Byron blamed for the *Edinburgh Review*'s devastating article on *Hours of Idleness*. Byron told Thomas Medwin that "in the duel-scene I had unconsciously made part of the ridicule fall on Moore."[34] "When LITTLE's leadless pistol met his eye" was the line that most provoked Moore, along with Byron's note: "In 1806, Messrs. Jeffrey and Moore met at Chalk Farm. The duel was prevented by the interference of the Magistracy; and, on examination, the balls of the pistols, like the courage of the combatants, were found to have evaporated. This incident gave occasion to much waggery in the daily prints." On 4 November 1811, the day of his first meeting with Moore, Byron wrote a new note to replace the one that offended Moore: "I am informed that Mr. Moore published at the time a disavowal of these statements in the newspapers as far as regarded himself, and in justice to him I mention this circumstance: as I never heard of it before, I cannot state the particulars, and was only made acquainted with the fact very lately" (*BCP* 1:407). This note was intended for the fifth edition, which Byron soon decided to suppress when he began to be accepted into the Holland House circle of Whig writers and politicians that he had mocked in his satire.

Byron happened to meet Moore at a time just before Moore's circle declared a war of satire against the Prince Regent and the Tories, and it was in the intimate company of Moore that Byron moved into the next stage of his poetic career. In the winter of 1811–12 Byron and Moore, setting aside the lyrical escapism of Little, became known instead as Whig poets.

"Our political malice"

Political Verse and Satires

In August 1824 William Maginn, in an article in *Blackwood's Edinburgh Magazine* entitled "Profligacy of the London Periodical Press," held up Byron and Moore as prime examples of the "natural filthiness of the Whig spirit." The article accused the two poets of being for many years the most "unsparing and . . . unfeeling" of the satirists and "libeller[s]" of the Tories. Moore was condemned for having written the "infamous" *Twopenny Post-Bag* and *The Fudge Family in Paris* (a "vile personal attack upon private life," "scraped up" from "all the rancorous records of political hate"), and for the "scurrilous and unmanly wit" of the many political squibs he wrote for the *Morning Chronicle*. Byron's chief offenses were said to be his "heartless rascality" about Castlereagh's suicide and his ridicule of Robert Southey and the other Tory Lakers in *Don Juan*. Maginn expressed his outrage over these publications, asking: "In a word, is there anything that has ever been said or feigned of the atrocity and recklessness of uncalled-for libel which cannot be matched from the writings of the two most eminent of the Whig poets?"[1]

To recover this image of Byron and Moore as "the two most eminent of the Whig poets"—as writers strongly identified with the Whig party and associated by their contemporaries as much for this fact as for their friendship and their art—is to begin to restore an important measure of historical context to the modern study of their works. In *England in 1819*, James Chandler observes that "Moore's extreme invisibility to modern readers, even to modern literary historians of the Romantic period, has made his role in . . . Byron's own satiric work—difficult to recognize."[2] Literary scholars today rarely look for connections between the topical and political satires of Byron and those of Moore, but it was common during Byron's lifetime for observers of the literary scene to refer to their similar subject matter and partisan motivation. Byron's dedication of *The Corsair* to Moore in 1814 ensured that Byron's declaration of his own poetical Whiggism occurred in the specific context of his personal relationship with Moore, a circumstance that firmly established the two poets as political allies in the public consciousness. Byron was always amused and sometimes inspired by Moore's political verse and learned to adapt elements of Moore's general satirical approach to his own writings. Both writers were pleased to be known as Whig poets and used their satires not only to attack the policies of the Prince Regent and his conservative allies but to ridicule them personally, even to the extent of mocking their physical defects, as in the case of the Regent's corpulence and Castlereagh's rumored impotence. The extent to which their similarly irreverent abuse of the Prince Regent united Byron and Moore in most people's minds is demonstrated by the editor's remark in an 1850s American edition of Moore's collected works: "George the Fourth has certainly as fair a chance of immortality as any sovereign that ever lived, since Byron and Moore, the two wittiest and most popular poets of his times have made him the subject of their unsparing sarcasms."[3] Byron's and Moore's congenial Whiggism was so well known that hostile critics sometimes accused the two poets of subversive collusion; in 1823, after reviewing Byron's anti–Holy Alliance satire "Age of Bronze" and noting that Moore's own satirical *Fables for the Holy Alliance* would soon be published, the *Literary Gazette* claimed that Byron and Moore formed "one poetical association or manufactory established on the same principles, and working together for the same purposes."[4]

Byron and Moore both began to practice their poetical "Whiggism" in earnest during Byron's years of fame in England. Moore first became widely known as a Whig poet (that is, one whose poetry was generally thought to be overtly informed by his Whig partisanship) in 1812, the year he wrote his privately circulated "Parody of a Celebrated Letter" and began writing political squibs for the *Morning Chronicle*. Byron had been known to be a Whig legislator since his debut in the House of Lords, but he was not generally considered to be a Whig poet until 1814, when he published *The Corsair* with its provocative dedication to Moore and its acknowledgment of Byron's authorship of the anti-Regent "Lines to a Lady Weeping." In the years before his exile Byron believed Moore to be England's best satirist, and he tried to write topical political satire of the type Moore was writing only to find his own attempts in this vein unsatisfactory. It was not until *Beppo* in 1818 and the first cantos of *Don Juan* in 1819 that Byron successfully incorporated the lessons of Moore's colloquial, Horatian, sociopolitical approach into his own distinctive satirical style and vision.

I

When Byron and Moore met in 1811, Moore was moving socially in the very midst of the Whig party's inner circle and was deeply interested in and knowledgeable about its machinations and strategies. Moore was friendly with some of the most prominent figures in the Whig party, including the moderate Whig leader Lord Holland, the Earl of Moira, the Marquis of Lansdowne, and the Duke of Bedford. His letters from the period are full of political reflection and speculation, and he sought political information from whomever he could get it. Byron was not politically ignorant at this time: he imagined himself as a future statesman; he joined the Whig club at Cambridge; he read parliamentary debates and history; and he attended parliament seven times before leaving on his grand tour. Yet as late as 15 January 1809 Byron, in reference to his entrance into the House of Lords, could still tell John Hanson, "I cannot say that my opinion is strongly in favor of either party" (*BLJ* 1:186). Three years later, Byron's strong identification with the Whigs and the development of his particular ideas about specific political issues as he began to pursue his parliamentary career in earnest were most likely positively influenced by his frequent conversations with Moore in 1811–12. Politics was a constant theme in the two poets' letters to each other, and at times Moore urged Byron to speak out in his role as a legislator. In his biography of Byron, Moore noted that in early 1814, when Byron had largely lost interest in speaking in Parliament, Moore "endeavored to persuade him to take a part in parliamentary affairs, and to exercise his talent for oratory more frequently" (*MLB* 1:531). On 16 February 1814 Byron replied to a letter from Moore, "I shall think about your *oratorical* hint; but I have never set much upon 'that cast'" (*BLJ* 4:63).

Moore's and Byron's political philosophies were very similar. In 1812 both were somewhat more liberal than the mainstream Whigs and somewhat more conservative than the Radical faction that was beginning to take shape.[5] Both poets romanticized and admired Napoleon, resented Wellington, and despised the Tories, the Prince Regent, Castlereagh, the Bourbon dynasty, and the political apostasy of the Lake Poets. They ridiculed the infirm Louis Dix-huit of France, Moore calling him "Louis des huîtres," which amused Byron, who was himself fond of calling him "Louis the Gouty."[6] Byron and Moore saw themselves as opponents of civil oppression and religious intolerance; Moore was Irish and culturally Catholic (although intellectually a skeptic like Byron), and so had encountered both forms of injustice at first hand. Both poets called themselves Jacobins in 1812 but, in practice, shunned all but what Byron called "the genteel part of the Reformers" (*BLJ* 7:44). Both strongly admired the aristocratic rebel Lord Edward Fitzgerald, whose biography Moore would publish in 1831.[7] They applauded revolutionary movements in foreign countries such as Italy and Greece, but shared a disdain for English radicals, whom Byron called "low designing dirty levellers" (*BLJ* 7:99). Byron made the distinction, "I am and have been for *reform* always—but not for the *reformers*" (6:166), a sentiment Moore shared, having himself often objected to the populist radicalism of the Irish separatist Daniel O'Connell. Both men were uneasily suspended between hatred of tyranny from above and fear of anarchy from below, and in this sense they personally struggled with the great clash between "genteel" and popular reform that would lead to crisis in the Whig party following passage of the Reform Act in 1832.

This political moderation is the reason why Byron and Moore were regarded by most people as "Whig poets" rather than "revolutionary poets," and the reason why they wrote such poems as *The Corsair* and *The Veiled Prophet of Khorassan,* which expressed ambivalence or even pessimism about revolution, rather than such unabashedly "Jacobinical" poems such as Percy Shelley's *Queen Mab* or *The Revolt of Islam.* The enduring myth of Byron as enthusiastic revolutionary that took root after Byron's "martyrdom" at Missolonghi has been largely dissipated in the twentieth century by critics such as David V. Erdman, Leslie Marchand, and Malcolm Kelsall.[8] Byron's preference for the practical over the ideal was another quality that made him retain his Whig "buff and blue"; this practicality also convinced him it was more useful to satirize real politicians and ministers in his poetry than to tilt at grand abstractions. In 1870 John Morley placed Byron "among the most essentially political" of "all English poets" because of what he called Byron's "quality of poetical *worldliness,* in its enlarged and generous sense of energetic interest in real transactions, and a capacity of being moved and raised by them."[9] Morley could just as easily have used the same words to describe Moore, whose scores of poems on the political issues of the month or even of the week are all far from the abstraction and idealism of a poem like *Prometheus Unbound.*

Byron and Moore each insisted on the moral superiority of great statesmen to great poets, but neither was able to achieve a satisfactory political role. The electors of Limerick offered Moore a seat in the House of Commons in 1832 (an offer made possible by Catholic Emancipation), but Moore was forced to decline because he insisted on the freedom to vote independently of the wishes of any party. Byron's own ambition for parliamentary success was quenched by the indifferent reception of his 1812 and 1813 speeches in the House of Lords and his conclusion that "the whole thing is a grand deception—and as tedious and tiresome as may be to those who must often be present" (*BLJ* 9:11). Quickly deciding that "parliamentary mummeries" (*BLJ* 3:206) were fruitless and frustrating, he turned to his poetry as a vehicle for his political sentiments. In 1818 he would recall that in the years following 1812 he "wrote from . . . the love of fame (not as an *end* but as a *means* to obtain that influence over men's minds—which is power in itself & in it's consequences)" (*BLJ* 6:61).

Prior to the period in late 1811 and early 1812 that marked the beginning of both Byron's parliamentary career and his friendship with Moore, Byron wrote poetry that, while political, nevertheless tended to avoid directly engaging the *specific* political issues and personalities of his time. *Hints from Horace,* finished on 12 March 1811, dealt with literary rather than political abuses.[10] Byron began *The Curse of Minerva* at Athens on 18 March 1811, but almost certainly did not compose any of its savage attack on English foreign and domestic policies (ll. 211–312) until around 17 November 1811, after he had met Moore and during a period when (by Moore's account) the two poets were seeing each other almost daily.[11] The first two cantos of *Childe Harold,* written and revised before Byron's return to England on 14 July 1811, had as their backdrop the Peninsular War and the Turkish domination of Greece, but treated the English role in contemporary events with a much greater degree of emotional distance and abstraction than he would employ in much of his later poetry. The poem's observations of the state of the modern world in cantos I and II are for the most part elegiac and melancholy rather than satiric, and therefore any sustained or detailed indictment of English politics or politicians is notably absent.[12]

Although Byron was tentative about introducing political allusions into his poems up until late 1811, the political content of Moore's poems steadily increased during the same period. In the five-year interval between the publication of *Epistles, Odes and Other Poems* in 1806 and his first meeting with Byron, the direction of Moore's art took a sharp turn away from erotics and toward politics. In 1807 Moore told his friend Lady Donegal:

> "To God's pleasure and both our comforts," . . . I am not writing *love-verses*. I begin at last to find out that *politics* is the only thing minded in this country, and that it is better even to *rebel* against government, than to have nothing at all to do with it; so I am writing politics: but all I fear is, that my former ill-luck will rise up against me in a new shape, and that as I could not write *love* without getting into ——, so I shall not be able to write politics without getting into *treason*. (*ML* 1:120–21)

In April 1808 the first of his new attempts at political art appeared in the form of the first two installments of his series *A Selection of Irish Melodies*. These two collections of songs boldly celebrated Irish nationalism and included laments for Lord Edward Fitzgerald and Robert Emmet, fallen heroes of the 1798 and 1803 Irish rebellions. Despite their political undertones, Moore's *Melodies* were a tremendous success and eight more installments were published between 1808 and 1834. They became a fixture in virtually every English or Irish home where the pianoforte was played or songs were sung, and Moore's impassioned performances of his music ensured that his presence at London parties was more in demand than ever.

In his 1810 dedication to the third number of the *Melodies*, Moore alluded to England's "bigotry and misrule," and to "the zeal with which [Ireland] has always loved liberty, and the barbarous policy which has always withheld it from her" (*MCP* 4:118), and he defended his songs against newspaper articles that had attacked their "mischievous" political tendency:

> To those who identify nationality with treason, and who see, in every effort for Ireland, a system of hostility toward England,—to those too, who, nursed in the gloom of prejudice, are alarmed by the faintest gleam of liberality that threatens to disturb their darkness . . . to such men I shall not deign to apologize for the warmth of any political sentiment which may occur in the course of these

pages. . . . [The *Irish Melodies* are purchased by] many, whose nerves may be, now and then, alarmed with advantage, as much more is to be gained by their fears, than could ever be expected from their justice. (4:129–30)

In his "Advertisement" for the fourth number (1811), Moore responded to a rumor that the Protestant Irish government had tried to prevent the publication of further installments, by wryly observing, "There is no truth to the report; and we trust that whatever belief it obtained was founded more upon the character of *the Government* than of *the Work*" (4:134).

As it was not safe for Moore's lyrics to refer directly to England's mistreatment of Ireland, Moore cleverly wrote many of his love songs in such a way that their references to abandoned or betrayed lovers would be read as metaphors for Ireland's plight. For instance, Moore told Power in June 1814 that his song "When first I met thee" was "on the *Prince's desertion of Ireland,* and done so as to appear like a Love-Song, in the manner of some other political ones in the Collection" (*ML* 1:317). This song was particularly daring as it was also generally understood to refer to the Regent's abandonment of Mrs. Fitzherbert, a low-born Roman Catholic whom he had secretly married and then divorced. As *Blackwood's Edinburgh Magazine* recalled in 1853, Moore in these years "had *two* formidable means of attack—the press and the piano: the public had the satire, the world of fashion had the song."[13]

In 1808, the same year that the first two numbers of the *Irish Melodies* appeared, Moore also published "Corruption and Intolerance, Two Poems," a pair of Juvenalian satires that attacked the secular and religious abuses afflicting English politics. At the time, Moore announced "Intolerance" to be only the first in a series of poems on the subject. The year 1809 brought "The Sceptic: A Philosophical Satire," in which Moore imagined the Whigs and Tories as the two biblical thieves with "Freedom's form hang[ing] crucified between" (ll. 75–76). In January 1810 the third number of *Irish Melodies* was published, and also in 1810 Moore published his first prose work, *A Letter to the Roman Catholics of Dublin,* in which he urged his countrymen not to ruin their chances for emancipation by demanding too much too soon. The following year brought the fourth *Irish Melodies* and the performance of his comic opera *M.P.; or, The Blue-Stocking,* which dealt with Sir Charles Canvas, an unscrupulous seeker and dispenser of parliamentary patronage. According to Moore, *M.P.* "underwent a very severe cutting from the Licensor for the very opposite quality to Courtiership" (*ML* 1:158). All of these works dealt with contemporary politics in one way or another, setting the stage for Moore's full emergence as a committed Whig satirist in 1812.

II

By the time of their first meeting in November 1811, Byron had barely written a line of political satire, whereas Moore had written political satires, a polemical tract, a political farce, and many perilously political lyrics. In his *Lord Byron as a Satirist in Verse,* Claude M. Fuess observes that "not until after . . . the beginning of his friendship with Moore, Hunt, and other active Whigs, did [Byron's] interest in politics revive and his pen become a party weapon."[14] Fuess's claim for Moore's stimulation of Byron's party writing is sound, although his claim for Hunt is less so; Byron did not meet Hunt until 20 May 1813, over a year after Byron had begun writing squibs for the Whig *Morning Chronicle.* In any event, Byron had the desire to write political satire and Moore had the experience, and their personal relationship and harmony of thought probably would have impelled both to write this type of poetry even if the period of their first acquaintance had been politically uneventful.

As it happened, however, it was the political events of the year 1812 that chiefly launched Byron and Moore upon their careers as allied Whig poets. The two poets met during a period of great anticipation on the part of the opposition Whigs, who had been (and would remain) out of power for the entirety of Byron's life. Early in 1811, following King George III's latest attack of madness, Parliament had recognized the Prince of Wales as acting sovereign, but had placed restrictions upon his power. These restrictions were due to expire on 5 February 1812, and since the Prince had been a Whig all his life the Whigs expected that February would bring a change of administration and their long-awaited elevation to power. The Prince was even said to have designed a new court uniform in the Whig colors of buff and blue. However, the timidity and indecision of the despised Prince ultimately led him to declare that he would leave the Tories in office. He announced this decision on 13 February 1812 in a letter to his brother the Duke of York, cynically protesting that a change of ministry might further damage the King's health.

The Whigs were stunned by the Prince Regent's unexpected betrayal. Byron's great contempt for the Regent dates from this period, but Moore had an even stronger reaction. Moore knew that the retention of the Tories meant that there was now no hope in sight for the emancipation of the Catholics or the freedom of the Irish. Moore was also angry because he had been hoping for years to gain political influence through his friendship with the Earl of Moira, whom everyone had expected to be made lord lieutenant of Ireland in a new Whig administration. That hope was now crushed. Moore was bitter, but he also felt liberated now that his slim but long-held hopes of political advancement were over. On 6 March 1812 he told his friend Mary Godfrey: "*I,* thank Heaven! (and it consoles me for my poverty) am free to call a rascal a rascal wherever I find him, and never was I better disposed to make use of my privilege" (*ML* 1:179).

In late 1811 Moore had experimented with at least one "*wickedly* political" poem and had thought of sending it to Leigh Hunt's *Reflector* (*ML* 1:158). Moore had already decided to abandon his attempts at what he called "the stately, Juvenalian style of satire," partly because "Corruption and Intolerance" and "The Sceptic" had had disappointing sales, the former only achieving a second printing and the latter not even that.[15] When the Regent betrayed the Whigs, Moore leapt to the attack, choosing, as he later recalled, a "lighter form of weapon" that was "not only more easy to wield, but, from its very lightness, perhaps, more sure to reach its mark" (*MCP* 3:vi). This change of style produced "Parody of a Celebrated Letter," a comical travesty of the Regent's letter to the Duke of York announcing the retention of the Tories. Moore tried to persuade his friend James Perry, editor of the Whig *Morning Chronicle,* to publish the "Parody" in his newspaper, but Perry was too frightened of possible prosecution. Eventually Moore convinced him to print several copies of the poem for private circulation[16] and then sent the anonymous poem off to his Whig friends. That evening, on 6 March 1812,[17] Moore went to a large dinner at Holland House and, without revealing his authorship to anyone but Lord Holland, quietly reveled in the delight and excitement at the poem expressed by all the other Whig luminaries in attendance. The poem quickly circulated throughout London; on 8 March Leigh Hunt published it in the *Examiner,* and at some point it was printed as a broadside headed by a Cruikshank print and retitled "A Parody on an Original Letter from a Certain Personage to a Bishop."[18]

"Parody of a Celebrated Letter" (probably composed sometime between 13 and 29 February)[19] was the first major shot fired in a barrage of Whig attacks upon the Regent and his government, and the beginning of what

Moore would refer to years later as "my long course of Anti-Tory warfare" (*MCP* 9:iv). Moore's 120-line poem was written in the persona of the Regent and used some phrases from the Regent's actual letter to the Duke of York:

> I need not remind you how cursedly bad
> Our affairs were all looking, when Father went mad;
> A strait waistcoat on him and restrictions on me,
> A more *limited* Monarchy could not well be.
> I was call'd upon then, in that moment of puzzle,
> To choose my own Minister—just as they muzzle
> A playful young bear, and then mock his disaster,
> By bidding him choose out his own dancing-master.   (ll. 19–26)

The poem mocked the Regent's superficiality and stupidity and implied that he was impatient for his father's death. The Regent was made to boast ironically that the neutrality of his temper kept him "royally free of all troublesome feelings" and "little encumber'd by faith in [his] dealings":

> I am proud to declare I have no predilections,
> My heart is a sieve, where some scatter'd affections
> Are just danc'd about for a moment or two,
> And the *finer* they are, the more sure to run through:
> Neither feel I resentments, nor wish there should come ill
> To mortal—except (now I think on't) Beau Br[u]mm[e]l,
> Who threaten'd last year, in a superfine passion,
> To cut *me*, and bring the old K[i]ng into fashion.   (ll. 87–94)

"Scatter'd affections" suggested to contemporary readers not only the Regent's political betrayals but his domestic ones as well: he had abandoned not only Mrs. Fitzherbert but also Queen Caroline, whom he left the day after their wedding. Brummel's falling-out with the Regent was real and well known, and the suggestion that the Regent's thoughts were more occupied with being "cut" by the dictator of English fashion than with the affairs of the nation or the war with Napoleon was entirely credible to Moore's readers.

Moore's decision to give up his former Juvenalian tone in favor of the more relaxed jesting of Horatian satire was as shrewd as it was important. It showed that Moore understood that the classical voice of public address was no longer appropriate for a society as riven by conflicting ideas and discourses as was Regency England. Though it would take time for Byron to accept this, Moore realized that magisterial pronouncements about church

and state had become too easy to dismiss or ignore, and that Augustan couplets—Moore called them "the Popish sing-song" (*MJ* 1:199)—had begun to
seem stale and inert. More important, as Gary Dyer points out in his *British
Satire and the Politics of Style, 1789–1832,* it was conservatives who were "the
most inclined toward Juvenalian writing," because a univocal and ex cathe-
dra style had the rhetorical effect of "reproduc[ing] their authoritarianism
formally."[20] The irresistible comedy of Moore's "Parody" and of the later
satires of the *Twopenny Post-Bag* established a more readable, more popular
and colloquial model for other liberal satires on the Regent and his allies
to follow. Moore's most important inspirations for this mode were probably
Christopher Anstey's *New Bath Guide; or Memoirs of the B—r—d Family* (1766)
and the anonymous *Groans of the Talents* (1809). The former volume presented a series of anapestic mock epistles from different ludicrous characters, a scheme Moore borrowed for his "Parody," the *Twopenny Post-Bag,* and
the *Fudge Family in Paris,* and both the Ansteyan versification and the structure of *Groans of the Talents* are employed by Moore in the *Post-Bag.* Several
satirists before Moore had imitated Anstey, but Fuess and other critics have
agreed that it was Moore who perfected the style; in his *Political Satire in English Poetry* C. W. Previté-Orton claims that Moore "must always retain the
credit of the invention of the rapid, sparkling style of satire."[21] Dyer catego-
rizes Moore's style as "Radical verse satire," meaning, essentially, that it tends
toward the "multi-voiced" or dialogic rather than the univocal, and that its
usually light tone conceals a very serious reformist purpose (a concealment
partly necessary because of the threat of prosecution). Dyer acutely notes
that always "behind Moore's apparent playfulness lie his disgust and anger."[22]

On 29 February 1812 Byron told Samuel Rogers: "Your epigrammatic example[23] has set Moore & me scribbling, I send you the fruits of *my* midnight
buffoonery, forgive me.—I don't know whether you have seen M[oore]'s
parody, it is without exception the best thing of ye kind I ever heard or read"
(*BLJ* 11:180). The "*parody*" was almost certainly "Parody of a Celebrated Letter."[24] It is likely that the poem Byron sent to Rogers was "Ode to the Framers
of the Frame-Bill," published two days later in the *Morning Chronicle* (Byron
could not have published it the next day because the *Chronicle* had no Sunday
issue). If this was indeed the case, perhaps the "Ode" was written during one
of Byron's and Moore's late nights at Watier's gambling club, or at Stevens's,
while Moore worked on his "Parody" (or some other poem) on the other side

of the table. Whatever poem Byron sent to Rogers, Byron's letter suggests that Byron and Moore began "scribbling" political poems for the purpose of amusing others as well as themselves. Moore wrote a letter to Byron suggesting that they begin a satirical correspondence (the letter is from sometime in January or February):

> I have a most immortalizing scheme to propose to you—or rather, what is better, a most amusing one—in the literary way—You & I shall write Epistles to each other—in all measures and all styles upon all possible subjects—laugh at the world—weep for ourselves—quiz the humbugs—scarify the scoundrels—in short do every thing that the mixture of fun & philosophy there is in both of us can inspire. . . . [I]t would bring out every thing we might publish or not, comme vous voudrez. (*ML* 1:176)

Moore's offer of a poetical partnership must have been flattering to Byron, who at that time had not yet published anything noteworthy except *Hours of Idleness* and *English Bards*. Moore's reference to humbugs and scoundrels indicates that he envisioned their epistles to be of a mostly political cast, most likely along the lines of the "Parody" and the satirical epistles that would comprise Moore's *Intercepted Letters; or, The Twopenny Post-Bag*, published a year later in 1813.

Starting in February or March 1812 Moore began publishing short, anonymous (or pseudonymous) political satires in the *Morning Chronicle*.[25] Moore republished eighteen of these widely read poems in his 1813 *Intercepted Letters; or, The Twopenny Post-Bag* and also included them in later editions of his collected works. Unsigned or initialed squibs appeared in the *Chronicle* almost daily during March, April, and May, and steadily in later months, and many of these poems were probably also written by Moore, although positively identifying many of them as Moore's is now difficult if not impossible.[26] Byron also contributed at least three poems to the *Morning Chronicle* that spring: "Ode to the Framers of the Frame Bill" (2 March), "Impromptu on a Recent Incident" (6 March),[27] and "Sympathetic Address to a Young Lady" (7 March). The "Young Lady" of the last poem was Princess Charlotte, who had supposedly burst into tears over the treachery of her father at a Carlton House banquet on 22 February where the Regent petulantly abused his quondam Whig allies. "Impromptu" also dealt with this episode. It may have been Moore who suggested that Byron submit these three poems, since Byron probably did not then know the editor James Perry, with whom Moore was on friendly terms (a year later Moore wrote to Perry, "Lord Byron has just called upon me & begs I will use my interest with you to insert the inclosed report of a Speech he has just spoken—as he considers my influence with you very great, you will oblige me by *confirming* him in the idea").[28] Leigh Hunt's publication of Moore's "Parody of a Celebrated Letter" in the *Examiner* on 8 March, the day after the appearance of Byron's "Address," must have pleased both poets.

There is some evidence that Byron's "Sympathetic Address to a Young Lady" could have been directly inspired by Moore's political indignation. In his 1824 *Recollections of the Life of Lord Byron,* Robert Charles Dallas suggested that Byron's hostility to the Regent in 1812 was partly due to the influence of a "newly-made friend," and he believed Byron's "harsh verses" against the Regent (probably the "Address") were "composed more to humour his new friend's passions than his own." Dallas also surmised that it was because of this person that Byron "fell into the habit of speaking disrespectfully of the Prince."[29] Moore seems a very likely candidate for this "new friend," since the "Address" was written at a time when Moore's "squib-warfare" was beginning in earnest and when by Byron's own account he and Moore were scribbling "buffooner[ies]." Moore read this passage of Dallas's book in 1824, and noted in his journal: "It occurred to me that by the 'newly-made friend,' he mentions who turned Lord B. out of the path of courtiership into which Dallas thinks he was so laudably entering at one time, he must have meant *me,* and so Lord Jersey thought. But Lord L[ansdowne], at dinner, said it was quite as likely to be Lady Jersey; and so, upon reconsideration, I have no doubt it is. A good deal of laughing with her about this" (*MJ* 2:775). Moore's professed change of mind about this may have been owing to his modesty or his desire to please Lady Jersey, with whom he was dining at the time. Moore's initial response, as well as that of Lady Jersey's husband, is perhaps more telling.

The identity of the "newly-made friend" must remain conjectural, since Dallas's account, as David Erdman points out, is deliberately left ambiguous.[30] If the "friend" was not Moore, the only other likely candidate is not Lady Jersey but rather Byron's lover, the liberal Lady Oxford. Still, Rowland E. Prothero endorsed the thesis that Moore was primarily responsible for Byron's Whig sentiments, suggesting that the "Address" "rather betrayed the influence of Moore than expressed [Byron's] own feelings at the time."[31] An interesting comment on the causes of Byron's political orientation during his

years of fame comes from Walter Scott, who, recalling his acquaintance with
Byron in the spring of 1815, observed that "on politics, he used to express a
high strain of what is now called Liberalism; but it appeared to me that the
pleasure it afforded him as a vehicle for displaying his wit and satire against
individuals in office was at the bottom of this habit of thinking, rather than any
real conviction of the political principles on which he talked" (*MLB* 1:616).
Doubtless Scott exaggerates, but nevertheless, if one enjoyed "displaying
[one's] wit and satire against individuals in office," taking up arms with Moore
and the Whigs at this moment was the perfect opportunity.

Byron's three *Chronicle* squibs were published without his name, and since
it became generally known that most of the anonymous satires in that newspaper were Moore's, the Prince Regent reportedly assumed that the "Sympathetic Address" was written by Moore (*BLJ* 4:51). Nevertheless, there were
rumors of Byron's involvement in the Whig "squib-warfare," as is demonstrated by a letter from Mary Berry to the Countess of Hardwicke on 16 March
(which also provides a vivid picture of the attacks on the Regent that spring):
"The author of the versification of the letter [the "Parody"] is little Anacreon, not avowedly, but certainly. You must see likewise a certain vision, said
to be by Lord Byron, as well as some lines on the Princess Charlotte's tears at
the *far-famed dinner*, and the *triumph of the whale* in the 'Examiner' of last Sunday. The prose squibs and abuse are endless. People begin to look grave at
the license taken."[32] (The "vision" may have been Moore's "Anacreontic. To a
Plumassier," published in the *Chronicle* the same day that Berry's letter was
written; "The Triumph of the Whale" was Charles Lamb's, printed in the
Examiner on 15 March.)

The Regent assigned advisers to monitor the newspaper attacks for opportunities to prosecute, and later in the year, after reading an especially vicious
article in the *Morning Chronicle*, one of these advisers warned the Regent, "I
have reason to think Lord Byron employs himself in this way."[33] It is possible
that Byron may have contributed other unsigned poems to the *Chronicle* in
1812 in addition to the "Ode," the "Impromptu," and the "Address" (as well
as "*Parenthetical Address*, by Doctor Plagiary," a nonpolitical satire published
on 28 October), although there is no direct evidence that he did. McGann
has suggested that Moore's poem "Lines on the Death of Mr. P[e]rc[e]v[a]l,"
which appeared in the *Chronicle* on 23 May 1812, might have been co-authored
by Byron, but this is extremely unlikely.[34] Moore's squibs continued to appear

intermittently in the *Morning Chronicle* throughout the year, some of them so personally insulting to the Regent that only their anonymity must have saved Moore from a charge of libel. For instance, in one untitled poem of Moore's printed on 27 March the Regent places the goddess Britannia, who has been starved by misrule, on a scale to be weighed against his fat elderly mistress the Marchesa of Hertford, in order to determine their relative importance (*ML* 1:183–84).[35]

Whereas Moore's squibs could be extremely cutting and comical at the same time, Byron's attempts at this kind of writing tended to be merely savage. Byron's "Ode to the Framers of the Frame-Bill" is written in anapests, like Moore's "Parody," but the humorous cantering rhythm of the "Ode" jars with the poem's evident vehemence of feeling and violence of imagery. In the "Parody," the moderate language Moore used to describe the government's neglect of English distresses did not interfere with the humor provided by the poem's meter: "No—let *England's* affairs go to rack, if they will, / We'll look after th' affairs of the *Continent* still; / And, with nothing at home but starvation and riot, / Find Lisbon in bread, and keep Sicily quiet" (ll. 83–86). When Byron described the same English hunger and want in his "Ode," his violent images conflicted with his versification and his casual diction: "Some folks for certain have thought it was shocking, / When Famine appeals, and when Poverty groans, / That life should be valued at less than a stocking, / And breaking of frames lead to breaking of bones" (ll. 25–28). Besides the groaning poor and the breaking bones, the poem also featured the image of weavers hanging "in clusters" around factories (l. 7) and the hope, at the end of the poem, that "the frames of the fools" who recommended hanging as a punishment "may be first to be *broken*" (l. 31). Byron had not yet learned how to write political satire without being, as he put it, "too *farouche*" (*BLJ* 4:80). In *Byron the Satirist,* Frederick L. Beaty correctly observes that the satires of Byron's London years "often . . . are so charged with the poet's antipathies that they lack the equanimity characteristic of the most skillful satiric art" (73). Byron was well aware of this shortcoming of the satirical political verse he wrote during this period.

Byron had at least two reasons for discontinuing his squib writing for the *Chronicle.* He was dissatisfied with his ability to write humorous satire (as he would later confess to Moore), and he was afraid that if he was known to be a squib writer other poets' anonymous verses would be attributed to him. Such misattribution caused Byron to worry in a letter to Murray of 29 November 1813 that he would be blamed for recent epigrams on J. W. Ward appearing in the *Chronicle:*

> The Regent is the only person on whom I ever expectorated an epigram or ever should—& even if I were disposed that way—I like & value Mr. W[ard] too well to allow my politics to contract into spleen—or to admire anything intended to annoy him or his. . . . I have said this much about the epigrams because I live so much in the *opposite camp* [the Whigs]—& from my post as an Engineer— might be suspected as ye. flinger of these hand Grenadoes—but with a worthy foe I am all for open war—& not this bush-fighting—& have [not] had nor will have anything to do with it—I do not know the author. (*BLJ* 3:182–83)

Of course Byron was being disingenuous if he meant to claim that he had not been involved at any point in the Whigs' satirical "bush-fighting."

In October Byron again attempted to write a satire that was both cutting and playful, and again achieved only mixed results. *Waltz,* though versified, as Byron explained, in the Popeian "old style" of *English Bards and Scotch Reviewers* (*BLJ* 2:228), nevertheless often recalls the light tone of bantering ridicule that had already become the hallmark of Moore's satire. In the "Parody" Moore had portrayed the Regent childishly exulting over his increased power: "A new era's arriv'd—though you'd hardly believe it—/ And all things, of course, must be new to receive it. / New villas, new fêtes (which ev'n Waithman attends)—/ New saddles, new helmets, and—why not *new friends?*" (ll. 57–60). Byron's *Waltz* referred to the same period of the Regent's ascendancy in much the same way:

> Blest was the time Waltz chose for her debût;
> The Court, the R———t, like herself were new;
> New face for friends, for foes some new rewards,
> New ornaments for black—and royal guards;
> New laws to hang the rogues that roared for bread;
> New coins (most new) to follow those that fled;
> New victories—nor can we prize them less,
> Though Jenky wonders at his own success;
> New wars, because the old succeed so well,
> That most survivors envy those who fell;
> New mistresses—no—old—and yet 'tis true,
> Though they be *old,* the *thing* is something new;
> Each new, quite new—(except some ancient tricks)
> New white-sticks, gold-sticks, broom-sticks, all new sticks!   (ll. 161–74)

Fuess observes that in *Waltz* "Byron for the first time manifests the ability to deal with political questions in a lighter vein, in a manner something like that of Moore" (105). *Waltz* had a humorous preface and like Moore's poems comically mocked the Regent's corpulence and his taste for large, elderly mistresses, but Byron's attempt to reproduce Moore's light touch was nevertheless not entirely successful. As William Childers has noted, the poem is marred by "an uneven tone, a mixture of humor and bitter mockery," a quality exemplified by the above quotation, in which a violent image of hanging and roaring is placed incongruously in the middle of an otherwise gracefully lighthearted passage (165). Moore thought *Waltz* "full of very lively satire," but that the poem fell "far short of what was . . . expected from [Byron] by the public" (*MLB* 1:388).

Waltz was not ready for publication until the spring of 1813, during which time, on 20 March, Moore published his *Intercepted Letters; or, The Twopenny Post-Bag*. The *Post-Bag* was a triumphant success despite being expensive for its size (5s. 6d. for just over a hundred pages); the volume reached its fifth edition in less than a month (*ML* 1:250), went through at least eleven editions within the year, and reached its seventeenth by 1822.[36] Moore's fictional editor Thomas Brown the Younger claimed in a preface that the volume contained versifications of letters purchased from an agent of the Society for the Suppression of Vice, who had picked them up after they had been dropped by the Twopenny postman.[37] The Society had found the letters useless, because "it turned out, upon examination, that the discoveries of profligacy which it enabled them to make, lay chiefly in those upper reaches of society, which their well-bred regulations forbid them to molest or meddle with" (*MCP* 3:88). In these epistles Moore once again delighted in mocking the Regent. In one letter the Countess of Cork tells a friend she can no longer invite the Regent and his lover to her parties because

> The Marchesa and he, inconvenient in more ways,
> Have taken much lately to whispering in doorways;
> Which—consid'ring, you know, dear, the *size* of the two—
> Makes a block that one's company *cannot* get through;
> And a house such as mine is, with doorways so small,
> Has no room for such cumbersome love-work at all.— (ll. 18–23)

Moore portrayed the Regent and his intimates as sybaritic philistines, in one scene gorging themselves in celebration of Leigh Hunt's recent imprisonment. In addition to the eight epistles, the *Post-Bag* also printed the "Parody"

along with eighteen of Moore's *Chronicle* poems and an appendix that purported to present extracts from a new melodrama starring the Regent. The
conservative reviews were furious, the *Antijacobin Review* calling the volume
"the splenetic effusions of some opposition muse"[38] and the *Satirist* claiming
that Moore, "the slanderer of a Prince," intended "to degrade our government, to lower the head of the executive in the estimation of his people, and
bring the laws into contempt."[39] Moore refused to admit openly that the *Post-
Bag* was his, wisely fearing the possibility of prosecution. Nonetheless, the
book was so popular that Moore for a while considered writing a collection
of "Convivial and Political Songs," which would doubtless have combined the
political content of songs like "When first I met thee" with the bantering
mockery of the *Post-Bag* (*ML* 1:256–57).

In his journal entry for 22 November 1813 Byron marveled, "By the by,
what humour, what—every thing, in the 'Post-Bag!' There is nothing M[oor]e
may not do, if he will but seriously set about it"; he also praised Moore's "honour, principle, and independence" (*BLJ* 3:215). Byron began quoting the *Post-
Bag* in his letters, and on 22 May 1813 he wrote to John Murray offering to
review the volume for Murray's *Quarterly Review*, but Murray was apparently
uninterested in publishing what would doubtlessly have been a panegyric on
a collection of anti-Tory poems in his own staunchly Tory magazine. On 19
May 1813 Byron wrote an anapestic verse epistle to Moore in the style of the
epistles in the *Post-Bag*, beginning:

> Oh you, who in all names can tickle the town,
> Anacreon, Tom Little, Tom Moore, or Tom Brown,—
> For hang me if I know of which you may most brag,
> Your Quarto two-pounds or your Twopenny Post Bag.   (ll. 1–4)

Byron wrote this epistle in reply to an invitation by Moore to join him in a
visit to Horsemonger Lane Gaol in order to express their political solidarity
with Leigh Hunt, recently incarcerated for libeling the Regent; Moore wrote
in his biography of Byron that Byron's "political view of the case coincided
entirely with my own" (*MLB* 1:401). Moore told Hunt that one of the reasons
Byron wanted to meet him was that Byron liked Hunt's politics.[40] Byron's
epistle continued:

> To-morrow be with me, as soon as you can, sir,
> All ready and dress'd for proceeding to spunge on
> (According to compact) the wit in the dungeon—

Pray Phoebus at length our political malice
May not get us lodgings within the same palace!   (ll. 6–10)

Byron ended his letter with the promise that "to-morrow, at four, we will both play the *Scurra* [buffoon], / And you'll be Catullus, the R[egen]t Mamurra" (ll. 15–16). This epistle is one of Byron's most deliberate imitations of Moore's satirical style, and it is regrettable that the manuscript version is lost, since Moore omitted a presumably indelicate and perhaps lengthy portion of the poem when he published it in his biography of Byron. The poem shows Byron's delight with the *Post-Bag* and illustrates Byron's identification of his own political satire with Moore's ("our political malice"). Byron also identifies Moore with Catullus, as he did formerly in *English Bards*, but this time because Moore satirizes the Regent as Catullus satirized the similar figure Mamurra, a powerful glutton and gambler (*BLJ* 3:50).

Moore's *Post-Bag* was the rage of London when Byron published *Waltz* anonymously in April. Byron also sent a new anti-Regent poem, "Windsor Poetics" (Moore called it "those bitter and powerful lines" [*MLB* 1:537]) in a letter to Lady Melbourne on 7 April 1813. Like Moore's squibs for the *Chronicle*, this short poem was inspired by an actual event involving the Regent, but Byron knew that "Windsor Poetics" was too insulting for the *Chronicle* or anyone else to publish without inviting prosecution. The poem satirized the Regent's recent visit to the tomb of Charles I and Henry VIII, calling the Regent "another sceptred *thing* . . . Charles to his people—Henry to his wife / The double tyrant" (ll. 3–6). Byron asked Lady Melbourne to give a copy of the poem to "Ld. Holland or anybody you like or dislike," and accordingly, like Moore's "Parody," the poem was widely circulated and read by both Whigs and Tories (*BLJ* 3:38). Although the poem was not published anywhere until 1818, by March 1814[41] Moore happily reported to Byron, "Your lines about Charles & Henry are, I find, circulated with wonderful avidity" (*ML* 1:387), and by June the poem's existence and authorship was generally known, as an article in that month's issue of the *Antijacobin Review* demonstrates.[42] On 21 September Byron sent another political squib to Lady Melbourne, the six-line poem beginning, "'Tis said *Indifference* marks the present time." This poem, very much in the style of the many poems entitled "Epigram" appearing in the *Chronicle* the previous year, expressed Byron's increasing frustration with the inertia of "patriots" as well as with the Tories and the Regent.

In December 1813 Byron began "The Devil's Drive," a harsh political satire that he never completed. This poem attacked not only the Regent but also other Tories such as Yarmouth, Eldon, and Castlereagh, all of whom Moore had previously satirized in the *Post-Bag*. In "Letter III" of Moore's volume the courtier Thomas Tyrwhitt is depicted as a dull-witted court jester upon whom the Regent inflicts juvenile practical jokes; in "The Devil's Drive" Tyrwhitt is "that standing jest, / To princely wit a Martyr" (115–16). Byron's poem also ridiculed the soporific quality of Castlereagh's speeches, as had Moore's very popular poem "The Insurrection of the Papers. A Dream," published on 23 April in the *Morning Chronicle*. Byron never showed "The Devil's Drive" to Moore, and when Moore finally saw Lord Holland's copy in 1829 he was "a good deal disappointed by it" (*MJ* 3:1222) and observed that it was "for the most part rather clumsily executed, wanting the point and condensation" of Southey's and Coleridge's "The Devil's Walk," the poem on which it was loosely based (*MLB* 1:470–71). Byron most likely abandoned the poem because, like Moore, he could see that the poem's cantering, irregular, ballad-style meter too often conflicted with the Juvenalian bitterness of its sentiments. Once again Byron's palpable anger had undermined his attempt to write satire with a lighter tone.

III

Since *Waltz* was published anonymously, "Windsor Poetics" circulated privately, and "The Devil's Drive" was set aside, it was not until the appearance of *The Corsair* on 1 February 1814 that the English reading public first began to read Byron's writings in the same highly partisan light that it read Moore's. *The Corsair* began with an effusive dedication to Moore in which Byron chose not only to praise Moore's writing and "puff" Moore's anticipated oriental poem (*Lalla Rookh*), but also to let it be known that Byron approved of Moore's political writings. At a time when the Tories were still seething over the *Post-Bag*, Byron declared the name of Thomas Moore to be "consecrated by unshaken public principle" and announced that "Ireland ranks [Moore] among the firmest of her patriots." Byron went on to claim that Moore, in writing of the East, would find parallels to "the wrongs of your own country, the magnificent and fiery spirit of her sons, the beauty and feeling of her daughters" (*BCP* 3:148–49). When Byron first showed this dedication to John Murray, Murray objected to the "expressions on Ireland" (*BLJ* 4:32) and asked Byron to rewrite the dedication. Byron complied, but ultimately retained his first dedication at Moore's request, telling Murray, "M[oor]e has seen & decidedly preferred the part your Tory bile sickens at—if every syllable were a rattle-snake or every letter a pestilence—they should not be expunged—let those who cannot swallow chew the expressions on Ireland" (*BLJ* 4:32). Murray argued that the dedication might do Moore "harm," but Byron saw through this pretended concern, telling Moore, "The fact is, [Murray] is a damned Tory, and has, I dare swear, something of *self*, which I cannot divine, at the bottom of his objection, as it is the allusion to Ireland to which he objects" (*BLJ* 4:18). Doubtless Murray's well-grounded fear was that his most popular writer, as well as he himself, would incur the wrath of the conservative press for giving aid and comfort to the Regent's premier literary enemy and implicitly endorsing the Irish cause with which Moore was closely associated.

As it happened, the Tories were provoked by the dedication and by the fact that Byron reprinted the much more offensive "Lines to a Lady Weeping" after the main text of *The Corsair*, thereby acknowledging the poem as his. The result of the dedication to Moore the "patriot" and Byron's avowal of the "Lines" was an explosion of abuse in the Tory newspapers. The offending poem was only eight lines long, but the public reaction colored readers' perceptions of Byron and his poetry for the rest of his career:

> Weep, daughter of a royal line,
>   A Sire's disgrace, a realm's decay;
> Ah, happy! if each tear of thine
>   Could wash a father's fault away!
>
> Weep—for thy tears are Virtue's tears—
>   Auspicious to these suffering isles;
> And be each drop in future years
>   Repaid thee by thy people's smiles!

The pointed reference to "these suffering isles" in the plural, so easy to miss today, "struck a blow for Ireland," as Carl Woodring has observed.[43] That Byron thought of this poem as a contribution to Moore's poetic war against the Regent is suggested by his letter to Moore on 9 April referring to "the Bag and my hand-grenade" as two of the best "invectives" against the Court (*BLJ* 4:92). As Peter J. Manning has observed, "certainly readers who first encountered *The Corsair* . . . placed between the dedication to Moore and '[Lines]

To a Lady Weeping,' apprehended the poem as modern readers by and large do not"; that is, they apprehended it as a more provocative combination of eastern revolution and contemporary English politics.[44] On the very day of the *Corsair*'s publication the dedication and the "Lines" became a focus of partisan combat in the newspapers. The *Morning Chronicle* of 1 February printed the dedication and approvingly called it an "elegant eulogium" of Moore; on the same day the Tory *Courier* ridiculed the dedication and condemned the "Lines" as "disgusting" and unpatriotic. The *Courier*, the *Morning Post*, the *Daily Herald*, and the *Sun* commenced a daily barrage of politically motivated prose and verse assaults on Byron that continued during the next two months, the *Courier* printing a series of articles entitled "Byroniana" in which Byron's respectful dedications to Lord Carlisle, Lord Holland, and Moore were contrasted with his mockery of all three in *English Bards*. These articles, which ironically referred to Byron's family motto, *Crede Byron,* put Byron in a very bad light and greatly embarrassed him.

Byron's dedication ensured that Moore suffered a good portion of the Tories' abuse. Since Byron had already been suspected of having cooperated with Moore in the anti-Regent "squib-warfare" of the spring of 1812, the Tory papers were now only too grateful for the excuse the dedication gave them to attack Byron and Moore together as poetical and political allies. On 3 and 4 February 1814 the *Post* printed outraged letters from "Hibernicus," who claimed to be an "Irish Gentleman" and who took Byron to task, protesting that it was unpatriotic for Moore to write the Irish Melody "Let Erin remember the days of old," "a trifling Song lamenting *Ireland's* being subject to an *English King*."[45] On 7 February the *Daily Herald* accused "Lord Byron, Anacreon Moore and Sam Rogers" of "work[ing] underground" to defame and discredit the Regent.[46] On the same day the *Post* excoriated Byron, calling the "Lines" "Irish trash" and warning both Byron and Moore not to "meddle with politics."[47] In the *Courier*'s third "Byroniana" article on 12 February, Moore was accused of "tuning his harpsichord to the key-note of a faction, and of substituting, wherever he could, a party spirit for the spirit of poetry." This article went on to condemn both poets for writing "vile and anonymous stuff" for the *Morning Chronicle,* and reprinted Byron's insulting lines and notes on Moore from *English Bards*.[48]

In the next "Byroniana" on 17 February, the *Courier* expanded its attack on Byron and Moore to include Rogers, who was (erroneously) accused of having "clubb'd with the Irish Anacreon in that scurrilous collection of verses," the *Post-Bag*. The writer claimed that he preferred Byron's acknowledgment of his authorship of "Lines to a Lady Weeping" to "the cowardly prudence of the author or authors of the *Twopenny Post-bag* lurking behind a fictitious name."[49] Also on the seventeenth, the *Post* printed a verse satire on Byron and Moore entitled "Patronage Extraordinary," beginning: "A friendship subsisted, no friendship was closer, / 'Twixt the heir of a Peer and the son of a Grocer." The poem accused Byron of having chosen Moore, "the low and indecent composer of jigs . . . the son of the seller of Figs," as his patron:

> Atheistical doctrines in verse we are told,
> The former sold *wholesale,* was daring and bold;
> While the latter (whatever *he* offered for sale)
> Like papa, he disposed of—of course by *retail!*
> First—*scraps* of *indecency,* next *disaffection,*
> Disguised by the knave from his fear of detection;
> To court party favour, then, sonnets he wrote;
> Set political squibs to the harpsichord's note.

The poem mocked Byron for "*daubing*" Moore "*thickly all over with praise*" and urged parents, including by implication the Regent, to shield their daughters from the works of "*these serpents*": "their *infernal attacks* from your *mansions* repel, / Where *filial affection* and *modesty* dwell."[50]

The "serpents" were also attacked by the conservative literary journals and in at least one book of satirical poems. The *British Critic*'s review of the *Corsair* mocked "our noble Author's favorite poet" and accused Moore of sympathizing with those "who live by libelling the Sovereign and his powers, and by disseminating the seeds of rebellion among an ignorant and deluded people [the Irish]." The reviewer then assailed Byron's "Lines," recognizing the newly explicit "Whiggism" of Byron's poetry: "Those vehicles of blasphemy and sedition, the Sunday papers, had rung all their libellous changes on this anecdote [of Princess Charlotte's tears] two years ago, and now the noble Lord brings up his *corps de reserve;* we feel no doubt that they will rejoice in such an ally, and may even employ him as an auxiliary in their service."[51]

The Irish wit Edmund Lewis Lenthal Swifte repeatedly assailed Byron and Moore over the *Corsair* controversy in his 1814 collection of poems entitled *Anacreon in Dublin,* which he ironically dedicated to Byron.[52] Swifte's eighteen-page dedication echoed the *Courier*'s charges against Byron's character: "Against Lord Carlisle and Lord Holland, your praise and your censure have fallen equally harmless:—but the Twopenny-Post-man and your Lordship!—Really, really, the revilers of the Sovereign must not quarrel at their petty calumnies on one another." Swifte's "Ode IX—The Melodist" was a satirical imitation of Moore's style that touched on Byron's dedication:

> Yes—mine is the Peer of the Misanthrope Lyre,
> With his headpiece of paper and bosom of iron;
> Who praises the Daughter to slander the Sire,
> And writes Dedications to me—*Crede Byron!*[53]

A note to the lines ridiculed Byron's "expressions on Ireland" as well:

[*The Corsair*] is very handsomely dedicated to [Byron's] brother-poet: praising the little man, of course, his patriotism and his genius; and likening the Papists of Ireland to the Parias of the East, her damp vapours to the vertical sun of Madras, and her Bogs to the plains of Bencoolen.—How this compliment was received, we know not:—but few honest men would be gratified by a panegyric on themselves at the opening of that book which ends with A LIBEL ON THE SOVEREIGN.[54]

In his hostile 1822 *Memoirs of the Life and Writings of the Right Honourable Lord Byron,* John Watkins noted the political character of the dedication and claimed that Byron wished to make "an alliance" with Moore.[55]

The publication of *The Corsair* was an important moment in Moore's career as well as Byron's. The two friends were forever after closely associated as fellow Whig poets. For instance, the only two poets featured in Henry Palmerston's 1819 *New Whig Guide,* which satirized leading Whig personalities, were Byron and Moore, several of whose *Hebrew* and *Irish Melodies* were travestied and given political lyrics.[56] In 1825 *John Bull* condemned the Whigs as "a party, of which the favorite poet is MR. THOMAS MOORE, author of '*Fanny of Timmoul,*' '*The Twopenny Post Bag,*' and other chaste and unpersonal compositions—of whom the great ornament was the late GEORGE LORD BYRON."[57] As late as 1840 the *Times* could summarize the spectrum of nineteenth-century English political opinion by referring to "the Liberalism of Lord Byron & Thomas Moore, [and] the Toryism of the Duke of Wellington and Sir Walter Scott" (qtd. in *MJ* 5:2168).

Until the end of Moore's life he would be popularly referred to as "the poet of all circles, and the idol of his own," a phrase from Byron's dedication, but at the time the politics of the dedication brought Moore mostly negative attention. Moore told James Corry around the end of February:

> [Byron] has got into a tremendous scrape with the Carlton House faction by the avowal of his 'Lines to the Young Princess'. . . . I have come in for my full share of the bespatterment. . . . Indeed, "The Courier" has taken the only method such dull dogs could hit upon for annoying Byron, by raking up all his past and *suppressed* abuse of those he is now friends with; and they have quoted the very passage upon which I called him to account (and from which sprung our intimacy), to contrast it with his present praise of me. (*ML* 1:302–303)

Moore seems to have been unconcerned about the abuse, telling Byron that "such things should be heard by both of us" with a "sacred silence and contempt" (*ML* 1:301), but Byron was embarrassed, and on 16 February 1814 he reaffirmed his loyalty to Moore:

> You may be assured that the only prickles that sting from the Royal hedgehog are those which possess a torpedo property, and may benumb some of my friends. . . . It is something quite new to attack a man for abandoning his resentments. . . . I did not know that it was wrong to endeavour to do justice to those who did not wait till I had made some amends for former and boyish prejudices, but received me into their friendship, when I might still have been their enemy. . . . I believe that most of our hates and likings have been hitherto nearly the same; but from henceforth, they must, of necessity, be one and indivisible,—and now for it! I am for any weapon,—the pen, till one can find something sharper, will do for a beginning. (*BLJ* 4:62)

Byron's desire to be "one and indivisible" with Moore as fellow Whig poet would remain strong for the rest of his life. Moore took Byron at his word in this instance and was quite willing to help take up "the pen" against their mutual enemies. In early March[58] Moore told him, "If you have any *libels* that you wish to see in print, I am going to add two or three things, (since published) to the Fourteenth Edition of the bag, and shall insert yours, as *from a friend*, with much delight—your lines about the bodies of Charles & Henry are, I find, circulated with wonderful avidity" (*ML* 1:387). Byron balked at the offer, on 12 March replying:

> I have nothing of the sort you mention but *the lines* (the Weepers), if you like to have them in the Bag. I wish to give them all possible circulation. The *Vault* reflection ["Windsor Poetics"] is downright actionable, and to print it would be peril to the publisher; but I think the Tears have a natural right to be bagged,

and the editor (whoever he may be) might supply a facetious note or not, as he pleased.

If Byron had been confident in his ability to write a satire humorous enough to place beside Moore's, he most likely would have seized this excellent opportunity to take his revenge on the Tories. But Byron was not confident and, perhaps for the first time, confessed his diffidence to Moore:

> I cannot conceive how the *Vault* has got about,—but so it is. It is too *farouche;* but, truth to say, my satires are not very playful. I have the plan of an epistle in my head, *at* him and *to* him [the Regent]; and, if they are not a little quieter, I shall imbody it. I should say little or nothing of *myself.* As to mirth and ridicule, that is out of my way; but I have a tolerable fund of sternness and contempt, and, with Juvenal before me, I shall perhaps read him a lecture he has not lately heard in the C[abine]t. From particular circumstances, which came to my knowledge almost by accident, I could "tell him what he is—I know him well." (*BLJ* 4:80)

Despite his show of bravado, Byron did not write the poem.[59] It is significant that Byron envisioned the satire he dreamed of writing as an "epistle" to the Regent, most likely along the lines of Moore's successful epistles, only harsher. Moore had been encouraging Byron to write an epistle to "scarify the scoundrels" since he proposed the "immortalizing scheme" of collaboration in his letter to Byron in early 1812.

Aside from Byron's fitful attempts at political satire, his strong desire to write "mirth and ridicule" during his years of fame is also reflected by the fact that he began a dramatic comedy sometime in 1813 before abandoning it in frustration. In his journal entry for 14 November 1813 Byron tersely noted: "This afternoon I have burnt the scenes of my commenced comedy" (*BLJ* 3:205). A month later Byron observed: "A comedy I take to be the most difficult of compositions" (3:237). Moore was perhaps more conscious than anyone else of Byron's early difficulty with humorous writing. Moore recalled in his biography of Byron that during these years a remarkable "slowness of self-appreciation" and "diffiden[ce] in his intellectual powers" led Byron "in the full flow of his fame" to doubt "his own aptitude for works of wit and humour" (*MLB* 1:175). In his notes for the biography Moore listed "his slowness in discovering his talent for humorous poetry" as an important fact about Byron.[60] Byron's confession to Moore that mirth and ridicule was "out of his way" was also in a sense a capitulation to Moore. Byron's attempts to write humorous, colloquial political satire began with his acquaintance with Moore, but Moore's repeated successes and Byron's own insecurity and perceived ineptitude may have finally convinced Byron to leave this sort of writing to Moore, at least for the next few years. The storm of abuse he endured over *The Corsair* may have strengthened this conviction by temporarily scaring him away from sharply partisan political poetry. Moore testified in his biography of Byron that the attacks "mortified and disturbed" Byron (*MLB* 1:549). Much as Byron wanted to join with Moore in his friend's unending poetical "anti-Tory warfare," he apparently did not consider his own political satires to be up to the comparison with Moore's that they would surely undergo; on 8 December 1813 Byron had told Moore, "I think no one equal to you . . . in satire" (*BLJ* 3:194). Byron did write a small group of poems dealing with Napoleon in 1815 for anonymous publication in the *Examiner,* but these were political without being satirical. One of them, "Napoleon's Farewell (From the French)," actually echoes the imagery, meter, and rhetorical style of many of Moore's political *Irish Melodies.*

Later in his career, after he had found his distinctive satirical voice, Byron would be pleased when Moore and he were mentioned together for their similar politics and satires. In 1820, when a fanciful article in *Blackwood's Edinburgh Magazine* imagined Byron and Moore laughing together at Southey and the other prominent poets of the day, Byron wrote Moore, "These rogues are right—*we* do laugh at *t'others*—eh?—don't we? You shall see—you shall see what things I'll say, an' it pleases Providence to leave us leisure" (*BLJ* 7:245). Moore too encouraged this association in latter years; he dedicated his satirical, anti-Tory *Fables for the Holy Alliance* to Byron in 1823, a decision that was doubtless political as well as personal.

Moore's disgust with the dominance of the Tories and the fall of Napoleon apparently provoked him to suggest to Byron in early April 1814 that they move to Paris and write together. Moore's letter is lost, but Byron's response survives:

> Your French scheme is good, but let it be *Italian;* all the Angles will be at Paris. Let it be Rome, Milan, Naples, Florence, Turin, Venice, or Switzerland, and 'egad!' (as Bayes saith), I will connubiate and join you; and we will write a new 'Inferno' in our Paradise. Pray, think of this—and I will really buy a wife and a ring, and say the ceremony, and settle near you upon the Arno, or the Po, or the Adriatic. (*BLJ* 4:93)

In the coming years Byron would often fantasize about "settling" somewhere near Moore and collaborating on political poetry or a newspaper, most often when he felt besieged by the rest of the world or frustrated by political developments. On 10 February 1815 Byron told Moore he had a plan for the two of them to take a year-long trip to Italy and Greece (with or without their wives) and for them to use the opportunity to "overflow" with poetry. On 28 January 1817, in the midst of social unrest in England, Byron dreamed of returning to England and writing Whig poetry with Moore:

> If there is a row, by the sceptre of King Ludd, but I'll be one; and if there is none, and only a continuance of "this meek, piping time of peace," I will take a cottage a hundred yards to the south of your abode, and become your neighbour; and we will compose such canticles, and hold such dialogues, as shall be the terror of the *Times* (including the newspaper of that name), and the wonder, and honour, and praise, of the Morning Chronicle and posterity. (*BLJ* 5:165)

Once again, it is significant that Byron was not primarily thinking like a revolutionary writing for the ages, but like a Whig writing for the British public. His mention of the Tory *Times* and the Whig *Morning Chronicle* shows that he was seeing the political conflict in terms of a clash between two political parties, rather than in a larger sense, such as a war between classes.

In the years 1818—19 the two poets had a minor disagreement, not over political principles but over the political significance of Venice as a symbol of republicanism. Byron wrote his 1818 *Ode on Venice* without Moore in mind, but Moore apparently felt impelled to write a response. In 1819 Moore composed a poem on Venice that is clearly a retort to Byron's. This poem was "Extract IV" of Moore's *Rhymes on the Road,* which was not published until 7 May 1823, when it appeared in the same volume with his satirical *Fables for the Holy Alliance* and a variety of other poems. It does not appear to have occurred to contemporary reviewers (or modern critics) to compare "Extract IV" and Byron's *Ode,* even though the "Extract" was followed by a poem whose subject is Byron himself,[61] or though the volume as a whole was dedicated to Byron.

Byron's poem was published with *Mazeppa* in June 1819 and lamented the fall and degeneration of Venice, which once united, according to Byron, glory, empire, and freedom: "godlike Triad!" (101–2). Byron included Venice, Holland, Switzerland, and America in the small group of glorious modern republics; of these, according to Byron, only America was still entirely free.

Byron's poem moves from a condemnation of the "gloomy errors" of northern nations (32), to the fatalistic declaration that "There is no hope for nations" because human nature itself "strikes us down" (56, 63), to an assertion that tyranny is only a "momentary [start] from Nature's laws" (94), to an concluding encomium upon America. The central image of Byron's poem is Venice itself, rotted and vanishing beneath the waves, its freedom swept away by a succession of foreign powers and corruption of which the Holy Alliance is only the latest manifestation.

Moore took issue with this interpretation of Venice's history, and probably said so to Byron himself during his visit in Venice in October 1819. After Moore left him, Byron wrote to Richard Belgrave Hoppner, "[Moore] *hated* Venice by the way, and swore it was a sad place" (*BLJ* 6:238). Most likely begun at the time of his visit or not long afterward, Moore's ode is dated "Venice, 1819," and begins in a stately and declamatory style:

> Mourn not for VENICE—let her rest
> In ruin, 'mong those States unblest,
> Beneath whose gilded hoofs of pride,
> Where'er they trampled, Freedom died.
> No—let us keep our tears for them,
>   Where'er they pine, whose fall hath been
> Not from a blood-stain'd diadem,
>   Like that which deck'd this ocean-queen,
> But from high daring in the cause
>   Of human Rights—the only good
> And blessed strife, in which man draws
>   His mighty sword on land or flood.   (ll. 1–12)

Byron had insisted that Venice's imperial conquests were of a different kind than those of the modern monarchies that he condemns: according to his poem, Venice's crimes

> Were of a softer order—born of Love,
> She drank no blood, nor fatten'd on the dead,
> But gladden'd where her harmless conquests spread;
> For these restored the Cross, that from above
> Hallow'd her sheltering banners, which incessant
> Flew between earth and the unholy Crescent,
> Which, if it waned and dwindled, Earth may thank
> The city it has clothed in chains.   (ll. 110–18)

Byron seems to have allowed his romanticizing of Venice to carry him into a position of crude and blatant hypocrisy, which Moore attacked at once:

> Vanish'd are all her pomps, 'tis true,
> But mourn them not—for vanish'd, too,
>   (Thanks to that Power, who, soon or late,
>   Hurls to the dust the guilty Great,)
> Are all the outrage, falsehood, fraud,
>   The chains, the rapine, and the blood,
> That fill'd each spot, at home, abroad,
>   Where the Republic's standard stood.   (ll. 29–36)

Moore also condemned Venice for being ruled by an oligarchy that only pretended to embrace democratic ideals. Byron claimed that the "sinful deeds" of the Venetians "Were but the overbeating of the heart, / And flow of too much happiness" (ll. 26–28), but Moore pointed to the city's history of assassinations, torture, and

> Thy all-pervading host of spies,
>   Watching o'er every glance and breath,
> Till men look'd in each others' eyes,
>   To read their chance of life or death.

Moore calls these "The stern machinery of [the] State" (l. 40). He concluded his poem with an exclamation of "moral vengeance" (l. 67):

> Thus perish every King and State,
>   That tread the steps which VENICE trod,
> Strong but in ill, and only great,
>   By outrage against man and God!   (ll. 69–72)

Moore's historical footnotes to his seventy-two-line poem take up more space than the poem itself and suggest how seriously he took this issue. His poem suggests that peoples' enchantment with the beauty of Venice might entrap them as it had Byron, who had excused Venice's own imperialism as conquest in the name of a good cause. Byron's uncharacteristic suggestion that Venice was justified in conquering Muslim peoples probably irritated Moore as well, since such religiously based bigotry was often employed in order to justify Protestant England's mistreatment of Catholic Ireland. Unfortunately, if Byron commented upon Moore's poem his comments have not survived.

Byron's interest in actually collaborating with Moore on political poetry revived in 1820, a year during which Byron praised Moore's political consistency, recalling Moore's triumphant reception by the city of Dublin in 1818 in his letter to *Blackwood's Edinburgh Magazine*: "Look at Moore—it will be long ere Southey meets with such a triumph in London as Moore met with in Dublin—even if the Government should subscribe for it & set the money down to Secret Service.———It was not less to the Man than to the poet, to the tempted but unshaken patriot—to the poor but incorruptible fellow Citizen that the warm hearted Irish paid the proudest of tributes."[62] On 25 December 1820 Byron wrote a long letter to Moore proposing in detail "for you and me to set up jointly a *newspaper*" in London that would print their poetry and "give the age some new lights on policy, poesy" and other departments. Byron offered to move to London and even to pay for Moore's own residence there with him. Byron's intention was apparently to make the newspaper chiefly political, like the *Morning Post* or *Morning Chronicle* (and to give it a defiant or democratic title like "Tenda Rossa" or "I Carbonari"), but he told Moore, "We will modify it into as literary or classical a concern as you please, only let us put our powers upon it, and it will most likely succeed" (*BLJ* 7:253–54). Teresa Guiccioli recalled that Byron's plan was partly motivated by his frustration over English newspaper reports that he had become more interested in Italian licentiousness than in liberal politics.[63]

Moore, who talked seriously about Byron's proposal with his close friend the Whig M. P. and future prime minister Lord John Russell (*MJ* 2:492), replied to Byron,

> With respect to the newspaper, it is odd enough that Lord [John] and myself had been (about a week before I received your letter) speculating upon your assistance in a plan somewhat similar, but more literary and less regularly periodical in its appearance. Lord [John], as you will see by his volume of Essays, if it reaches you, has a very sly, dry, and pithy way of putting sound truths, upon politics and manners, and whatever scheme we adopt, he will be a very useful and active ally in it. (*MLB* 2:436)

Although Moore was apparently interested in the plan, he was in exile in Europe for debt at the time and so may have ultimately seen it as unrealistic. Byron seems to have made little distinction between the terms *journal* and *newspaper*, telling Moore on 2 January 1821, "With regard to our proposed Journal, I will call it what you please, but it should be a newspaper, to make it *pay*. We can call it "The Harp" if you like—or any thing. . . . I wish you to think seriously of the Journal scheme—for I am as serious as one can be, in this world, about any thing" (*BLJ* 8:55). On 22 June 1821 Byron was still fantasizing about the newspaper to Moore: "Now, if we were but together a little to combine our 'Journal of Trevoux' But it is useless to sigh, and yet very natural,—for I think you and I draw better together, in the social line, than any other two living authors" (*BLJ* 8:140). On 5 July he wrote, "If we were together, I should publish both my plays [*Sardanapalus* and *The Two Foscari*] (periodically) in our joint journal. It should be our plan to publish all our best things in that way" (*BLJ* 8:147). He tried to spark Moore's interest yet again on 2 August: "Is there no chance of your return to England, and of *our* Journal? I would have published the two plays in it—two or three scenes per number—and indeed *all* of mine in it. If you went to England, I would do so still" (*BLJ* 8:166). Later, even though Byron was aware that Moore disapproved of his association with Leigh Hunt's *Liberal,* on 27 August 1822 Byron told Moore, "Leigh Hunt is sweating articles for his new Journal; and both he and I think it somewhat shabby in *you* not to contribute. Will you become one of the *properrioters?* 'Do, and we go snacks.' I recommend you to think twice before you respond in the negative" (*BLJ* 9:197). It would, of course, have been extremely foolish for Moore to have become associated with the *Liberal;* it would have meant that Moore by this time, living in England and within easy reach of his enemies, would have had to bear the whole brunt of the opprobrium that Byron's or Hunt's publications would regularly provoke. Moore warned Byron that by joining with others he was putting himself in the kind of situation in which "the bad flavour of one ingredient is sure to taint all the rest" (*ML* 1:514).

In his notes for his life of Byron, Moore mentioned Byron's propositions: "Had myself refused to join [Byron] in a journal, because I thought he ought to stand alone. Had often asked me to join him in undertakings, but I never would."[64] Moore probably feared being compared with Byron, as he had when he had declined Byron's offer to publish a poem with himself and Rogers in 1814. In spite of Byron's repeated proddings during 1821, the journal of policy and poesy never materialized. In that same year the liberal Whiggism of one of Moore's most vehement political poems directly inspired Byron to compose a poetic response in a similar style. Byron was delighted when he received on 3 May 1821 a letter from Moore containing "Lines on the Entry of the Austrians into Naples, 1821," a passionate, angry political poem on the failure of the Italians to effectively revolt against their Austrian oppressors. The poem (beginning "Ay—down to the dust with them, slaves as they are / From this hour, let the blood in their dastardly veins, / That shrunk from the first touch of Liberty's war, / Be wasted for tyrants, or stagnate in chains") was much more akin to Byron's Juvenalian tone of "sternness and contempt" than to Moore's own lighter Horatian approach. Byron wrote to Moore on the same day to thank him for the lines, exulting: "They are sublime, as well as beautiful, and in your very best mood and manner. They are also but too true. . . . Nothing . . . can be better than your poem" (*BLJ* 8:108–9). Byron also passed on a copy of the poem to at least one other correspondent, writing: "These lines are by Moore and in his very best vein. . . . [Jean Antoine] Galignani[65] was afraid to publish & only dared to print them" (*BLJ* 8:105).[66]

Aside from his approval of the sentiment of the poem, Byron also must have been pleased that Moore had written a political poem that more closely approximated the aggressive tone Byron himself tended to take when he tried to write political satire. Inspired and perhaps to some extent reinforced by Moore's successful use of this tone, Byron a few months later wrote "The Irish Avatar," an indignant poem attacking the Irish populace and politicians for a warm reception they gave to the Regent (now King George IV) on a state visit to Ireland. Byron sent his poem to Moore on 17 September 1821 and called it "a reply to your lines against my Italians" (*BLJ* 8:213). Later he explained to Moore that it was written "in 'the high Roman fashion,' and full of ferocious phantasy. As *you* could not well take up the matter with Paddy (being of the same nest), I have;—but I hope still that I have done justice to his great men and his good heart" (*BLJ* 8:225). According to Medwin, Moore told Byron that "'it saved him from writing on the same subject'"; Byron told Medwin that "'[Moore] would have done it much better.'"[67] Byron asked Moore to alter the poem if it needed improvement, and on 20 September Byron sent additional stanzas to Moore, who was then living in Paris, and excitedly urged him to "get me twenty copies of the whole carefully and privately printed off, as *your* lines were on the Naples affair. Send me *six*, and distribute the rest according to your own pleasure" (*BLJ* 8:219). While writing "The Irish Avatar," Byron again thought of writing political satire in tandem with Moore; referring to the trial of Queen Caroline the year before, on 27 September 1821 Byron ended his letter to Moore by exclaiming, "If the G. Rex marries again, let him not want an Epithalamium—suppose a joint concern of you and me, like Sternhold and Hopkins!" (*BLJ* 8:225). Some months after having "The Irish Avatar" privately printed at Paris, Moore advised Byron on 19 February 1822 that in future, if Byron had any more "political catamarans to explode, [Paris] is your place," and reminded him that "boldness, and even licence, in politics, does good,—actual, present good" (*ML* 1:503).

"The Irish Avatar" is, like Moore's poem, written in anapestic quatrains, and it condemns the Irish in the same tone and for the same basic reason that Moore's had condemned the Neapolitans. The version of the poem privately printed in Paris ended with a tribute to Moore:

> Or, if aught in my bosom can quench for an hour
>   My contempt for a nation so servile though sore,
> Which though trod like the worm will not turn upon Power—
>   'Tis the glory of GRATTAN and the genius of MOORE!

In a surviving manuscript version the final line is even more effusive: "Twere the heart—the free Spirit—the genius of Moore!" (ll. 125–28). Byron might have written the poem partly in response to an attack on Moore in the 5 August 1821 number of *John Bull*.[68] In any event the poem reached Moore in Paris on 3 November 1821, and he enthusiastically wrote in his diary: "Received Lord Bs. tremendous verses against the King & the Irish for their late exhibition in Dublin—richly deserved by my servile & hollow-hearted countrymen" (*MJ* 2:501). A decade after Byron's death, Moore proudly recalled: "Byron felt [the shame of the Irish adulation of George IV] as if he was himself an Irishman, and so his Poem on the subject shows" (4:1612). The two poets' appreciative responses to each other's poems are an example of the strong and enduring appeal the idea of a poetico-political "dialogue" between them always held.

IV

Echoes of both the style and content of Moore's Regency political satires are apparent in Byron's, and at least until his exile Byron tended to view the political dimension of his identity as a poet in relation to Moore's reputation as a Whig and as a supporter of liberal causes. Although he perhaps overstates the case slightly, Fuess is basically correct in noting that "it was not until the formation of this friendship [with Moore] that Byron began to take any active part in current politics; during the rest of his life, however, he was linked with Moore as a satirist on the Whig side and was, to a considerable extent, influenced by his work" (96). But in what particular way did this influence manifest itself in the latter part of Byron's career as a satirist: the period between 1818 and 1824 during which Byron wrote his most important sociopolitical satires, *Beppo*, *Don Juan*, and *The Vision of Judgment?*

For Byron's satire, Fuess calls the period between *The Curse of Minerva* in 1811 to *Beppo* in 1818 "plainly transitional" because it marks "the gradual change in Byron's satiric method from the formal vituperation of *English Bards* to the colloquial raillery of *Beppo*. Little by little [Byron] forsakes the heroic couplet for other measures; more and more he diverges in practice from the principles of his masters, Pope and Gifford" (93). William Ruddick has argued that this gradual change in Byron's attitude toward Popeian satire and his increasing acceptance of the informal, colloquial mode owed a great deal to Moore. Ruddick's remarks warrant quoting at length:

> [Moore] showed Byron how the kind of impromptu-seeming, rapid, diverse poems he had till then thought of as mere vehicles for the entertainment of close friends could be fit media for satirical public statements. Byron learned from Moore that the standards of Pope could be embodied in verse whose tone and range of reference accorded closely with the fashionable culture of Regency England. . . . It was from Moore, indeed, that Byron learned how to give the man of the world who constantly features in his letters a local habitation and a tone of voice within his satires. And finally, even before he tried the *ottava rima* stanza, Byron had discovered from Moore's work that a lighter, more rapid rhythm such as Moore's favorite anapest was a better medium for contemporary satire than the . . . heroic couplet.[69]

Ruddick is right to draw special attention to the tonal qualities of Byron's later satires. The example of Moore's satires seems to have helped Byron not only to discover a more congenial verse form but also to replace his generally Juvenalian tone of "sternness and contempt" with the urbanity and good-natured mockery of the Horatian approach. It is a short step from the gossipy, chatty personae of Moore's verse epistles to the urbane, conversational narrator of *Don Juan*.

Ruddick finds evidence of Moore's influence in the many colloquial, jocular verses that Byron often sent in letters to Moore and other correspondents. These poems often resembled Moore's verse epistles, and Ruddick considers them to have been productive experiments by means of which Byron slowly gained proficiency and confidence in writing a more colloquial, relaxed form of satire. The extent to which the back-and-forth satirical verse-writing of Byron's and Moore's letters encouraged the changes in Byron's own satire would probably be much more obvious if the great majority of Moore's letters to Byron had not been lost or destroyed. Several of Byron's letters to Moore feature such poems, but a letter from Moore to John Hunt written on 24 December 1822 indicates that Moore's letters to Byron contained perhaps as many. Concerned about Byron's involvement with Leigh Hunt's journal *The Liberal,* Moore told Hunt's brother John in 1822: "I have, from time to time, in my letters to Lord Byron inserted some hasty verses, chiefly satirical, which it struck me he might, from thoughtlessness or *fun,* let, some time or other, escape among the minor pieces of the Liberal, and I have often intended to give him a little caution on the subject, but have always forgot it" (*ML* 2:508).

Insofar as it is known, none of these verses survives, with two notable exceptions. In a letter to Moore of 5 November 1820, written during the trial of Queen Caroline, Byron wrote: "I am glad of your epigram. It is odd that we should both let our wits run away with our sentiments; for I am sure that we are both Queen's men at bottom. But there is not resisting a clinch—it is so clever!" (*BLJ* 7:218). This "epigram" was most likely the six-line poem that Moore included in his journal entry for 5 October:

> It is strange, but amusing to think, of the strife
> Which the Alphabet often has caus'd in this life.
> At Constantinople, as histories mention,
>   (See Gibbon, Vol. 8—if it don't too much trouble you)
> A *dipthong* was once the great cause of contention,
>   And now we see England all in arms for a W.

Moore added, "I had rather this joke had cut the other way—for I wish *her* success (W. or not) with all my soul" (*MJ* 1:349–50). (The Queen's grievances against her husband became a cause célèbre for the Whigs, and both Byron and Moore supported her.) Byron's comments suggest that in this instance Byron invited Moore's lines on the Queen with some of his own. Moore had recently been delighted by Byron's "*excellent* epitaph" on Castlereagh, sent to him in a letter of 2 January 1820 whose arrival had apparently been delayed by eight or nine months.[70]

At some point, probably in 1821,[71] Moore responded with an epitaph for Southey, which Byron then showed to Thomas Medwin. Byron gave Medwin permission to copy the lines and Medwin printed them in his 1824 *Conversations of Lord Byron,* saying that they were written by "a correspondent of Lord Byron's" who was in Paris. Most of Medwin's readers would have deduced from this that they were Moore's, and Medwin confirmed that they were, in a note intended for a later edition. The poem does not appear in Moore's 1840–41 *Collected Works,* and only appears, under the title "Epitaph on a Well-Known Poet," and in a somewhat altered form, in an 1831 Philadelphia edition of Moore's works. Medwin's version, probably taken directly from Moore's letter, is as follows:

> Beneath these poppies buried deep,
>   The bones of Bob the Bard lie hid;
> Peace to his manes! may he sleep
>   As soundly as his readers did!
>
> Through every sort of verse meandering,
>   Bob went without a hitch or fall,
> Through Epic, Sapphic, Alexandrine,
>   To verse that was no verse at all;
>
> Till Fiction having done enough
>   To make a bard at least absurd,
> And give his readers *quantum suff.,*
>   He took to praising George the Third:
>
> And now in virtue of his crown,
>   Dooms us, poor Whigs, at once to slaughter;
> Like Donellan of bad renown,
>   Poisoning us all with laurel water.
>
> And yet at times some awkward qualms he
>   Felt about leaving honour's track;
> And though he has got a butt of Malmsey,
>   It may not save him from a sack.
>
> Death, weary of so dull a writer,
>   Put to his works a *finis* thus.
> O! may the earth on him lie lighter
>   Than did his quartos upon us![72]

Moore's poem would, of course, have delighted Byron; it recalls the spirit and tone of the dedication to *Don Juan*, as well as those of Byron's epigrams on Castlereagh. Most importantly, it was written in the sort of demotic cadence that was Moore's constant response to Tory formalism. If more of Moore's letters to Byron were extant, the two poets' correspondence might somewhat more closely resemble the series of "scoundrel-scarifying" satirical epistles that Byron and Moore had always talked of writing to each other.

In his biography of Byron, Moore included fragments ("the only parts producible") of a "long rhyming Epistle, full of jokes and pleasantries upon every thing and every one around him" (*MLB* 1:561), that Moore had received from Byron in London in June 1814, in the midst of the "crowded desert" he called "the summer of the sovereigns" (*BLJ* 4:125). This epistle was written in the bantering anapests of Moore's *Post-Bag*, like Byron's earlier epistle to Moore regarding their visit to Leigh Hunt. Also as in the case of the earlier epistle, this one was written from a Whig point of view. It mocked the Regent, who was celebrating the defeat of Napoleon and his own hour of glory, and also abused Southey and the tsar of Russia. The epistle was obviously much longer than the fragments Moore printed, and doubtlessly Byron went on to ridicule some of the various monarchs, generals, and society figures in London at that time. The epistle described the "the fusses,/The fêtes, and the gapings" going on at the London parties in a gossipy manner that immediately recalls the *Post-Bag*, especially "Letter III. From G[eor]ge Pr[in]ce R[e]g[en]t to the E[arl] of Y[armou]th," in which the Regent himself gossips about the various Tories present at the previous night's banquet. As in Byron's verse epistle to Moore the year before, in which Byron celebrated his and Moore's "political malice," in this poem Byron once again employed the image of himself and Moore together in order to counter that of the Regent: "I saw him, last week, at two balls and a party,—/For a prince, his demeanor was rather too hearty./You know, *we* are used to quite different graces"; unfortunately Moore omits the remainder of this section.

Ruddick demonstrates that the comical, versified rejection letter beginning "Dear Doctor, I have read your play" that Byron sent to John Murray on 21 August 1817 was patterned after Moore's "Letter VII. From Messrs. L[a]ck[in]gt[o]n and Co. to ———, Esq.," from the *Post-Bag*. Moore's poem purported to be a rejection letter from the famous bookseller James Lackington to a hopeful author and was the only satire in the *Post-Bag* that was not political. Byron's poem was not political either, and was written in reply to

Murray's request for a "civil declension" to give to John Polidori's tragedy
(*BLJ* 5:258–61). Byron wrote his poem in an irregular mixture of lines between eight and ten syllables in length rather than in the twelve-syllable lines
of Moore's poem, and in iambic rather than anapestic meter, but Ruddick
calls it "the best of all Byron's imitations of Moore," because it demonstrates
how Byron, by this point, had "mastered the characteristics of Moore's satirical style and then surpassed the already considerable achievement of his
master."[73] In this poem Byron duplicated the rapid pace and deft rhyming of
Moore, but heightened the interest and comedy by satirizing himself along
with Polidori. The self-consciousness of the narrator in Byron's late satires is
an important dimension that Moore's satires lack; although Moore's epistle
writers are often memorable characters, they are not able to reflect on their
relationship with their readers (that is, Moore's readers) in the way that
Byron's narrators are able to reflect on theirs. James Chandler has also noted
the similarities in voice and rhyme between Moore's satires and *Don Juan,*
concluding, "Indeed, of the many 'sources' that have been identified as contributing to Byron's style in [*Don Juan*]—Pope, Pulci, Sterne—it is surprising
how little attention has been paid to the immensely popular satirical verse of
Byron's close friend and confidant."[74]

In *Don Juan* Byron persisted in fighting the same fight against the same
Tories that Moore and he used to abuse in Byron's London years, and often
had Moore in mind while he was doing it. There are several echoes of Moore's
satires in political passages of *Don Juan;* among them, Irene Lurkis Clark has
traced several images of Castlereagh back to their origins in Moore's *Post-Bag*
and *Morning Chronicle* squibs.[75] Byron's contemptuous reference to King
George IV as "Fum the Fourth" is traceable back to Moore's poem "Fum and
Hum, the Two Birds of Royalty. A Fragment," published in the *Morning Chronicle* and reprinted in the 1818 *Fudge Family in Paris.* Moore's poem depicted
the Regent surrounded by his risible Chinoiscrie in Brighton Pavilion, and it
enraged the Tories by describing him as a "cackling and ravenous creature,"
"half way / 'Twixt the goose and the vulture, like Lord c[a]stl[erea]gh"
(ll. 8–9). Moore provoked the outrage of *John Bull* and other government
mouthpieces by speaking of "The p[rinc]e just in bed, or about to depart
for't, / His legs full of gout, and his arms full of h[e]rtf[or]d," (ll. 28–29).

Byron probably received a copy of Moore's second hugely successful collection of political verse epistles, *The Fudge Family in Paris* (published 20 April
1818) around the time he began *Don Juan.* Byron told Medwin that "'The

Fudge Family' pleases me as much as any of [Moore's] works" and that Moore's poem "Epistle from Tom Crib to Big Ben . . . ," included with the volume, was based on an actual letter given to Moore by Byron and Douglas Kinnaird.[76] By presenting a series of verse epistles from four different travelers, *The Fudge Family in Paris* cleverly alternated verse written in Moore's normal jocular style with absolutely fierce and anguished denunciations of the European powers, specifically condemning England's role in the oppression of Ireland and of the spirit of liberty generally. Moore's brilliant new book may have served as a valuable reminder to Byron of the techniques of his friend's satire, but Byron had already published *Beppo* on 28 February and had doubtless already learned the most important lessons Moore's satire had to offer him. In any event, the style of Italian comic poets like Pulci and the immediate example of John Hookham Frere's *Whistlecraft* were more important as immediate formal models for *Beppo* and *Don Juan* than anything Moore wrote. Yet in the case of *The Vision of Judgment* Dyer correctly identifies a close kinship between what he calls the Radical styles of Byron's poem and Moore's *Fudge Family in Paris*, arguing that both accomplish a deceptively casual undercutting of Tory authority (both political and rhetorical) that is more damaging than any formal jeremiad, and that their "apparent mildness or equanimity" therefore delivers deeper wounds.[77] It should be remembered that even in Byron's last great satire he was a Whig poet: he told Moore while working on *The Vision of Judgment* that his intention was to "put . . . [King] George's Apotheosis in a Whig point of view" (*BLJ* 8:229).

In contributing to Byron's sense of his identity as a Whig poet and in exposing Byron to a more informal, colloquial, relaxed, and ultimately, for Byron, more appealing approach to political and social satire, Moore encouraged and helped Byron to construct his own unique satirical voice. This voice potently combined a more all-encompassing and digressive version of the Horatian *sermo merus* style with (in *Don Juan*) the attitude of the proud but outcast and outdated Whig gentleman who retained his "buff and blue" in spite of the rapid disappearance of the Regency culture of his youth. Byron's particular brand of "political malice" and his bantering Horatian style as they are displayed in his late satires are both qualities that grew, not exclusively but significantly, out of his personal and artistic relationship with Thomas Moore.

"That's my thunder, by G—d!"

Nationalism, Music, and Poetry

When Byron began writing poems to be set to music in the spring of 1814, Moore was England's most popular and accomplished song-writer, his songs ubiquitous in London society and his collections of melodies indispensable to anyone who entertained guests, sang, or owned a musical instrument. In 1813 the *Monthly Review* declared that the beauties of the *Irish Melodies* placed Moore "indisputably at the head of our living song-writers; and . . . [enabled] him on some occasions proudly to contend for pre-eminence with Burns himself."[1] Separate installments of Moore's *A Selection of Irish Melodies* had appeared in 1808, 1810, 1811, and 1813, and Byron was an ardent admirer of them, both for their lyrical beauty and for the romantic nationalism they expressed. For these reasons Byron's *A Selection of Hebrew Melodies*, his 1815 collaboration with the Jewish composer and singer Isaac Nathan, could not help being written and published under the shadow of Moore. But the formal and ideological similarities between Byron's *Melodies* and Moore's reveal more about Byron as an artist than merely his obvious delight in his friend's "mixture of politics and poetry."[2]

In essence *Hebrew Melodies* was Byron's first published collection of lyric poems since *Hours of Idleness*. Just as he followed Moore in his earlier volume, eight years later in *Hebrew Melodies* Byron the lyricist was still looking to Moore, a circumstance that demonstrates that, far from rapidly growing beyond Moore's influence, as some critics have suggested, Byron used Moore's poems as his primary lyrical models at least until he left England in 1816. Leslie Marchand correctly notes that Byron's "facility in some of the lyric measures he learned from Moore was one of the chief merits of his occasional verse," and he suggests that this learned facility bore its most important fruit in the *Hebrew Melodies*.[3] The characteristic balanced mixture of passionate feeling and stylized sentiment so typical of Moore's lyric poetry is as observable in Byron's *Melodies* as it is in his juvenile lyrics. Yet in Byron's lyrics of 1815, he was able, like Moore, to overcome his misgivings about being "a melodious advocate of lust" by employing his sensuous lyricism in the service of the more serious and "manly" Whig ideals of liberty, tolerance, and romantic nationalism. The fact that this second stage of Byron's lyric poetry so obviously takes its cue from the second stage of Moore's (and for the same reasons) demonstrates that during his years of London fame Byron felt the influence of Moore's lyric poems just as strongly as he did the influence of Moore's colloquial satires.

I

In his journal of 24 November 1813 Byron placed Moore with Campbell in the third rank of his "Gradus ad Parnassum" after Scott and Rogers, but with this caveat: "I have ranked the names upon my triangle more upon what I believe popular opinion, than any decided opinion of my own. For, to me, some of M[oor]e's last *Erin* sparks—'As a beam o'er the face of the waters'—'When he who adores thee'—'Oh blame not'—and 'Oh breath not his name'—are worth all the Epics that ever were composed" (*BLJ* 3:220). Byron wrote effusively of his enjoyment of the *Melodies* in a letter to Moore of 8 December 1813:

> You cannot doubt my sincere admiration, waving personal friendship for the present, which, by the by, is not less sincere and deep-rooted. I have you by rote and by heart; of which "ecce signum!". . . . I have a habit, in passing my time a good deal alone, of—I won't call it singing, for that I never attempt except to myself—but of uttering, to what I think tunes, your "Oh breathe not," "When the last glimpse," and "When he who adores thee," with others of the same minstrel;—they are my matins and vespers.

Byron went on to tell Moore he was "indebted" to him for the songs and concluded: "A man may praise and praise, but no one recollects but that which pleases—at least, in composition. . . . I think no one equal to you in that department, or in satire,—and surely no one was ever so popular in both"

(*BLJ* 3:193–94). Byron told Medwin, "Moore is one of the few writers who will survive the age in which he so deservedly flourishes. He will live in his 'Irish Melodies;' they will go down to posterity with the music; both will last as long as Ireland, or as music and poetry."[4]

Byron often expressed these sentiments; he told Lady Blessington, "No one writes songs like Moore. . . . Sentiment and imagination are joined to the most harmonious versification, and I know no greater treat than to hear him sing his own compositions; the powerful effect he gives to them, and the pathos of the tones of his voice, tend to produce an effect on my feelings that no other songs, or singer, ever could."[5] Byron recalled in 1821 that he knew "Tho' the last glimpse of Erin with sorrow I see" "by heart in 1812" (*BLJ* 8:46). He used a quatrain from "As a Beam o'er the Face of the Waters may glow" as the epigraph to *The Giaour* and often quoted the *Melodies* in his letters. Summarizing Moore's artistic virtues in his journal of 1813–14, Byron observed: "M[oor]e has a peculiarity of talent, or rather talents,—poetry, music, voice, all his own; and an expression in each, which never was, nor ever will be, possessed by another" (*BLJ* 3:215). He told Moore that "When first I met thee" was "one of the best things you ever wrote" (*BLJ* 4:263), and Moore recalled that he had watched Byron "[give] himself up to the . . . natural sentiment of the song with evident emotion" (*MLB* 1:597). In his 1820 letter to *Blackwood's Edinburgh Magazine* Byron claimed that Moore, "as the Burns of Ireland, possesses a fame which cannot be lost."[6] His particular love of "Oh breathe not his name," Moore's tribute to his executed friend Robert Emmet, led him to ask Moore in 1820 to write a song about him if he was killed in an Italian revolution, so that his ghost could "have the satisfaction of being plaintively pitied—or still more nobly commemorated, like 'Oh breathe not his name'" (*BLJ* 7:218–19). Byron also enjoyed other of Moore's songs besides the *Melodies;* Moore recalled that the "Lusitanian War-Song" from *National Airs* "seemed especially to please him," partly because of "the national character of the music" (*MLB* 1:597), and Mary Shelley wrote that, along with "When he who adores thee" (*MJ* 3:1034), Byron sang Moore's "Tyrolese Song of Liberty" so often that it was "inextricably linked" with her memory of him.[7] Both the Lusitanian and Tyrolese songs are rousing calls to battle in the cause of liberty.

Moore's *Melodies* were phenomenally popular, and would have been performed at many if not most of the parties and social gatherings Byron attended. Evidence of Byron's enjoyment of the *Melodies* in performance is plentiful. In a letter to Moore of 25 July 1813 Byron mentioned a party at which Mrs. Edward T. Dalton sang one of Moore's "best songs so well, that, but for the appearance of affectation, I could have cried" (*BLJ* 3:79). Certainly Byron had heard Moore sing the *Melodies* in person on several such occasions. Byron wrote to Moore on 4 May 1814 to tell him that at the previous night's party "that plaguy voice of yours made me sentimental, and almost fall in love with a girl who was recommending herself, during your song, by *hating* music" (*BLJ* 4:114). In a letter to Byron of 31 January 1815 Lady Melbourne reported Moore's sensational performance of his new song "When first I met thee," remarking that the lines of the song "have acquired great celebrity, by its being known, that You Wept when they were Sung to you," and asking if the story was true.[8] Byron responded with satisfaction: "It rejoices me to hear of Moore's success—he is an excellent companion as well as poet—though I cannot recollect that I 'wept' at the song you mention—I ought to have done so—but whether I did nor not—it is one of the most beautiful and touching compositions that ever he penned—and much better than ever was compounded by any one else" (*BLJ* 4:262).

In a letter of 9 June 1820, Byron told Moore that he preferred hearing his songs to reading them, because the musical notations "confound the words in my head, though I recollect [the *Melodies*] perfectly when *sung*" (*BLJ* 7:117). Moore himself testified in his biography of Byron: "I have, indeed, known few persons more alive to the charms of simple music; and not unfrequently have seen the tears in his eyes while listening to the Irish Melodies" (*MLB* 1:597). Moore told Walter Scott that, although Byron "knew nothing of music," he "still had a strong feeling of some of [the *Melodies*]—particularly "When he who adores thee"—that I have sometimes seen the tears come into his eyes at some of my songs—Another great favorite of his was 'Though the last glimpse of Erin,' from which he confessedly borrowed a thought for his Corsair, & said to me 'It was shabby of me, Tom, not to acknowledge that theft'" (*MJ* 2:849).

Byron's appreciation of Moore's singing probably had much to do with his passionate love of acting and self-dramatization generally. Moore's singing was highly dramatic and was often compared to a chant or bardic recitation. The firsthand account by the American poet Nathaniel Parker Willis provides a good picture of Moore's unique style of performance:

He makes no attempt at music. It is a kind of admirable recitative, in which every shade of thought is syllabled and dwelt upon, and the sentiment of the song goes through your blood, warming you to the very eyelids, and starting you to tears, if you have soul or sense in you. . . . We all sat around the piano, and after two or three songs of Lady Blessington's choice, he rambled over the keys for awhile and sang "When first I met thee," with a pathos that beggars description. When the last word had faltered out, he rose and took Lady Blessington's hand, said good-night, and was gone before a word was uttered. For a full minute after he had closed the door, no one spoke.[9]

Mary Shelley was fascinated by Moore's singing, and called it "something new & strange & beautiful."[10] Moore believed that in singing, all considerations were secondary to the communication of emotion, and it is easy to imagine the extent to which Byron, who was moved almost to convulsions by the passion of Edmund Kean's acting, could enter emotionally into the spirit of Moore's performances.

Moore's songs held two obvious attractions for Byron's particular poetic sensibility. First, their usually mournful tone and their preoccupation with tragic love are qualities that are featured in the majority of Byron's own short lyric poems. Moore meant his love songs to be capable of both a literal and an allegorical interpretation (love of a woman equaling love of Ireland, the betrayal of a lover equaling the treachery of England, and so on), but whereas Moore was primarily interested in their allegorical dimension, Byron was doubtless moved by their literal meaning. Second, the romantic nationalism of the *Melodies* would also have resonated with Byron, whose enthusiasm for the struggles of oppressed peoples was a major trait of his character and art from his first grand tour to his final days in the Greek war of independence. Leith Davis observes that the popularity of the *Irish Melodies* meant that the songs "provided a universal prototype for Romantic nationalism in a defeated country."[11] Byron recognized too that the music of "primitive" peoples was a powerful and affecting medium through which their sorrows and aspirations could be conveyed. Canto II of *Childe Harold's Pilgrimage*, composed in 1810, featured Byron's own imagined version of a Suliote war song, and in his notes to the poem Byron reproduced and translated two genuine Albanian songs. From the summer of 1816 Mary Shelley recalled Byron howling forth an Albanian song during one of their circle's boating excursions on Lake Geneva (*MLB* 2:24).

II

Byron made some abortive attempts at songwriting in 1813 before becoming confident enough in his abilities finally to agree to write for Isaac Nathan in late 1814. At some point during 1812, George Thomson, a publisher of Scottish, Welsh, and Irish airs, had written to Byron to request that he compose some lyrics that Thomson could set to music. Byron initially said he would, but in January 1813 Murray wrote to Thomson to tell him that Byron had decided not to contribute, "because Mr. Moore wrote verses for the same airs."[12] Long afterward, on 10 September 1813, Byron wrote apologetically to Thomson, explaining that he had

> repeatedly tried since you favoured me with your first letter . . . without being able to satisfy myself. . . . It is not a species of writing which I undervalue—on the contrary Burns in your country—& my friend Moore in this—have shewn that even their splendid talents may acquire additional reputation from this exercise of their powers—You will not wonder that I decline writing after men whom it were difficult to imitate—& impossible to equal. . . . [B]elieve me I have again & again endeavoured to fulfil my promise without success—nothing but my most decided conviction that both you & I would regret it could have prevented me from long ago contributing to your volume. (*BLJ* 3:114)

Despite his misgivings, in the spring of 1814 and in the full glow of the public's ecstatic reception of *The Corsair,* Byron again began gradually turning his attention to songwriting. Impelled by his own persistent desire to write lyric poetry and inspired by both the great public demand for songs and the brilliant example of Moore's *Melodies,* Byron began to overcome his qualms. Byron's serious songwriting efforts seem to have begun with the lyric "I speak not, I trace not, I breathe not thy name," which he sent to Moore on 4 May 1814, in response to a request from Moore that Byron write a poem that he could set to music. Byron called the song an "experiment" and confessed that, as it had cost him "something more than trouble" to write it, it would probably be unsuitable, in which case he urged Moore to "throw it into the fire without *phrase*" (*BLJ* 4:114). That Byron was willing to submit his first "experiment" of the kind to the very man whose songs he despaired of imitating or equaling is evidence of the trust he placed in Moore's tact and friendship. Moore must have responded with encouraging words, because on 6 May, two days later, Moore told James Power, "Lord Byron has done *two* Songs already for me,"[13] though the identity of this second song remains unknown.

In June 1814 Isaac Nathan wrote to propose that Byron write a series of songs on Old Testament themes that Nathan could then adapt to ancient Hebrew music, a project that would eventually evolve into the *Hebrew Melodies*. Byron initially declined, but on 15 September 1814 Byron's friend Douglas Kinnaird wrote to on behalf of Nathan, and Byron changed his mind and agreed to participate. By 20 October 1814, as Byron told both Augusta Leigh and Annabella Milbanke, he had already completed "nine or ten" songs, a few of which he had probably written before he agreed to Nathan's proposal (*BLJ* 4:220).

However, although he was now writing for Nathan, Byron still wanted to give Moore what songs he could, and on 2 March 1815 he sent Moore the lyric "There's not a joy the world can give," remarking, "You once asked me for some words which you would set. Now you may set or not, as you like." Moore sent Byron his approval of the verses, and Byron replied on 8 March:

> I am very glad you like them, for I flatter myself they will pass as an imitation of your style. If I could imitate it well, I should have no great ambition of origi-nality—I wish I could make you exclaim with Dennis, "That's my thunder, by G——d!" I wrote them with a view to your setting them, and as a present to Power, if he would accept the words, and *you* did not think yourself degraded, for once in a way, by marrying them to music. (*BLJ* 4:279–80)

In an undated letter of 1815 Moore told Power, "Lord Byron has sent me a song to set—very beautiful, but devilish hard to put to music."[14] Later in the year, Moore found what he called "a very pretty Irish air" to which the words to "There's not a joy the world can give" went "remarkably well." He offered to set Byron's words to the tune and to include the song in the next number of the *Irish Melodies*.[15] On 4 November Byron responded, "If you think the verses worth it, I would rather they were embalmed in the Irish Melodies, than scattered about in separate song—much rather" (*BLJ* 4:330). Moore ac-cordingly asked Power if he would agree to the song's inclusion, but appar-ently he did not.[16] Instead, Power published the lyric separately with music by Sir John Stevenson, who had provided the music for many of the *Irish Melodies* (*BCP* 3:462–63).

As late as 12 December 1821, Byron sent Moore an unsolicited song, writing, "I enclose you some lines written not long ago, which you may do what you like with, as they are very harmless. Only, if copied, or printed, or set, I could wish it more correctly than in the usual way, in which one's 'nothings are monstered,' as Coriolanus says" (*BLJ* 9:80–81). The song is the one beginning, "Oh, talk to me not of a name great in story," written in four anapestic quatrains and expressing the speaker's preference for youth and love over fame and age. It is not a very accomplished poem, but its concern with aging and the relationship between worldly glory and love, as well its formal structure, clearly reveal its kinship to many of Moore's songs. The poem could in fact very easily be mistaken for one of the *Irish Melodies*, its phraseology and tone sounding more like Moore than like Byron:

1.

Oh! talk not to me of a name great in story
The days of our Youth, are the days of our Glory,
And the myrtle and ivy of sweet two and twenty
Are worth all your laurels though ever so plenty.

2.

What are garlands and crowns to the brow that is wrinkled?
Tis but as a dead flower with May-dew besprinkled,
Then away with all such from the head that is hoary,
What care I for the wreaths that can *only* give Glory?

3.

Oh! Fame!—if I e'er took delight in thy praises—
'Twas less for the sake of thy high-sounding phrases
Than to see the bright eyes of the dear One discover
She thought that I was not unworthy to love her.

4.

There chiefly I sought thee, *there* only I found thee,
Her Glance was the best of the rays that surround thee.
When it sparkled o'er aught that was bright in my story,
I knew it was love, and I felt it was Glory.

Moore, apparently not setting this song to music, reproduced it in his biography of Byron without critical comment (*MLB* 2:566–67). The song is not based upon any one Moore lyric, but below, for purposes of comparison, is an *Irish Melody*, published in 1815, whose diction, message, and anapestic meter are similar to that of Byron's song as well as being characteristic of many of Moore's lyrics. The rhyme scheme is different, and the lines alternate between twelve and eleven syllables rather than roughly approximating a constant twelve, as in Byron's song, but "I saw from the beach" provides a good generic example of the type of lyric that Byron was modeling his songs upon:

> I saw from the beach, when the morning was shining,
>> A bark o'er the waters move gloriously on;
> I came when the sun o'er that beach was declining,
>> The bark was still there, but the waters were gone.
>
> And such is the fate of our life's early promise,
>> So passing the spring-tide of joy we have known;
> Each wave, that we danc'd on at morning, ebbs from us,
>> And leaves us, at eve, on the bleak shore alone.
>
> Ne'er tell me of glories, serenely adorning
>> The close of our day, the calm eve of our night;—
> Give me back, give me back the wild freshness of Morning,
>> Her clouds and her tears are worth Evening's best light.
>
> Oh, who would not welcome that moment's returning,
>> When passion first wak'd a new life thro' his frame,
> And his soul, like the wood, that grows precious in burning,
>> Gave out all its sweets to love's exquisite flame.

The spirit of elegant sentiment that attracted the young Byron to *Little's Poems* made itself felt in certain of the *Irish Melodies* as well, and obviously still appealed to one aspect of Byron's artistic sensibility even in his "mature" years.

III

The first installment of Byron's *A Selection of Hebrew Melodies, Ancient and Modern* was published by Nathan in May 1815 (one more would appear in November).[17] Like each number of the *Irish Melodies*, each of Byron's collections consisted of twelve songs, and Joseph Slater has noted that "physically the book was made almost a facsimile of Moore's Irish volumes."[18] Reviewers were quick to draw parallels between Byron's songs and Moore's, especially since Byron's dedication of *The Corsair* to Moore the previous year had closely linked the two poets in the public's mind. On 11 June 1815 Francis Jeffrey, writing to Moore that he had just read the *Hebrew Melodies* for the first time, complimented Moore by remarking, "There is rather a monotony in the subjects, but a sweetness of versification to which I know but one parallel."[19] The *Theatrical Inquisitor* observed: "With less brilliance of expression, and less voluptuousness of feeling than the verse of Moore, these songs have more of thought and energy. It is the stern manliness of the Corinthian order, compared with the lighter elegance of the Ionic. Yet it must be confessed that Moore's genius and style are better adapted to this species of poetry."[20]

Byron's melodies "often reminded" the *Eclectic Review* of "the compositions of his friend More [*sic*],"[21] whereas the *Critical Review* remarked that the taste and felicity of expression of Byron's lyrics were "not excelled, scarcely equalled, by any other writer of the day, excepting Moore. . . . In one respect Lord Byron is superior to Moore, and that is in the energy and strength of his style. . . . [But] if Moore cannot attain his height, Lord Byron cannot maintain his flight."[22] *Blackwood's Edinburgh Magazine* drew a harsher comparison in an 1820 "Essay on Song Writing": "Among the English lyrists . . . [Moore] is unrivalled. He is worthy of the melodies of Ireland, and they of him. After these, Byron's Hebrew Melodies must not be named. To say the truth, they are neither Hebrew nor melodies."[23] The two collections were also explicitly associated in the "English Melodies" section of the 1819 *New Whig Guide,* wherein songs from both the *Irish* and *Hebrew Melodies* were parodied.[24]

Moore was apparently greatly irritated by Byron's entry into the field of national melodies. Byron's Eastern tales had already spoiled Moore's plans to blaze a new poetic trail with *Lalla Rookh,* which in 1815 still remained unpublished after years of toil. Moore knew that if Byron's melodies proved successful Byron would become a direct threat to his position as England's preeminent songwriter. Even worse, by the time Moore first heard of Byron's intention to publish his *Hebrew Melodies,* Moore had already made plans with his publisher to produce his own collection of *Sacred Songs* on biblical subjects. As early as 25 January 1814 Moore had announced to the composer Edward Dalton, "My appearance as a 'sweet singer of Israel' is near at hand" (*ML* 1:297), but as it happened Moore's *Sacred Songs* were not actually ready for publication until June 1816, by which time they had ironically come to seem like an imitation of Byron's *Hebrew Melodies.* A bitter letter written in 1815 to Power expressed the depth of Moore's annoyance: "It is very amusing to think of Byron becoming a 'sweet singer of Israel,'—but you will find but little of the poetry actually his."[25] In May Moore wrote to Power on the subject of the contrast between his work's advertisement and Byron's: "Did you see the mention of my work and its price in the Chronicle last week? How Lord Byron must curse that fellow Nathan, who is puffing off his Jewish wares in all sorts of quackish ways. He had a Puff about them the other night directly under the Lottery Squibs, in the small type part of the Courier." After the publication of the *Hebrew Melodies* Moore exclaimed to Power with an uncharacteristic petulance, "Was there ever any thing so bad as the Hebrew Melodies? Some of the words are of course good, tho' not so good as might have been expected—but the Music! 'O Lord God of Israel!' what stuff it is! and the price! If the Angel on the title page had *four crowns* instead of *one* and the odd shilling tucked under his wing, it would be four times as emblematical than it is."[26]

While Byron was still working on the *Melodies,* Moore apparently made some disparaging remarks about the project in a letter to Byron. Moore's criticisms were doubtless disappointing, but in a letter of 22 February 1815 Byron tried good-naturedly to laugh them off: "Curse the Melodies and the Tribes, to boot. [John] Braham is to assist—or hath assisted—but will do no more good than a second physician. I merely interfered to oblige a whim of K[innaird]'s, and all I have got by it was 'a speech' and a receipt for stewed oysters" (*BLJ* 4:274). Apparently Moore did not let the matter rest, and so on 8 March Byron retorted, "Sunburn N[athan]!—why do you always twit me with his vile Ebrew nasalities? Have I not told you it was all K[innaird]'s doing, and my own exquisite facility of temper? But thou wilt be a wag, Thomas" (*BLJ* 4:280). In his biography of Byron, Moore attempted to explain this exchange of letters by confessing that he had written to Byron and had taken "the liberty of laughing a little at the manner in which some of his Hebrew Melodies had been set to music" (*MLB* 1:607). Interestingly, however, the first number of the *Melodies* was not published until May, so Moore could not have been "twitting" Byron about Nathan's music unless Byron had shown him an advance copy of the settings.

The nature of the influence of the *Irish Melodies* upon the *Hebrew Melodies* was essentially twofold. First, Moore's lyrics exerted a degree of specific formal and verbal influence upon Byron's. As Leslie Marchand has noted, "some of [Byron's] harps and minstrels and waters" cannot help but recall Moore.[27] Second, and more important, Byron based his entire conception and execution of his task upon the general strategy Moore employed in writing his own "national" melodies. Thomas L. Ashton, author of *Byron's Hebrew Melodies*, correctly observes that Moore "helped create the national-melodies style, and Byron learned that style and its meaning from him."[28] Moore carefully crafted his collections, alternating despairing with defiant laments, hoping to generate a sense of emotional sympathy for the sorrows of his countrymen while also working to transform the image of the Irish from that of a brutish, dirty, drunken race into that of a valorous, artistic, sensitive people worthy of respect and humane treatment. In his preface to the third number of his *Melodies,* Moore characterized the music of the Irish as expressing "the tone of defiance, succeeded by the languor of despondency," and vice versa (*MCP* 4:118). Byron's "Hebrew" lyrics aimed to convey the same senses of sorrow and valorous dignity, and in the same way, through an alternation of delicate laments and stirring martial songs. Marilyn Butler asserts that Byron's attraction to the "politicized tone" of Moore's songs led him to craft a similar "blend of lamentation and fierce patriotic assertion," although Byron's "more aggressive temperament" resulted in a "louder" tone of "ferocity."[29] Frederick Burwick and Paul Douglass, editors of the facsimile edition of the *Hebrew Melodies,* write that Byron "learned to imitate that verve of proud nationalism which resounds in the *Irish Melodies.*"[30]

By writing songs that purported to express the feelings of the Jews, a people at least as oppressed and defeated as the Irish, Byron was enabled, like Moore, to indulge his penchants both for melancholy poetry and for the advocacy of the downtrodden. Byron had in fact explicitly compared the oppression of the Irish with that of the Jews in his 1812 Roman Catholic Claims speech before Parliament,[31] and Isaac Nathan very tellingly observed that while collaborating with Byron, he observed that Byron's "liberality of sentiment . . . was not confined to the Jews alone, but his Lordship often regretted the truly distressed state of Ireland" as well.[32] The identification of Irish Catholics with Jews was a frequent rhetorical device of liberal reformers as well as an old Irish tradition.[33] Moore himself drew a comparison between the two "conquered and broken" nations in his song "The Parallel," included in the eighth number of the *Irish Melodies* (1821), in which song, Moore commented in his journal, "England [is], of course, Babylon" (*MJ* 1:340). Ashton notes that the *Hebrew Melodies* were to a large extent a marriage of Byron's enthusiasms for Old Testament stories and for Moore's brand of romantic Irish nationalism: "From Moore, Byron learned about nationalism and the national-melodies style. . . . Byron joined the national-melodies style he learned from Moore and the Jews he read about in the Bible to write the Jacobin airs of old Zion."[34] Slater writes that pious purchasers of Byron's *Melodies* must have been surprised to find an essentially "secular" book, in which "nationalism rather than religion is the burden" of the songs.[35] In Marchand's words, Byron "associated the militant Zionism of the *Hebrew Melodies* with the struggles for freedom with which he later allied himself."[36]

Burwick and Douglass suggest that Byron preferred Moore's national melodies to those of his many imitators because, while other melody-writers' songs tended to be loaded with sentiment and stereotype, "Moore's melancholy and nostalgia were informed by strength and integrity protesting against a history of Irish oppression and subjugation." They assert that "Byron reveals again and again in his collaboration with Nathan" "his conviction that Moore's way was the right way," and they note that Byron's "contemporaries immediately recognized the similarity between 'The Harp the Monarch Minstrel Swept' and Moore's 'The harp that once through Tara's halls.'"[37] The themes and images of these two lyrics are indeed quite similar. Both poems are laments for a nation's lost glory and degenerated culture. Moore's poem specifically concerns the Hill of Tara, seat of the high kings of Ireland until the sixth century A.D.:

> The harp that once through Tara's halls
>   The soul of music shed,
> Now hangs as mute on Tara's walls,
>   As if that soul were fled,—
> So sleeps the pride of former days,
>   So glory's thrill is o'er,
> And hearts, that once beat high for praise,
>   Now feel that pulse no more.   (ll. 1–8)

Byron's poem took as its central image the silencing of the harp of King David:

> The harp the monarch minstrel swept,
>   The King of men, the loved of Heaven,
> Which Music hallowed while she wept
>   O'er tones her heart of hearts had given,
>   Redoubled be her tears, its chords are riven!   (ll. 1–5)

The harp of Ireland is said to have praised "chiefs and ladies bright," while the harp of Israel "told the triumphs of our King" and "wafted glory to our God" (ll. 11–12) Both poems end on a wistful but somewhat hopeful note: in Moore's poem, the melody of freedom is nearly dead, but the breaking chords of indignant hearts show that "still she lives"; in Byron's poem, the harp of ancient Israel is "heard on earth no more," but can still sound in dreams engendered by devotion and love (ll. 16–17). Byron's poem was the second of the twelve printed in the first number of the *Hebrew Melodies* (the first was "She Walks in Beauty"), a position which effectively established the silenced harp as the controlling metaphor of the entire collection. This was further emphasized by the title page of the second number, which featured the first verse of "The Harp the Monarch Minstrel Swept" over an illustration of David playing his harp. Moore had placed "The harp that once, thro' Tara's halls" in the center of his twelve-song first number, and continually used the harp as a symbol for Ireland in his *Melodies'* engravings.

Byron's "Bright be the Place of Thy Soul" echoes "Oh! breathe not His Name," one of Byron's favorite *Irish Melodies*. The conclusion of Moore's poem compared the tears wept by Irishmen over the execution of Robert Emmet to the "night-dew that falls on the grass o'er his head":

> But the night-dew that falls, though in silence it weeps,
> Shall brighten with verdure the grave where he sleeps;
> And the tear that we shed, though in secret it rolls,
> Shall long keep his memory green in our souls.   (ll. 5–8)

Moore's poem was surely on Byron's mind as he composed the final lines of his own poem:

> Light be the turf of thy tomb!
>   May its verdure like emeralds be:
> There should not be the shadow of gloom,
>   In aught that reminds us of thee.
> Young flowers and an evergreen tree
>   May spring from the spot of thy rest;
> But not cypress nor yew let us see;
>   For why should we mourn for the blest?   (ll. 9–16)

Ashton speculates that "Oh! breathe not his name" also "probably suggested Byron's lines beginning 'I speak not, I trace not, I breathe not thy name,'" but in this case Moore's poem most likely only supplied Byron with his opening line.[38] Still, it is revealing that the first line of the first song he sent to Moore (or anyone else) happened to echo the first line of one of Moore's most famous songs.

In Moore's "Tho' the last glimpse of Erin with sorrow I see," an Irishman flees his country, which has been conquered by "the cold-hearted Saxon." In the first two verses he takes one last look back at Ireland as he prepares to begin his exile:

> Tho' the last glimpse of Erin with sorrow I see,
> Yet wherever thou art shall seem Erin to me;
> In exile thy bosom shall still be my home,
> And thine eyes make my climate wherever we roam.
>
> To the gloom of some desert or cold rocky shore,
> Where the eye of the stranger can haunt us no more,
> I will fly with my Coulin, and think the rough wind
> Less rude than the foes we leave frowning behind.   (ll. 1–8)

Byron's "On the Day of the Destruction of Jerusalem by Titus" expresses the same theme of sorrowful exile from a conquered homeland:

> From the last hill that looks on thy once holy dome
> I beheld thee, Oh SION! when rendered to Rome:
> 'Twas thy last sun went down, and the flames of thy fall
> Flashed back on the last glance I gave to thy wall.
>
> I look'd for thy temple, I look'd for my home,
> And forgot for a moment my bondage to come;
> I beheld but the death-fire that fed on thy fane,
> And the fast-fettered hands that made vengeance in vain.   (ll. 1–8)

Ashton asserts that there is "no doubt" that Moore's song "is the source" of Byron's.[39] As we have seen, Moore's song, referred to as "When the last glimpse" by Byron, was one of the lyrics that Byron had memorized and often sung to himself. Certainly in writing his song Byron could not help but recall the many songs of Moore dealing with Irish men and women exiled like the Jews from their native land.

Moore's "Erin! the tear and the smile in thine eyes" first compares the mixed sorrow and gaiety of the Irish to the blended colors of a rainbow, and then in the second verse expands the simile to hope for a day when "like the rainbow's light / [Ireland's] various tints unite" and form "one arch of peace" (ll. 9–12). Byron's "I Saw Thee Weep" is similarly constructed: it also is a two-stanza poem, in which a woman weeps and smiles in the first stanza, the "living rays" of her eyes outshining the blue and violet of a sapphire; in the second stanza her intertwined emotions are likened to an harmonious intermingling of clouds and sunshine that can bring joy to the "moodiest mind." Byron's "All is Vanity, Saith the Preacher" is very similar in tone and theme to "As a beam o'er the face of the waters may glow," one of the darkest of all the *Irish Melodies.* Moore's poem laments a mysterious thought that "in the midst of enjoyment will stay," reducing the "cold heart to ruin" even in the happiest of moments:

> One fatal remembrance, one sorrow that throws
> Its bleak shade alike o'er our joys and our woes,
> To which life nothing darker or brighter can bring
> For which joy has no balm and affliction no sting.   (ll. 5–8)

(Byron used this stanza as the epigraph for *The Giaour,* as we have seen.) The speaker in Byron's *Hebrew Melody* has "fame, wisdom, love, and power," but every moment of his life is spoiled by a secret sorrow "coil[ed] around the heart," that "stings for evermore / The soul that must endure it" (ll. 1, 19, 23–24).

Moore's "When first I met thee" was a barely veiled and devastating assault upon the Prince Regent, and one of his most popular songs in performance, with Byron and with the rest of Moore's public. The political dimension of this song has been examined in the preceding chapter. Its brilliance lay in charging the Regent by implication with several craven betrayals at once: his betrayal of the Irish; of Catholics; of liberal reformers including the Whigs; of his legitimate wife, Queen Caroline; and of his cast-off mistress and clandestine wife, the Catholic Mrs. Fitzherbert. Byron made his own attempt at this type of stealthy attack in two poems: "Herod's Lament for Mariamne," which was included in the *Hebrew Melodies,* and "To Belshazzar," which he left out of the collection, probably on the advice of William Gifford. In the former poem, Herod is, as McGann observes, "a veiled *figura* of the Prince Regent" (*BCP* 3:471). Herod grieves over his wife Mariamne, she "who shared my diadem," and who has been murdered on his own orders (l. 17). He is shown to be a creature of impulse, who has doomed himself to bitter remorse through his "phrensy's jealous raving" and who has "earn'd those tortures well" (ll. 10, 23). The poem doubtless should be read as a condemnation of the Regent for deserting Mrs. Fitzherbert, which he did not hesitate to do once he realized that marriage to her threatened his royal authority. "To Belshazzar" is much harsher and attacks the Regent even more obviously than does Moore's "When first I met thee." Moore depicted the Regent as an aged, treacherous, foolish deceiver, surrounded by pomp and flattery and lost in "pleasure's dream." In Byron's poem, in the guise of Belshazzar, he is a "sensual" tyrant, "weakest, worst of all," "a mass of earth," old and vain, "Unfit to govern, live, or die" (ll. 2, 7, 20, 24). Like Moore, Byron hinted at the Regent's future downfall.

Byron strove to capture the tone of Moore's defiant war songs as well. This tonal similarity can be heard by comparing such poems as Byron's "Thy Days are Done" with poems like Moore's "Remember the glories of Brien the brave." Moore's soaring song exhorts Irishmen to remember the heroes of their past, such as the eleventh-century King Brien Boru (Moore spells his last name "Boromhe" in a note):

> Remember the glories of Brien the brave,
>   Tho' the days of the hero are o'er;
> Tho' lost to Mononia and cold in the grave,
>   He returns to Kinkora no more.
> That star of the field, which so often hath pour'd
>   Its beam on the battle, is set;
> But enough of the glory remains on each sword,
>   To light us to victory yet.   (1–8)

Moore's song declares that the Irish will "never resign" freedom, urging them to remember the heroes who soaked the moss of the battlefield with their blood, who "stirr'd not, but conquer'd and died." The Danes represent the English: "Go, tell our invaders, the Danes, / That 'tis sweeter to bleed for an age at [freedom's] shrine, / Than to sleep but a moment in chains" (13–16). Byron's "Thy Days are Done" celebrates a fallen, unnamed (presumably) Jewish war hero[40] who will inspire future victories:

> Thy days are done, thy fame begun;
>   Thy country's strains record
> The triumphs of her chosen Son,
>   The slaughters of his sword!

> The deeds he did, the fields he won,
> The freedom he restored!

The poem promises to remember the blood the hero shed and to fight for freedom in his honor.

Comparing the imagery and themes of Byron's and Moore's *Melodies* is much easier than comparing the lyrics' prosody. This latter approach is made nearly impossible by a fundamental but often overlooked difference between the specific type of lyric writing each poet was engaged in: Moore painstakingly wrote his lyrics to fit particular pieces of Irish music, whereas in Byron's case Byron wrote his lyrics without music, and only after he was finished did Nathan attempt to set them to melodies. This is one reason why, when heard, the overall superiority of Moore's songs to Byron's immediately becomes apparent to nearly all listeners; Moore was in almost total control of both aspects of his compositions, whereas Nathan's music sometimes altered the entire emotional content of Byron's words. As Hobhouse observed, "it is not precisely the same thing to have music made to one's poems, and to write poetry for music."[41] Slater points out that "it is quite true that the songs never achieve the inevitable marriage of words and music which is to be found in the work of Burns and Moore and that sometimes they form a most imperfect union."[42]

Hoover Jordan has demonstrated at length the ways in which Moore's task differed from the task of the lyric poet who does not write specifically for music, and how brilliantly Moore succeeded in joining poetry and song.[43] Moore himself considered his songs "compound creations, in which the music forms no less essential part than the verses," and he cringed to see the lyrics printed without their accompanying melodies in collected editions of his works, because those "occasional breaches of the laws of rhythm, which the task of adapting words to airs demands of the poet, though very frequently one of the happiest results of his skill, become blemishes when the verse is separated from the melody" (*MCP* 5:xix–xx). Jordan illustrates Moore's concerns by showing how often a seemingly predictable rhythm indicated by the rhyme scheme in Moore's lyrics is not at all the same rhythm that appears when those lyrics are sung to their appropriate melodies. Additionally, Jordan reveals how in the *Melodies* a word that would count as one syllable in a poem is often purposely held for more than one note when it is sung. Since Byron essentially wrote his lyrics as he would write any other poem, they are more easily judged according to the traditional rules and expectations of poetry. To judge Moore's lyrics in this way exclusively is to apply an inappropriate set of standards. Though Moore was in all of his works an assured master of prosodic technique, he himself wrote that the fact that the *Melodies* were "intended rather to be sung than read" might "exempt them from the rigors of literary criticism."[44]

Although Byron's and Nathan's collections of *Hebrew Melodies* were clearly modeled upon the *Irish Melodies* and, in commercial terms, represented an attempt to capitalize on the popularity of the national melodies style that Moore largely created, Byron's songs were just as clearly intended for a narrower audience than were Moore's. The early numbers of the *Irish Melodies* sold for between eight and fifteen shillings each, with copies of individual songs selling for around two shillings; they were intended to be purchased and enjoyed by the middle as well as the higher classes of society. Moore flattered his readers in the preface to the third number by claiming that his songs were chiefly "found on the piano-fortes of the rich and the educated" (*MCP* 4:130), but the *Melodies* also made their way into the homes of the less well-off, even including those of the poverty-stricken Irish. In 1820 *John Bull* complained that Moore's songs were "to be seen on the piano-forte of every young lady in the bills of mortality."[45] The Austrian Prince von Pückler-Muskau, traveling through the Irish countryside in 1828, described his guide, a "half naked boy of about eleven," "scrambling over the rocks like a squirrel, singing all the while bits of 'Tommy' Moore."[46] By 1839 the Vicomte de Montalembert could tell Moore that during his trip through Ireland the *Melodies* were "sung & really felt, in every priest's house and every peasant's cabin where I halted" (*MJ* 5:2076). In contrast, each number of Byron's and Nathan's *Hebrew Melodies* appeared in a large folio format and sold for a guinea, a price that Moore (and probably many other readers) found prohibitively expensive. Moore was catering to an audience that he knew would include poor Irish patriots as well as fashionable Londoners, whereas Byron was essentially still writing for the same upper-class audience that had patronized his expensive *Childe Harold* and oriental poems.

In commencing an 1818 review of the sixth and seventh numbers of the *Irish Melodies*, the *Monthly Review* presented an overview of Moore's work and observed:

> We find it . . . difficult to compare Mr. Moore with Lord Byron; for really there seems to be such an amicable sort of mutual plagiarism between them, that in the comparatively few lyric productions of Lord Byron he is often the *alter idem* of Mr. Moore; and, in return, Mr. Moore has not infrequently in his latest compositions poached on the manor of his Lordship. *Poached*, on second thoughts, may appear too strong a word; for we believe that, in most of these cases, the game originally strayed out of Mr. Moore's paddock; and, by the laws of fair and gentlemanly sporting, it may, we suppose, be pursued till it is bagged, alive or dead, by the original proprietor.[47]

By "latest compositions" the reviewer doubtless meant Moore's *Sacred Songs,* the first number of which appeared in June 1816. As has been mentioned, *Sacred Songs* inevitably appeared to be a partial imitation of the 1815 *Hebrew Melodies,* although Moore had begun composing the songs for his collection before Byron's volume appeared. Moore's "Sound the loud timbrel" certainly seems to recall Byron's "The Destruction of Semnacherib." Moore's song featured the lines,

> Sing—for the pride of the Tyrant is broken,
>   His chariots, his horsemen, all splendid and brave—
> How vain was their boast, for the LORD hath but spoken,
>   And chariots and horsemen are sunk in the wave.   (ll. 3–6)

The similarity of Moore's poem to Byron's well-known lyric, in which the mighty Assyrian host is laid low by divine will, is readily apparent:

> And the widows of Ashur are loud in their wail,
> And the idols are broke in the temple of Baal;
> And the might of the Gentile, unsmote by the sword,
> Hath melted like snow in the glance of the Lord!   (ll. 21–24)

Also, as Ashton notes, Moore's "Weep not for those" seems to be a reply to Byron's "Oh! Weep for Those."[48] Moore's "Like morning, when her early breeze," in which David "swept" his "sacred lyre," reworks Byron's "The Harp the Monarch Minstrel Swept."

Apart from the two poets' interaction as national melodists, there was one other significant moment in their careers in which poetry set to music played a role. When Byron was about to leave England forever in April 1816, he wrote the first two stanzas of his famous poem to Moore beginning, "My boat is on the shore, / And my bark is on the sea; / But, before I go, Tom Moore, /

Here's a double health to thee!" Rogers wrote to Moore about his last moments in England with Byron: "I see him now as he looked when I was leaving him one day, and as he cried out after me, with a gay face and a melancholy accent, 'Moore is coming, and you and he will be together, and I shall *not* be with you.' It went to my heart, for he loves you dearly."[49] Byron completed the lyric over a year later and sent it to Moore in a letter of 10 July 1817 (*BLJ* 5:250–51). Considering the circumstances under which Byron left England—"cut" by most of his acquaintances, hounded by bailiffs, and abandoned by the society that had worshiped him months before—Byron's tribute to Moore's friendship is all the more poignant:

> Here's a sigh to those who love me,
>   And a smile to those who hate;
> And, whatever sky's above me,
>   Here's a heart for every fate.
>
> Though the ocean roar around me,
>   Yet it still shall bear me on;
> Though a desert should surround me,
>   It hath springs which may be won.
>
> Were't the last drop in the well,
>   As I gasp'd upon the brink,
> Ere my fainting spirit fell,
>   'Tis to thee that I would drink.
>
> In that water, as this wine,
>   The libation I would pour
> Should be—peace to thine and mine,
>   And a health to thee, Tom Moore.

Moore's reaction to this poem has not survived, other than a remark in the biography where he calls it "that most cordial of farewells" (*MLB* 1:669).

The tribute to Moore was set to music by Henry Bishop and published by Power, probably at Moore's instigation (*BCP* 4:480). According to McGann, this first printing appeared in 1818, but Byron's words were printed three years later in the *Times* and the *Examiner,* and both newspapers referred to the verses as being "in circulation among a few of Mr. Moore's select friends," insisted that they were genuine, and referred to the poem as if it had never been made public before.[50] At any rate, at some point Bishop's setting became popular; for the rest of Moore's life people would sing it to him and bands would sometimes strike up the song in Moore's presence. The song fixed the image of Byron and Moore as close comrades even more firmly in the public mind.[51] Unlike many of the *Hebrew Melodies,* this lyric owes little or nothing to Moore's poetry, and is more typical of Byron's "Romantic" mode: the expressions are direct, forceful, and clear, and the tone is that of Byron's particular mixture of sadness mitigated by a wistful acceptance of process and change.

Byron's "amicable plagiarism" of Moore in his *Hebrew Melodies* was, like his earlier imitation of the Thomas Little lyrics and his fitful attempts at topical Whig satire, a natural result of his admiration for Moore's work. It also resulted from a combination of Byron's love of tragic lyrics, of his identification with the struggles of the oppressed, and his desire to give the public something other than the oriental tales of which he was already growing tired. Knowing the current fashion for national melodies, Byron could reasonably expect that such poetry from a pen as popular as his would be a popular success. Even if Byron had not been such close friends with Moore, nor had enjoyed Moore's melodies so much himself, he would naturally have closely studied the master of the medium when undertaking a form of writing that he had never previously attempted. When Moore protested to Power that he would find "but little of the poetry" of the *Hebrew Melodies* actually Byron's, he was complaining that his friend had taken imitation uncomfortably far. Ironically, only two years later, as Moore had always feared, many readers, including Byron, would object to Moore's own *Lalla Rookh* for precisely the same reason.

"An humble follower—
a Byronian"

Lalla Rookh and Byron's Oriental Poetry

O n 28 August 1813, three months after Byron's great success with his first oriental poem, *The Giaour* (published 5 June), Byron urged Moore to go ahead with his own plans for an oriental work:

> Stick to the East;—the oracle, [Madame de] Staël, told me it was the only poetical policy. The North, South, and West, have all been exhausted; but from the East, we have nothing but Southey's unsaleables,—and these he has contrived to spoil, by adopting only their most outrageous fictions. His personages don't interest us, and yours will. You have no competitor; and, if you had, you ought to be glad of it. The little I have done in that way is merely a "voice in the wilderness" for you; and, if it has had any success, that also will prove that the public are orientalizing, and pave the path for you. (*BLJ* 3:101)

It would be another four years before Moore's *Lalla Rookh, an Oriental Romance* would at last make its appearance, but in all that time Byron's interest in and eagerness for his friend's poem never flagged. Although a long oriental poem from Moore would place him in direct competition with Byron for both readers and acclaim, Byron always went out of his way to encourage Moore to "stick to the East," even using the dedication of his *Corsair* to advertise Moore's forthcoming poem. However, when Byron finally read Moore's long-awaited magnum opus in 1817, he saw aspects of his own style reflected back to him, and, rather than being proud of Moore's achievement, he seems to have been mortified. Byron's reading of *Lalla Rookh,* coinciding with an important turning point in the evolution of his critical opinions, crystallized a negative view of his own oriental poems that he had been developing over the past few years. The great majority of Moore's readers immediately detected Byron's influence upon *Lalla Rookh,* although they saw the work as a great accomplishment nevertheless. However, Byron, who had been in the position of imitating Moore directly or indirectly since his very first efforts at poetry, was evidently deeply unsettled by the unexpected role reversal. Moore was now imitating Byron, but Byron had come to see the qualities of his art that Moore was imitating as particularly egregious symptoms of a "wrong revolutionary poetical system" unworthy of either poet (*BLJ* 5:264). By 1817, Moore had moved as close to Byron's style as Byron had moved away from it, a circumstance that disturbed Byron and that demonstrates better than any other the changing nature of the artistic relationship between the two poets.

I

The enormous popularity of Byron's series of narrative oriental poems—his so-called Turkish tales—was constantly on Moore's mind during the five years that he spent working on *Lalla Rookh.* From the earliest stages of his labors, he always expected that his oriental poem, when it finally appeared, would inevitably be compared to Byron's tales. Unlike Byron, Moore could make no claim to firsthand knowledge of Eastern manners or scenery, and compounding this anxiety was his conviction that his own particular talent as a poet lay more in the realm of short lyric poems than in that of long narrative epics. Byron produced no less than six oriental tales during the composition of *Lalla Rookh,* and it is evident from Moore's letters that Moore kept a keen critical eye on all of them, assessing their artistic merit and their reception by the poetry-buying public, always with the aim of deciding what form his poem should take so as to ensure its ultimate success. Byron the oriental poet was an unavoidable, palpable, and crucial presence to Moore during these years of work, and therefore by 1817 Moore's poem could probably not help but exhibit some of those qualities of Byron's tales that Moore and the public had found the most appealing and impressive.

Moore first began work on his oriental romance sometime in 1811 or 1812, expecting that it would not take him very long to complete it. In a letter written to Mary Godfrey on 11 September 1811, Moore complained about the treatment his farce *M.P.; or, The Blue-stocking* had just received from the critics, but he concluded: "I shall now take to my poem, and do something, I hope, that will place me above the vulgar herd both of worldlings and of critics; but you shall hear from me again, when I get among the maids of Cashmere, the sparkling springs of Rochabad, and the fragrant banquets of the Peris. How much sweeter employments these than the vile joke-making I have been at these two months past!" (*ML* 1:160). On or around 22 March 1812 he told his mother that he hoped soon to "have leisure to finish a long poem I have in hand . . . [and] get a good sum for it" (*ML* 1:186). Moore was doubtless encouraged by the enormous success of the first two cantos of Byron's *Childe Harold's Pilgrimage*, published on 10 March, which proved that the public was hungry for narrative poems with Eastern settings. On 7 May Moore told the publisher Thomas Longman that his hectic town life was delaying the poem's completion, but that it would soon be done (*ML* 1:191–92).

At some point Moore showed the poem to Samuel Rogers, whose criticisms apparently led Moore to make major changes. By 13 August, Rogers had once more criticized the poem, and Moore wrote somewhat dejectedly to Lady Donegal:

> He left me rather out of conceit with my poem, "Lalla Rookh" (as his fastidious criticism generally does), and I have returned to it with rather a humbled spirit; but I have already once altered my whole plan to please him, and I will do so no more, for I should make as long a voyage of it as his own "Columbus" if I attended to all his objections. His *general* opinion, however, of what I have done is very flattering; he only finds fault with *every part* of it in detail. (*ML* 1:203–4)

In February 1813 Moore told James Power that Walter Scott's newly published narrative poem *Rokeby* had given him "a renewal of courage for my poem"; perhaps *Rokeby*'s generally cool reception from critics and readers convinced Moore that he could do better. He also told Power that he was refusing to show Rogers the poem until it was finished, as his criticisms had "twice upset all I have done" (*ML* 1:245).

The success of Byron's *Giaour* in June 1813 spurred on Moore's efforts to finish his poem. In July he wrote Leigh Hunt that he had "started afresh with my Poem—(as the Sailors term it) 'taken a new departure' and I like myself much better this time of setting out than I did before" (*ML* 1:273–74). It would be very interesting to know to what extent this presumably major alteration of his poem might have been due to the example of *The Giaour,* but

Moore gives no specific indication of this. He had undoubtedly read Byron's poem carefully, closely watching its reception; he asked his correspondents for news of the poem's fortunes and told his mother on 22 July, "[Byron's] last thing, the Giaour, is very much praised, and deservedly so; indeed, I think he will dethrone Walter Scott" (*ML* 1:270). In his biography of Byron, Moore called the poem "wild and beautiful," and he praised its "fragment" form as being particularly congenial to Byron's talents (*MLB* 1:388–89). By August, as Moore told Power, his "whole heart and industry [were] at last fairly set" on the completion of *Lalla Rookh*, "and for this reason, because, *anticipated* as I have already been in my Eastern subject by Lord Byron in his late poem, the success he has met with will produce a whole swarm of imitators in the same Eastern style, who will completely *fly-blow* all the novelty of my subject. On this account I am more anxious than I can tell you to get on with it, and it quite goes between me and my sleep (*ML* 1:271–72). Also in August Moore confessed to Mary Godfrey that Byron's success had made him feel "down-hearted" about his poem:

> Never was anything more unlucky for me than Byron's invasion of this region, which when I entered it, was as yet untrodden, and whose chief charm consisted in the gloss and novelty of its features; but it will now be over-run with clumsy adventurers, and when I make my appearance, instead of being a leader as I looked to be, I must dwindle into an humble follower—a Byronian. This is disheartening, and I sometimes doubt whether I shall publish it at all; though at the same time, if I may trust my own judgment, I think I never wrote so well before. (*ML* 1:275)

By the end of the month, Byron wrote his encouraging letter to Moore urging him to "stick to the East," and he began sending Moore reference works dealing with the countries of the Levant. Byron also mentioned that he had thought about writing a story about a Peri (a spirit from Persian mythology) in love with a mortal, a circumstance that alarmed Moore, as Moore had already begun writing an episode of his poem that dealt with the very same subject. Moore somewhat nervously asked Byron to inform him at once if he decided to deal with Peris at all in his forthcoming poems, so that he might choose "whether I shall be desperate enough to go on, with such a rival, or at once surrender the whole race [of Peris] into your hands" (*MLB* 1:424). On 1 September Byron assured Moore that he had no intention of writing about Peris, and he added, "Your affectation of dislike to encounter me is so flattering, that I begin to think myself a very fine fellow. But you are laughing at me . . . and, if you are not laughing at me, you deserve to be laughed at. Seriously, what on earth can you, or have you, to dread from any poetical flesh breathing?" Byron once again graciously told Moore that he did not consider himself Moore's competitor:

> It may be, and would appear to a third person, an incredible thing, but I know *you* will believe me when I say that I am as anxious for your success as one human being can be for another's—as much as if I had never scribbled a line. Surely the field of fame is wide enough for all; and if it were not, I would not willingly rob my neighbor of a rood of it. Now, you have a pretty property of some thousand acres there, and when you have passed your present Inclosure Bill, your income will be doubled . . . while my wild common is too remote to incommode you, and quite incapable of such fertility. (*BLJ* 3:105)

On 16 September 1813 Moore was predicting that he would soon finish his poem;[1] in the same month Moore informed Power that John Murray was interested in publishing his work, although Moore had told Murray that "the highest bidder shall have it."[2] On 30 November Byron wrote to Moore, "I have scribbled another Turkish story—not a Fragment—which you will receive soon after this. It does not trench upon your kingdom in the least, and, if it did, you would soon reduce me to my proper boundaries" (*BLJ* 4:184). *The Bride of Abydos* was published only two days later, and on that day Moore gloomily reported to Power, "You see [Byron] has another poem in the Turkish Style coming out—I wish I could write so fast, but this campaign (the Spring one, I mean) I am *determined* to be ready" (*ML* 1:287). By "Spring campaign," Moore meant the London publishing "season."

When Moore read *The Bride of Abydos* he must have been horrified; once again Byron had inadvertently stolen one of Moore's ideas. As he recalled in his biography of Byron, "Among the stories intended to be introduced into Lalla Rookh . . . there was one which I had made some progress in, at the time of the appearance of 'the Bride,' and which, on reading that Poem, I found to contain such singular coincidences with it, not only in locality and costume, but in plot and characters, that I immediately gave up my story altogether, and began another one on an entirely new subject, the Fire-worshippers." Moore "immediately communicated" this fact to Byron, and may have asked him for advance information on future oriental plots, so that nothing of the sort would happen again. Moore had even given the hero of his aborted tale the name "Zelim," which was nearly identical to the "Selim" of Byron's poem. Moore had intended to "shadow out . . . the national cause of Ireland" in his poem and told Byron, "I chose this story because one writes best about what one feels most, and I thought the parallel with Ireland would enable me to infuse some vigour into my hero's character. But to aim at vigour and strong feeling after *you*, is hopeless;—that region 'was made for Cæsar'" (*MLB* 1:433). By the end of the month Moore told Mary Dalby, "Lord Byron's last poem *did give* me (I am sorry to tell you) a deep wound in a very vital part—my story; and it is singular enough, for he could not know anything about it. . . . He *could not* write anything bad, but [*The Bride*] would have been much finer if he had taken more time about it. He is half-way or more through *another* poem, 'The Corsair'" (*ML* 1:289). On 23 December Moore was hoping for "a more uninterrupted spell at [his] Poem."[3] Byron tried to set his mind at ease about *The Corsair* by writing, on 6 January 1814, "When do you come out? I am sure we don't *clash* this time, for I am all at sea, and in action,—and a wife, and a mistress, &c. &c." (*BLJ* 4:17). Also in January, Moore mentioned to Power, "Lord Byron is about another poem. He is one of the very few men that write quick and well too."[4]

With each new appearance of Byron's oriental tales, Moore felt more pessimistic about the prospects for *Lalla Rookh*. Byron knew of these misgivings and in his dedication of *The Corsair* (published 1 February 1814), he tried to rally Moore's spirits. Besides declaring his political solidarity with his friend, Byron also took the opportunity to "puff" *Lalla Rookh:*

> It is said among [your] friends, I trust truly, that you are engaged in the composition of a poem whose scene will be laid in the East; none can do those scenes so much justice. The wrongs of your own country, the magnificent and fiery spirit of her sons, the beauty and feeling of her daughters, may there be found. . . . Your imagination will create a warmer sun, and less clouded sky; but wildness, tenderness, and originality are part of your national claim of oriental descent, to which you have already thus far proved your title more clearly than the most zealous of your country's antiquarians. (*BCP* 3:148–49)

Generous and self-effacing to a fault, Moore was always pleased to discover the same qualities in others and was delighted with the dedication, feeling "very proud and happy," calling his prospective competitor a "profuse, magnificent-minded fellow" and telling Rogers that there were "few more *generous* spirits than Lord Byron's" (*ML* 1:293–94). With regard to the *Corsair* itself, Moore gave Byron his candid opinion: "I may perhaps, as God-father, be suspected of undue partiality for this child, but certainly any thing more fearfully interesting, more wild, touching and 'negligently grand,' I never read even from *your* pen—you are careless, but you can afford to be so, and, whenever you slumber, it is like the albatross, *high in the air* and *on the wing*[5]— the blood upon Gulnare's cheek is terrifically fine" (*ML* 1:305).

On 3 March, after a month of conservative newspaper attacks on both Byron and Moore over the dedication to *The Corsair* and "Lines to a Lady Weeping," Byron again tried to encourage Moore, asking,

> How proceeds the Poem? Do not neglect it, and I have no fears. I need not say to you that your fame is dear to me,—I really might say *dearer* than my own; for I have lately begun to think my things have been strangely overrated; and, at any rate, whether or not, I have done with them for ever. I may say to you, what I would not say to every body, that the last two were written, the Bride in four, and the Corsair in ten days,—which I take to be a most humiliating confession, as it proves my own want of judgment in publishing, and the public's in read- ing things, which cannot have stamina for permanent attention. . . . I have no dread of your being too hasty, and I have still less of your failing. (*BLJ* 4:77)

Moore, however, was so discouraged about Byron's success and his own lack of progress (and undoubtedly stunned and shamed by Byron's rapidity of composition), that he told Byron in a letter written sometime between 3 and 12 March[6] that he was setting aside *Lalla Rookh* for the time being:

> As to my Poem, which you ask about, after many frights and miscarriages, it is at last in a fair way of being born and I think my Wife & I will lie in about the same time June—but that is so late for a poetical parturition, and I am so very willing that the public *not* forget (for what will the public *not* forget?) the very powerful impressions you have just made upon all their faculties, that I shall have no objection to let it sleep quietly over the summer, and try and fatten it up with hot-and-hot sunbeams in the dog-days. (*ML* 1:387)

Byron responded on 12 March by exhorting Moore to "*Think again* before you *shelf* your Poem." He told Moore that he had spoken with Henry Gally Knight, who had visited the Levant and was preparing to publish his own vol- ume of Eastern tales, "one in *each measure*," at Byron's own suggestion:

> The best way to make the public "forget" me is to remind them of yourself. You cannot suppose that *I* would ask or advise you to publish, if I thought you would *fail*. I really have no literary envy; and I do not believe a friend's success ever sat

nearer another than yours do to my best wishes. . . . I wish you to be out before Eastern subjects are again before the public. (*BLJ* 4:80–81)

Moore was probably doubly appalled by this letter, first because Byron had not mentioned anything about Knight's forthcoming volume of "Eastern Tales" even though he had known about it for months, and second, because Moore intended *Lalla Rookh* itself to be a collection of tales told "one in *each measure.*" This was a fact Moore had carefully kept secret, most likely hoping that the mixture of "measures" was a feature that would distinguish his poem from Byron's tales, but now Moore discovered that he had been anticipated even in this plan, and by a newcomer whose volume might appear at any moment. Within a week of receiving Byron's letter Moore told Power, "I am in a sad quandary about my Poem; work as I will I cannot get it ready to put to press till June, and that is quite too late for the season—and yet I hear of more Persian tales likely to come out, which may do me very great detriment, and makes me feel very unhappy at the delay." Frustrated, Moore blamed his nervousness and his delay with the poem on Rogers's "making me begin it all over again so often."[7] As it happened, the first of Knight's poems, *Ildirim, a Syrian Tale,* did not appear until 1816 and did not significantly resemble *Lalla Rookh,* but the prospect of the hordes of "clumsy adventurers" appearing on the horizon must have agitated Moore further.

In May 1814, when the two poets were together in London, Byron communicated to Moore Murray's proposal to purchase *Lalla Rookh* for two thousand guineas, a figure suggesting Byron's influence on his publisher (*ML* 1:321). Moore, however, decided to wait until his poem was finished before selling his copyright. In the meantime, Byron was preparing to publish *Lara,* a sequel to *The Corsair.* On 8 July Byron told Moore that he and Rogers were still deciding whether to publish *Lara* and Rogers's *Jacqueline* together, and Moore recalled that sometime after this letter Byron "proposed that I should make a third in this publication; but the honour was a perilous one, and I begged leave to decline it" (*MLB* 1:567). Moore probably felt that if he was going to be compared to Byron, it had better be on the basis of his grand poem or not at all. On 11 July 1814 Byron lent Moore the proofs of *Lara* to read, and the poem was published jointly with Rogers's *Jacqueline* the following month. On 12 August Byron advised Moore, "Now is your time. The people are tolerably tired of me" (*BLJ* 4:157). Even Moore was a bit tired. Although he told Byron he was "enraptured" with *Lara* (*MLB* 1:568), he gave a more honest opinion to Mary Godfrey: "I agree with you that a great part of 'Lara' is very prosy and somnific; but it has many striking parts, and the death is very fine. 'Lara's' waiting-maid, poor 'Jacqueline,' is in general, I find, thought rather *niaise* than otherwise; which I am sorry for" (*ML* 1:334).

Moore wrote Rogers on 29 October 1814 to propose a rather desperate stratagem that reveals the extent of his insecurity about *Lalla Rookh,* which was now destined to be a group of four tales rather than one extended narrative:

> I am more anxious than ever that you should keep my secret about the *plan* and the *title,* as I really am so nervous upon the matter, that I have serious thoughts of passing off a pious fraud upon the public, and saying, when I publish these Tales, that they have merely sprung out of the poem I have been employed upon, and that I reserve *that* for publication at some future period. This will not only take away all air of pretension from the Tales, but it will keep indulgence alive by giving a hope of something better unproduced. Don't betray me;—no one but yourself and Bessy [Moore] knows the truth; and I will not venture to ask your opinion upon the *morality* of the step, lest you should say something to scare me out of it. For my own part, I think every possible trick fair with that animal *ferae naturae,* the Public.

Moore immediately followed this with, "How do 'Lara' and 'Jacqueline' get on? I see them on every table; so I suppose they prosper" (*ML* 1:326–27). Since the general public had long anticipated *Lalla Rookh,* and since Moore would of course have no further Eastern poems ready to produce after the publication of his "Tales," his ploy was extremely unwise and impractical on its face, and surely the reviewers would have seen through it and punished him mercilessly for any such insecurity about his work. Rogers doubtlessly advised Moore to ignore his fears and press on. Accordingly, by December 1814 Moore had signed a contract with the Longmans publishing firm to be paid three thousand pounds upon delivering "a poem the length of Rokeby" (*ML* 1:343). Moore had refused the Longmans' earlier stipulation that they first have the opportunity of reading the manuscript; apparently this refusal was partly due to Moore's fear that they might be disappointed to receive four poems linked by prose interludes, rather than one long poem. For this reason on 22 May 1815 Moore would again warn Rogers not to refer to the poem as his "Tales": "There will of course be a revision of the contract, and perhaps a retraction, when I disclose the real nature of the work. . . . Pray keep my secret about it with your accustomed fidelity. You calling it 'my tales' in your letter quite startled me—I felt as if the whole thing were known,—for I never call it anything but my poem" (*ML* 1:364).

In the latter part of 1814 Byron and Moore had both kept a watchful eye out for the appearance of Scott's latest narrative poem, *The Lord of the Isles.* Byron saw Scott as Moore's competition, and doubtless Moore did too. *The Lord of the Isles* was generally seen to be the last chance for Scott's poetry to regain the popularity it had lost in the wake of Byron's fresher and more sensational tales. James Hogg mentioned the suspense over Scott's poem in a letter to Byron of 11 October: "The public, I perceive, are hanging in a curious suspense—good reason has [Scott] to be anxious about [the poem's] fate. By it he is established or falls."[8] When Scott's poem appeared in January 1815 it met with only a lukewarm reception from readers and critics. Byron sent Moore a letter on 10 January telling him that he had received an early copy through Murray. Moore printed this letter in his biography of Byron, replacing with asterisks a section in which Byron clearly gave his opinion of the poem. Moore's omission indicates that Byron's remarks must have been negative and likely to offend Scott, who was a friend of Moore's and to whom Moore dedicated the biography. Immediately after the omitted section, Byron wrote,

> Now is *your* time;—you will come upon them newly and freshly. It is impossible to read what you have lately done (verse or prose) without seeing that you have trained on tenfold. ** [Knight?] has floundered; ** [Scott?] has foundered. *I* have tired the rascals (i.e. the public) with my Harrys and Larrys, Pilgrims and Pirates. Nobody but S[outhe]y has done any thing worth a slice of bookseller's pudding; and *he* has not luck enough to be found out in doing a good thing. Now, Tom, is thy time. (*BLJ* 4:252–53)

Moore was doubtless relieved by Scott's failure; he thought Scott's poem "wretched stuff—the bellman all over" (*ML* 1:358).

Moore, however, continued to delay throughout 1815, and by 26 December he was predicting to Samuel Rogers that *Lalla Rookh* would not be ready until May 1816. He informed Rogers that he had finished three tales, but that he planned for the finished work to consist of five, all of which he vowed to take his time with: "I have formidable favourites to contend with, and must try to make up my deficiencies in *dash* and vigour by a greater degree, if possible, of versatility and polish" (*ML* 1:380–81). Moore was certainly referring to Byron's oriental poems in this instance, and the contrast between Byron's "dash and vigour" and Moore's "versatility and polish" would almost become a critical commonplace. Moore seems to have finished his poem by the fall of 1816, but, as he recalled decades later, "The state of distress to which England was reduced, in that dismal year, by the exhausting effects of the series of wars she had just then concluded, and the general embarrassment of all classes both agricultural and commercial, rendered it a juncture the least favourable that could well be conceived for the first launch into print of so light and costly a venture as Lalla Rookh" (*MCP* 6:ix).

Eighteen sixteen was the fabled "year without a summer," when record low temperatures and consequent agricultural disaster combined with widespread unemployment to produce a postwar economic depression. Faced with a severe shortfall in the demand for luxury items like *Lalla Rookh,* Moore asked the Longmans if they would prefer to delay publication until 1817, and on 9 November they said they would, agreeing with Moore that "the times are most inauspicious for 'poetry and thousands;' but we believe that your poetry would do more than that of any other living poet at the present moment" (6:x). Moore's anxieties probably did not lessen when he read the third canto of *Childe Harold;* on 24 December 1816 he told Murray simply, "The 3rd Canto of the Childe is magnificent—no man living can write up to it" (*ML* 1:407). Moore was always an excellent judge of his own strengths and weaknesses as a writer, and when he said "no man living," he certainly meant to include himself in that assessment.

By March 1817 Murray mentioned to Byron that Moore had decided on *Lalla Rookh* as a title, and on 25 March Byron happily chatted to Moore about his choice, comparing his own titles to Moore's:

> I am glad of it,—first that we are to have it at last, and next, I like a tough title myself—witness the Giaour and Childe Harold, which choked half the Blues at starting. . . . I wish you had not called it a *"Persian Tale."*[9] I am very sorry that I called some of my own things "Tales," because I think that they are something better. Besides, we have had Arabian, and Hindoo, and Turkish, and Assyrian Tales. But, after all, this is frivolous in me; you won't, however, mind my nonsense. Really and truly, I want you to make a great hit, if only out of self-love, because we happen to be old cronies; and I have no doubt you will—I am sure you *can.* (*BLJ* 5:186–87)

Byron repeated these thoughts in a letter to Murray, adding, "*tale* is a word it repents me to have nick-named poesy." Byron had subtitled *The Giaour* "A Fragment of a Turkish Tale," *The Bride* "A Turkish Tale," and both *The Corsair* and *Lara* "Tales"; perhaps Byron anticipated that if Moore subtitled his poem "A Persian Tale," it would seem to the public as if Moore were inviting comparison with Byron. Byron also told Murray, "I feel as anxious for Moore as I could do for myself for the soul of me" (*BLJ* 5:192).

II

Lalla Rookh, an Oriental Romance was finally published on 22 May 1817, five or six years after it was begun, and in its final form it consisted of a prose narrative linking four poems: *The Veiled Prophet of Khorassan, Paradise and the Peri, The Fire-worshippers,* and *The Light of the Haram.* The linking narrative tells the story of Lalla Rookh, princess of Bucharia, who is being taken in a ceremonial procession to Cashmere in order to marry the newly ascended young emperor of Persia, whom she has never seen. On the way she is entertained by a bard named Feramorz, who sings her the four tales that make up *Lalla Rookh.* She falls in love with him, and to her joy, at the end of their journey he is revealed to be her intended husband. The "critical and fastidious" eunuch Fadladeen, chamberlain of the harem, also accompanies Lalla Rookh and (since he is also ignorant of Feramorz's true identity) severely criticizes each of Feramorz's tales as soon as it is finished. By this method Moore comically anticipated exactly the sorts of criticisms that he expected to encounter from the actual reviewers of *Lalla Rookh,* thereby taking the wind out of those reviewers' sails.

The *Veiled Prophet* and *The Fire-worshippers* are long, tragic, bloody, and the more obviously Byronic of the four poems in tone, subject, and versification. Both have violent revolution as their subjects, and both are partly intended as political allegories: *The Veiled Prophet* is in large part a statement about the French Revolution, and *The Fire-worshippers* is closely based on the struggles of Catholic Ireland against the English, especially with regard to the disastrous Irish uprising of 1798. Marilyn Butler calls the two stories "fables of contemporary imperialism,"[10] and, although the political dimension of these two poems is rarely acknowledged today, it was immediately apparent to Moore's first readers. *Paradise and the Peri* and *The Light of the Haram* are both far shorter and lighter in tone, and they allowed Moore to exhibit his characteristic lyrical gifts more freely than did the two longer poems. By balancing these more sentimental tales of love and piety against martial tales of revolt and duty, Moore was working in feminine and masculine modes at the same time and offering both to his readers, presumably in hopes of pleasing them all.

When Hobhouse read *Lalla Rookh,* he wrote laconically in his diary, "It is all Byron."[11] As Moore had always predicted, many readers and reviewers noted the influence of Byron's oriental poems upon *Lalla Rookh.* Most of these praised Moore's volume as a work of genius, yet still chastised him for attempting to copy his friend and rival. The *Literary Gazette* noticed that the poems that made up *Lalla Rookh,* especially *The Veiled Prophet of Khorassan,* were

> the most direct imitation we have yet seen, of Lord Byron's style, both in thought and expression. The same ambition to analyse the human heart, and to pourtray its innermost emotions; and the same carelessness of diction, and harshness of metre, are evidently attempted in this work. The trial was an arduous and a dangerous one. First, because imitation is at all times difficult; secondly, because elegance and tenderness of sentiment are Mr. Moore's peculiar characteristics; and lastly, because the public expected from him, at least his usual refinement and correctness of language. That he could not equal Lord Byron in the terrible, was as clear as that Lord Byron could not have equalled him in the graceful. When, therefore, he resolved to cope with his Lordship on his own territory, he ought to have recollected that there still remained another weapon by which he might have made amends for the disadvantage, namely, correctness and harmony of numbers; but this weapon he has disdained to use. He has even affected more roughness than his Lordship.[12]

(By "roughness" this reviewer meant Moore's liberal use of the run-on or enjambed couplet, as well as metrical variation and other prosodic effects, some of which techniques will be examined later.) The Edinburgh *Sale-Room* hoped that *Lalla Rookh* would enhance Moore's reputation but complained that "there are too many points of similarity to Lord Byron, who is heavy metal to meddle with."[13] The *British Review* closely linked Byron and Moore in its notice, and "heartily wish[ed] that [Moore] could be persuaded to leave that morbid path, in which he is treading in the *footsteps* of Lord Byron, and in which there are no new laurels to be won." This reviewer lamented that "the sickly pages of our epicurean poets" had become devoted to the "dirt and debauchery" of the "squalid population of the Mahometan world," adding that Moore's only excuse for continuing the trend was that "the laziness, luxury, lust, and cruelty, which have overspread the Mahometan world have been found so captivating in Lord Byron's poetry . . . that the indigenous products of a mere English fancy have in a great measure lost their odour and their flavour."[14]

A reviewer for the *New Monthly Magazine* regretted that Moore had uncharacteristically "exerted the powers of his fancy to depict villainy and to paint distress," and, like the *British Review,* employed the image of Moore following in Byron's footsteps:

> In this it is evident that Mr. Moore has purposely gone out of his own flowery path, amidst all that can enchant the senses and soften the heart, to follow his friend Lord Byron in painting the fiercer passions, and giving them a terrible effect. Much therefore as we have been amused by these poems, and sometimes delighted, yet, upon the whole, the perusal has left an impression of concern that an author of so much originality of conception, and vigour of intellect, should have condescended to become in any degree the imitator of another, and that too a living bard.[15]

The *Critical Review,* after presenting extracts from *The Veiled Prophet,* remarked that in that tale "the reader will discover an obvious imitation of a noble poet . . . so obvious, that particular instances are unnecessary to point it out. It is successful to a certain extent; but though the story is as horrid, and the character of Mokanna as disgusting as even the feverish and morbid imagination of Lord Byron could picture, we look in vain . . . for the fervid energy of his Lordship's poetry."[16] John Wilson of *Blackwood's Edinburgh Magazine* declared that Azim, the protagonist of *The Veiled Prophet,* resembled the now-familiar Byronic hero: "There is nothing like plagiarism or servile imitation about Mr. Moore, but the current of his thoughts has been drawn into the more powerful one of Lord Byron's mind; and, except that Azim is represented as a man of good principles, he looks, speaks, and acts, exactly in the style of those energetic heroes who have already so firmly established themselves in the favour of the public."[17]

Although most reviewers considered *The Veiled Prophet* the most Byronic of Moore's tales, a few singled out *The Fire-worshippers* for comparison instead. The *Monthly Review* found the closest parallel with Byron in the latter poem: "a large portion of the tale of 'the Fire-worshippers' seems to our fancy to have fallen into the manner of Lord Byron; more particularly as that manner has been exhibited in the Bride of Abydos." The reviewer continued: "Indeed, this is not the only instance, by many, in which we have perceived the same vein of thought, and even an apparently studied imitation of style, in the brother-poets of the day. Mr. Moore, in this work, has, we imagine, frequently imitated Lord Byron; and Lord Byron, we are sure, of late has constantly *sunken* into the manner (if it can be called a *manner!*) of Mr. Wordsworth."[18] The *British Critic* excerpted a section of *The Fire-worshippers* and concluded, "Mr. Moore has imitated his friend Lord Byron in these lines with much success; they are superior perhaps to any of his master's."[19]

Jeffrey, in the *Edinburgh Review*, wrote a long and laudatory essay on *Lalla Rookh*, declaring at the outset, "There is a great deal of our recent poetry derived from the East: But this is the finest orientalism we have had yet." Such a ringing statement must have surprised and delighted Moore; it was almost an explicit judgment from the most prominent critic of the age that Moore's poem had surpassed Byron's oriental tales—at least as an example of "orientalism." Jeffrey noted approvingly that while the "descriptions of external objects" of Moore's East were perfectly rendered, the "characters and sentiments" of his tales were derived from the "poetical imagination" of "rational, honourable, considerate, and humane Europe" rather than from the actual "childishness, cruelty, and profligacy of Asia." This distinction suggests that, for Jeffrey, the best "orientalism" elided the more unpleasantly violent or sensual aspects of Eastern culture, rather than seeking to offer the more unvarnished authenticity that readers thought they found in Byron's tales. However, since Moore's two "Byronian" poems actually contained much more violence and cruelty than did any of Byron's tales, Jeffrey's comments in this regard remain somewhat puzzling. Other critics thought that it was the savagery and eroticism of *Lalla Rookh* that rendered it more convincing and "authentic" than poems like Southey's Eastern epics; George Brandes echoed such critics in 1906 when he wrote: "It required an Irishman . . . Thomas Moore, a colourist with Celtic blood in his veins . . . to reproduce the nature of the East in a style loaded with jewels and barbaric ornaments . . . . [Southey's] *Thalaba* . . . is tame in comparison with *Lalla Rookh*, and as moral as an English sermon."[20]

In addition to praising *Lalla Rookh*, Jeffrey even granted Moore a sweeping pardon for the moral laxity of his early works, conceding that the 1806 review that had led to his abortive duel with Moore had been written "perhaps with unnecessary severity." Since 1806 Moore and Jeffrey had become cordial friends, and Moore had even written reviews for the *Edinburgh* at Jeffrey's request, but nevertheless, Jeffrey's approval of *Lalla Rookh* had been by no means certain. Moore had taken a terrible risk in creating the character of Fadladeen, as he must have anticipated that the pedantic, moralizing, hypocritical eunuch would be widely interpreted as a satirical portrait of Jeffrey himself.[21] Also, the critic Allan Cunningham may have been voicing a common suspicion when he wrote in 1834 that Fadladeen's comical "remorse and contrition, when he discovers, to his mortification that he has been criticising a true prince instead of a peasant minstrel, was suggested, it is supposed, by the change which came over the mood of the *Edinburgh Review* when it was discovered that Byron was a Whig."[22] In the end Jeffrey may have elected to play along with Moore's joke, as he declared himself pleased with Fadladeen's criticisms, finding them "by no means solemn, stupid, and pompous, as was to have been expected," but rather, "very smart, snappish, and acute." Alternatively, perhaps Jeffrey chose to interpret the character of Fadladeen as the *Eclectic Review* described him: "a kind of concentration, we presume, of certain Fadladeens of the North," in other words, a synthesis of more than one writer for the *Edinburgh Review* or *Blackwood's Edinburgh Magazine*.[23]

Whatever he thought of Fadladeen's criticisms and their relation to himself or to Byron, Jeffrey could not very well conclude his remarks on *Lalla Rookh* without mentioning Byron at least briefly. While praising Moore's originality, near the end of his review Jeffrey nonetheless made a passing reference to the echoes of Byron:

> Mr. Moore, in the volume before us, reminds us oftener of Mr. Southey and Lord Byron, than any other of his contemporaries. . . . It is in his descriptions of love, and of female loveliness, that there is the strongest resemblance to Lord Byron—at least to the larger poems of that Noble author. In the powerful and condensed expression of strong emotion, Mr. Moore seems to us rather to have imitated the tone of some of his Lordship's smaller pieces—but imitated them as only an original genius could imitate—as Lord Byron himself may be said, in his later pieces, to have imitated those of an earlier date.[24]

The similar degree and kind of eroticism displayed in Byron's and Moore's poetry was of course often remarked upon, and Jeffrey's observation that the two poets' depictions of love and "female loveliness" were akin was a common one. His brief remarks about Moore's debt to Byron in this instance fail to illuminate the much deeper significance of this element of "imitation" or emulation to *Lalla Rookh.*

The Veiled Prophet and *The Fire-worshippers* were, like Byron's *Bride of Abydos, Corsair,* and *Lara,* concerned with violent revolutions or uprisings against tyranny. Like all of Byron's Eastern tales, Moore's two stories of revolution take place in atmospheres of frantic, despairing hopelessness that intensify as they draw to a close. Both of Moore's tales feature protagonists who are forced to choose between duty and love, and thereby set in motion chains of events that lead to their lovers' deaths; this fatalistic view of the incompatibility of the two imperatives is also one of the central messages of *The Corsair.* Moore's heroes, Azim and Hafed, are in one sense Byronic: both are gloomy, obsessive warriors whose hearts have been hardened by disillusionment and tragedy, though they are not as morally ambiguous as is Byron's typical protagonist; a brief portrait of an even more obviously Byronic character appears in *Paradise and the Peri. The Veiled Prophet* and *The Fire-worshippers* were so strikingly different in tone, style, and message from anything Moore had previously written that the easiest explanation for these new qualities of Moore's work seemed to contemporary reviewers to be that Moore had imitated Byron's tales. This is of course far too simplistic a view of Moore's achievement in these poems, but it is also undeniable that through a combination of his desire to please the public and his pleasure in Byron's work, Moore did imbibe something of his friend's manner and style, thereby producing Byronic passages and situations.

Although the critic for the *Literary Gazette* asserted that Moore clearly "could not equal Lord Byron in the terrible," surely in *The Veiled Prophet* Moore not only equaled Byron but surpassed him. *The Veiled Prophet* tells the story of the Muslim lovers Azim and Zelica (the names are curiously similar to Selim and Zuleika, the lovers of Byron's *Bride of Abydos*), who are swept up in the revolution waged against the autocratic caliph Al Mahdi by Mokanna, the veiled prophet. Mokanna is a Satanic figure who conceals his horrifically disfigured face behind a silver veil, telling his followers that the veil hides features so holy that mortals must not look upon them. The rallying cry of his revolution is "Freedom to the World," and the young, the idealistic, and the oppressed flock to his banner from all of the Levantine nations, deceived by his promises to rid the world of all forms of tyranny and to establish a new golden age. Mokanna is in actuality a hedonistic sadist who hates the human race and revels in carnage. To inspire his troops he makes the beautiful Zelica his high priestess, but in order to bond her to him he forces her to swear an oath of allegiance by drinking blood in a charnel house, after which he apparently rapes her.

Zelica originally joined Mokanna's crusade because she had been driven half-mad by the reported death of Azim, who had left her some years previously to fight against the Greeks, promising to return. Unknown to her, Azim had not been killed but had been taken prisoner, and during his imprisonment he became a convert to the cause of liberty. At the beginning of the poem, when Azim arrives to volunteer for Mokanna's supposedly noble cause, Mokanna orders Zelica to seduce him. After recognizing and confronting Zelica, Azim sees that Zelica is controlled by Mokanna, and he switches sides and helps the caliph rout Mokanna's forces in a series of savage battles. Defeated and besieged, Mokanna invites his chieftains to a climactic banquet, at which Mokanna poisons them and unveils himself as they die in agony. Mokanna then leaps into a pool of acid, leaving Zelica to put on his veil and impale herself on Azim's spear as Azim and his allies storm the stronghold. Years later, after Azim has grown old praying by Zelica's grave, he receives a vision that tells him that Zelica's soul has been accepted into paradise; he dies content and is buried by her side.

Since Azim and Zelica are relatively powerless before their fate, the only really vital character in the poem is Mokanna, whose chilling and ferocious speeches about the folly of mankind read like extreme and intensified expressions of the cynicism and misanthropy possessing Byron's antiheroes. The character of Mokanna also owes much to Milton's Satan, since, although malevolent, he is also portrayed as a fearless, daring, and masterful exploiter of the evil that is already present within human beings. Mohammed Sharafuddin notes that Moore focuses his attention on Mokanna in order to undertake "a multi-level exploration of the nature and origin of his tyranny," and believes that in this tale Moore attempted to put the "emphasis . . . on the tyrant," whereas "in 'The Fire-worshippers' the emphasis is on the *tyrannized.*"[25] Some commentators have called Mokanna a *figura* of Napoleon, but such an interpretation is reductive. Like Byron, Moore was an admirer of Napoleon's energy and brilliance, and Moore's continuing admiration for

Napoleon made itself felt in his *Fudge Family in Paris,* published in 1818, the year after *Lalla Rookh.* Mokanna's crusade certainly represents an incarnation of the revolutionary French cause, but Mokanna himself is fundamentally motivated by hatred for mankind, a form of evil that Moore would no more attribute to Napoleon than would Byron. Mokanna is more accurately seen as a personification of the most radical form of uprooting, demagogic Jacobinism, beautiful in theory but secretly animated by greed, lust, and the desire for vengeance.

Certain scenes and incidents of *The Veiled Prophet* recall moments from Byron's tales. Azim's reunion with Zelica begins with a mournful four-quatrain song sung by Zelica; in *The Corsair* Medora sings a similarly sad four-quatrain song at the beginning of her reunion with Conrad. Zelica's grief over the apparent loss of Azim and over her own sexual degradation drives her to a state of Ophelia-like insanity similar to that of the heroine of *Parasina,* who goes mad because of her incest and the condemnation of her lover Hugo. Moore's poem concludes with a coda in which the aged Azim is shown praying for the remainder of his life over Zelica's grave; similarly, *The Giaour* ends with its remorseful hero spending the rest of his days pining over the dead Leila.

Contemporary reviewers ascribed the "roughness" of Moore's handling of the heroic couplet in *The Veiled Prophet* to Byron's influence. Moore had used the heroic couplet before, in his 1806 *Epistles, Odes and Other Poems*—as well as in his 1808–9 juvenalian satires *Corruption, Intolerance,* and *The Sceptic*—and in these instances he had hewn fairly closely to Augustan standards of execution, keeping, for example, his stress patterns regular and not varying the number of syllables per line. In *The Veiled Prophet,* however, Moore broke with his previous practice and allowed himself much more freedom to create new prosodic effects. Miriam Allen DeFord points out that in this poem Moore sometimes employed a "bold manipulation of dactyls and anapests that lifts the lush verse above its usual self and strikes a note of true music. In this metric form, later to be used with so much distinction by Shelley, Moore was a pioneer."[26] Wallace Cable Brown explains that between the traditional neoclassical couplet and Leigh Hunt's alternative use of the form,[27] "Keats later, and Tom Moore and Shelley in particular, evolved a kind of compromise couplet that retained its form." According to Brown, "the so-called enjambed or run-on couplet appears to best advantage in the work of Moore, Keats, and Shelley," as particularly evidenced by two stanzas from *The Veiled Prophet:*

> Technically it represents a loosening, a relaxing, of the form in the direction of blank verse. The cæsura may occur almost anywhere—or not at all. Metrical substitution becomes more frequent. In meaning and stress, the rhymes tend to be de-emphasized. And, most important of all, the syntax becomes dominantly oblique rather than parallel, so that balance and antithesis are the exception rather than the rule. The dominance of these characteristics represents a final step in the decline of the heroic couplet.[28]

Moore's energetic use of the enjambed couplet in *The Veiled Prophet* gives his lines a flowing quality that increases the pace of the narration during the frenzied battle scenes and during Mokanna's ranting speeches. It also lends a floating, dreamlike quality to the long scene, full of sinuous motion, in which Azim is tempted by the sensuality of Mokanna's harem. Fadladeen turns up his nose at these innovations and others, such as the occasional use of more than ten syllables in a line, as actual critics had many times in the course of dissecting Byron's tales. He declares:

> Then, as to the versification, it was, to say no worse of it, execrable . . . [and] appeared to him, in the uneasy heaviness of its movements, to have been modelled upon the gait of a very tired dromedary. The licenses, too, in which it indulged, were unpardonable;—for instance this line, and the poem abounded with such;—
>
> > Like the faint, exquisite music of a dream.
>
> "What critic that can count," said Fadladeen, "and has his full complement of fingers to count withal, would tolerate for an instant such syllabic superfluities?" (*MCP* 6:148)

In Moore's time many critics wrote reviews that were often little more than lists of lines and couplets that violated the rules of regular versification, and Moore's joke is, of course, that any critic who spent all of his time counting syllables on his fingers was entirely missing the point of poetry. Moore often voiced this opinion, as in his poem "Genius and Criticism" (*MCP* 8:132)

The prosody of Byron's *Corsair* and *Lara* features some of the qualities Brown ascribes to verse employing the enjambed couplet, but these qualities appear less frequently in these two poems than in *The Veiled Prophet*. Wolfson and Manning note *The Corsair*'s use of "racy enjambment, unorthodox caesurae, and feminine and slant rhymes."[29] According to Byron, the irregularities of his versification resulted more from haste than from a conscious design; he told Moore that these "faults, whatever they may be, are those of negligence, and not of labour" (*BLJ* 9:171). As we will see, Byron thought Moore seemed "not so much at home in his versification" of *The Veiled Prophet,* so perhaps Byron felt that while he himself was straying too far from the polish of Pope's verse, Moore was straying further still. Moore's remarks to Byron about the "carelessness" and "negligence" of *The Corsair* suggest that Moore disapproved of this sort of looseness of versification, but by the time he wrote *The Veiled Prophet* he must have changed his mind. Perhaps Moore, like many more traditionally minded readers, saw that Byron's relaxed employment of the heroic couplet form allowed him to infuse his tales with a greater degree of urgency and vigor. By 1819 Moore could register his distaste for Popeian "sing-song" couplets in his diary: "Milton . . . is the truly musical poet, and Milton was a Musician, which neither Pope nor any of his monotonous imitators are—The genuine music of poetry is to be found in the olden time, & we, in these days, would revive its note, if the lovers of the Popish sing-song would let us" (*MJ* 1:199). Byron would return to a more strictly neoclassical heroic couplet as late as his 1823 *Age of Bronze,* but after 1809 Moore would only seriously return to this kind of verse in one more instance, in the angry letters of Phelim Connor in the 1818 *Fudge Family in Paris.*

The luscious, octosyllabic prosody of Moore's second tale is much more typical of Moore's usual style, yet Byron's artistic presence still makes itself felt. The vignette of the "man of crime" featured in *Paradise and the Peri* is clearly indebted to the criminal heroes of Byron's Eastern tales. A peri, searching the world for the one gift that will open the gates of Paradise for her, conceals herself and watches a murderous man regard an innocently pious child:

> She saw a wearied man dismount
>   From his hot steed, and on the brink
> Of a small imaret's rustic fount
>   Impatient fling him down to drink.
> Then swift his haggard brow he turn'd
>   To the fair child, who fearless sat,
> Though never yet hath day-beam burn'd
>   Upon a brow more fierce than that,—

Sullenly fierce—a mixture dire,
Like thunder-clouds, of gloom and fire;
In which the Peri's eye could read
Dark tales of many a ruthless deed;
The ruin'd maid—the shrine profan'd—
Oaths broken—and the threshold stain'd
With blood of guests!—*there* written, all,
Black as the damning drops that fall
From the denouncing Angel's pen,
Ere Mercy weeps them out again.

.   .   .   .

And how felt *he,* that wretched Man,
Reclining there—while memory ran
O'er many a year of guilt and strife,
Flew o'er the dark flood of his life,
Nor found one sunny resting-place,
Nor brought him back one branch of grace.   (ll. 412–29, 459–64)[30]

Stephen Gwynn calls this character "a Byronic sinner."[31] Indeed, the fierce
brow, the gloom, the sullenness, the comparison to thunderclouds, the gaze
that reflects "ruthless deeds," and the self-tormenting memory are all characteristics shared by Byron's giaour and corsair, and Moore's readers (who of
course were also Byron's) would have instantly identified them as such. Compare, for instance, the last six lines of the quotation above with a similar
moment of introspection from *The Giaour:*

But in that instant, o'er his soul
Winters of Memory seemed to roll,
And gather in that drop of time
A life of pain, an age of crime.
O'er him who loves, or hates, or fears,
Such moment pours the grief of years—
What felt *he* then—at once opprest
By all that most distracts the breast?
That pause—which pondered o'er his fate,
Oh, who its dreary length shall date!   (ll. 261–70)

While watching the child at prayer, Moore's "man of crime" becomes repen-
tant in a climactic conversion that was doubtless one of the special attractions
of "Paradise and the Peri" for the more pious readers of *Lalla Rookh,* both

during the Regency and on into the Victorian era. Perhaps many readers who enjoyed Byron's poetry and yet felt uneasy about the near-amorality of the Byronic hero felt a particular satisfaction in seeming to witness that hero's salvation in Moore's poem.

Moore recalled that he began work on his third tale in 1813, immediately after discarding an earlier poem whose plot and characters had been too similar to Byron's *Bride of Abydos*. However, Moore probably retained something of his original plan, because, as the *Monthly Review* seems to have noticed, the central emotional conflict of *The Fire-worshippers* recalls that of the *Bride*.[32] According to the *Literary Speculum*, the characters of Moore's poem "have, indeed, nothing original in them: Hafed and Hinda closely resemble Byron's Selim and Zulieka [*sic*]; but the freeborn loftiness and gallantry of the hero, and the exquisite tenderness of the maid, are more fully and not a whit less poetically developed by the genius of Moore."[33] *The Living Poets of England* (1827) echoed these observations: "[*The Fire-worshippers*], which is a happy mixture of grace and energy, has more than one affinity with Lord Byron's *Bride of Abydos*. Hafed is another Selim, Hinda another Zuleika; but Moore can afford to sustain a comparison of this description."[34] In Byron's poem, Selim, who is secretly the leader of a band of revolutionary pirates at war with the wicked Pacha Giaffir, falls in love with the Pacha's daughter Zuleika. Selim reveals the truth about Giaffir's evil to Zuleika and urges her to join him as her lover, forcing Zuleika to choose between her loyalty to her father and her love for her father's enemy. In the climax of the poem Zuleika decides to go with Selim only moments before he is discovered and killed, after which Zuleika herself dies of grief.

The plot is similar in *The Fire-worshippers,* in which Hinda, the daughter of the tyrannical Emir Al Hassan (a name borrowed from the villain of Byron's *Giaour*), falls in love with Hafed, a warrior who steals into her chamber one night. Hafed's proud, gloomy isolation recalls Byron's heroes; in one striking instance, Hafed, "warm in love . . . fierce in ire," is likened to "some unhallow'd child of air, / Some erring Spirit cast from heaven" (ll. 230–31), which is almost the same description Byron used for Lara: "a stranger in this breathing world, / An erring spirit from another hurled" (I., ll. 315–16). Hinda does not realize that Hafed is the leader of the rebel Fire-worshippers and that he entered her room thinking it was that of Hassan, whom he had come to assassinate. Hafed returns to her on a later night and reveals that it is not the Fire-worshippers who are evil, as she has been taught from infancy, but her father, the bloodthirsty Emir, Hafed's mortal enemy. Hafed leaves her in order to rejoin his comrades in a last stand against the Emir atop a mountain stronghold, but at length Hinda finds him again, warns him that he has been betrayed by one of his followers, and begs him to flee with her. Hafed refuses and dies after a ferocious battle. Hinda, witnessing his body's immolation from afar, is stricken with grief, leaps into the ocean, and drowns. In both Byron's and Moore's poems, the righteousness of the vengeful hero-rebel is partially proven by his ability to win the love of the daughter of his greatest enemy.

Both of Moore's "Byronian" tales are similarly fatalistic about the relationship between love and duty and about the possibility of a revolution against despotism that is both principled and successful. In Byron's *Bride,* Selim's plan to avenge his murdered father is ruined by his love for Zuleika, which compels him to swear that he will not harm Giaffir; Selim dies because he looks back at Zuleika instead of concentrating on escaping from Giaffir's men. Similarly, Moore's Hafed vows that he will not harm Hinda's father, and gives up his plan of assassination for her sake. Ultimately Hafed resists the temptation to abandon his duty and flee with Hinda; unlike Selim he does not allow his love to interfere with his war with the enemy. But as in Byron's tale, love and duty are antithetical, and one cannot choose the one without rejecting the other, and suffering the destructive consequences. In this respect the theme of *The Fire-worshippers* is also similar to that of Byron's *Corsair,* in which Conrad chooses duty over love, which dooms Medora, and honor over expediency, which dooms his rebellion.

The element of political allegory present in Byron's tales became less thickly veiled and more obvious in both of Moore's two "Byronian" poems, but especially in *The Fire-worshippers.* At least since 1813 it had been Moore's intention to "shadow out . . . the national cause of Ireland" in one of his tales (*MLB* 1:433). Byron knew this, and consequently in the dedication to *The Corsair* he emphasized the ancient link traditionally believed to exist between Ireland and the East, claiming that an Irishman would find a special inspiration in oriental materials. Decades later Moore recalled that before beginning *The Fire-worshippers* he had abandoned several stories half-finished, including the one that Byron's *Bride of Abydos* had spoiled, and had become frustrated with his task:

Had this series of disheartening experiments been carried on much further, I must have thrown aside the work in despair. But, at last, fortunately, as it proved, the thought occurred to me of founding a story on the fierce struggle so long maintained between the Ghebers, or ancient Fire-worshippers of Persia, and their haughty Moslem masters. From that moment, a new and deep interest in my whole task took possession of me. The cause of tolerance was again my inspiring theme; and the spirit that had spoken in the melodies of Ireland soon found itself at home in the East. (*MCP* 6:xvi)

Moore called this spirit "that most home-felt of all my inspirations, which has lent to the story of The Fire-worshippers its main attraction and interest" (*MCP* 6:xv). Moore set his story in Iran, whose very name suggested "Erin" to his readers, and Moore made it clear that the defeated, colonized, but defiant Ghebers, whose ancient religion had been outlawed by their Muslim oppressors, represented the Catholic Irish. Moore made his purposes perfectly plain in a footnote at the outset of the poem: "Voltaire tells us that in his Tragedy, 'Les Guebres,' he was generally supposed to have alluded to the Jansenists. I should not be surprised if this story of the Fire-worshippers were not found capable of a similar doubleness of application" (*MCP* 6:201). Fadladeen's "almost speechless horror" at Feramorz's "profane and seditious story" and at his "sympathy with Fire-worshippers" leads him to resolve to alert the government in hopes that Feramorz will be whipped or imprisoned; this was Moore's way of satirizing the reactions of the Tory press to Moore's Irish writings (*MCP* 6:201, 282).

In essence, *The Fire-worshippers,* which Moore had already begun by the time Byron's dedication to *The Corsair* was written, ultimately proved to be an epic tale of Irish resistance to England that Moore could not have written any other way without risking severe condemnation or imprisonment. The American *Lady's and Gentleman's Weekly Museum* noted that in the poem Moore "has given, as far as he dare, an outline of the persecutions of Ireland."[35] Byron Porter Smith describes Moore's characters as "patriotic Irishmen in disguise,"[36] and Howard Mumford Jones sees the tale as a direct allegory of the Irish rebellion of 1798, for his participation in which Moore's friend Robert Emmet was executed. According to Jones, "Hafed is a Persian Robert Emmet, Hinda the unfortunate Sarah Curran [Emmet's lover], and the traitor a composite portrait of government spies."[37] (The traitor is probably more specifically modeled upon Thomas Reynolds, the spy who informed upon

Lord Edward Fitzgerald and his fellow conspirators in 1798.[38]) Emmet cast a long shadow over Moore's life as a man and a poet, becoming a central figure not only in this, Moore's greatest long poem, but also in the *Irish Melodies* and in his biography of the Irish rebel Lord Edward Fitzgerald, in which Moore argued that Emmet was a hero who was forced into treason by England's "bigotry and misrule."

Moore attacked the religious and civil tyranny in a different way in *The Veiled Prophet*. Although Mokanna is a manipulator and charlatan, the autocratic power against which he is fighting is also said to be tyrannical and cruel. Also, although Mokanna's initial Satanic soliloquy about his hatred for mankind is sadistic and malign, his charges against the hypocrisy of conventional religions actually ring true, and almost certainly express some of the skeptical Moore's own beliefs. For example, in his November 1814 *Edinburgh Review* article on the church fathers, Moore had scoffed at the early Christian writers' "puerile and pernicious absurdities, [which] open a wide field of weedy fancies for ridicule to skim, and good sense to trample upon."[39] Fehmida Sultana acutely observes that Mokanna serves a twofold function: "On the one hand he is represented as a living symbol of falsehood and fanaticism, on the other he is a mouth-piece whereby Moore can show his defiance of religion in general as well as of Christianity." He is, as Sultana expresses it, "Moore's whip to lash" at religious excesses both orthodox and unorthodox:[40]

> "Ye too, believers of incredible creeds,
> "Whose faith enshrines the monsters which it breeds;
> "Who, bolder ev'n than Nemrod, think to rise,
> "By nonsense heap'd on nonsense to the skies;
> "Ye shall have miracles, aye, sound ones too,
> "Seen, heard, attested, every thing—but true.
> "Your preaching zealots, too inspir'd to seek
> "One grace of meaning for the things they speak;
> "Your martyrs, ready to shed out their blood,
> "For truths too heavenly to be understood;
> "And your State Priests, sole vendors of the lore,
> "That works salvation;—as, on Ava's shore,
> "Where none *but* priests are privileg'd to trade
> "In that best marble of which Gods are made;
> "They shall have mysteries—aye, precious stuff

"For knaves to thrive by—mysteries enough;
"Dark, tangled doctrines, dark as fraud can weave,
"Which simple votaries shall on trust receive,
"While craftier feign belief, till they believe.
"A Heav'n too ye must have, ye lords of dust,—
"A splendid Paradise,—pure souls, ye must:
"That Prophet ill sustains his holy call,
"Who finds not heav'ns to suit the tastes of all;
"Houris for boys, omniscience for sages,
"And wings and glories for all ranks and ages.
"Vain things!—as lust or vanity inspires,
"The heav'n of each is but what each desires,
"And, soul or sense, whate'er the object be,
"Man would be man to all eternity!
"So let him—Eblis! grant this crowning curse,
"But keep him what he is, no Hell were worse."   (ll. 537–67)

(Robert Birley quotes the concluding couplet of the above excerpt, and observes, "Byron might have written those lines."[41]) Moore certainly meant "State Priests" to recall the Anglican Church, while Mokanna's other remarks suggest the supposedly characteristic abuses of dissenters and Catholics. Immediately prior to this tirade, Mokanna mocks "Sages," "learn'd slaves" who shall reap "honours—wealth" for "trumpet[ing] along" Mokanna's cause "In lying speech, and still more lying song . . . Their wits bought up, their wisdom shrunk so small, / A sceptre's puny point can wield it all!" (ll. 528–36). The satire of these lines may apply to the legion of philosophers who cheered on the progress of the French Revolution, but Mokanna's argument is even more directly applicable to the despised Robert Southey, who, in Moore's opinion as well as Byron's, defended the tyranny of the state for the honors and wealth that the position of poet laureate brought him.

The specter of Robert Southey in Moore's poem is important, because, along with Byron's tales, Southey's *The Curse of Kehama* (1810) was an influence on *Lalla Rookh*, and in a way, Moore was using his oriental poem to frame a political response to Southey, just as Byron first used *The Giaour* for the same purpose. In her important article "Byron and the Empire in the East," Marilyn Butler explains how fictions like Southey's deliberately helped encourage a new, middle-class, pious, proselytizing ideology by emphasizing the supposed despotism, fraud, and cruelty of Eastern religions. Butler demonstrates how Byron attempted to controvert Southey's "'missionizing'" mind-set in his *Giaour* (1813) by establishing a moral equivalence between the pair of representatives of the Christian West, the giaour and the monk, and the pair of representatives of the Islamic East, Hassan and the fisherman. Butler sees Byron's anticolonial attitude toward the East as typical of his position as a political liberal; since, as Butler observes, "religious systems uphold state systems," the British liberal had to include the state religion in any critique of the reigning political order in England. Byron's natural liberal skepticism regarding the motives that underlay the calls of Southey and others for the mass conversion of oriental peoples was augmented by Byron's firsthand experience of those peoples and his consequently heightened sympathy for them.[42]

Moore's defense of the rights of the Persian Ghebers against the colonizing Moslems in *The Fire-worshippers* is sincere and literal, as well as being an allegorical defense of the Irish Catholics against the colonizing English. If Byron had good reasons for writing oriental tales that problematized colonialism, Moore had still better: Moore was an actual member of a people who had been colonized by the British, and whose religion had been proclaimed by the state to be barbaric and fraudulent. There are no Christians in Moore's two Byronian tales, but by strong and unmistakable implication, establishment Christianity, the state power it upholds, and the colonizing ideology it legitimizes are all criticized and finally condemned. The boldness of this most important aspect of Moore's oriental tales took its cue from Byron's, but by portraying the active agency and heroism of his oppressed peoples, Moore refused to present them as silenced victims, as Byron did with the Greek Leila in *The Giaour.* Moore's natural anger over colonialism, fueled partly by his reaction to the systematic British slandering of his executed friend Emmet, is vigorously expressed in this passage:

> Rebellion! foul, dishonouring word,
>   Whose wrongful blight so oft has stain'd
> The holiest cause that tongue or sword
>   Of mortal ever lost or gain'd.
> How many a spirit, born to bless,
>   Hath sunk beneath that withering name,
> Whom but a day's, an hour's success
>   Had wafted to eternal fame!

As exhalations, when they burst
From the warm earth, if chill'd at first,
If check'd in soaring from the plain,
Darken to fogs and sink again;—
But, if they once triumphant spread
Their wings above the mountain-head,
Become enthron'd in upper air,
And turn to sun-bright glories there!   (ll. 546–61)

The intensity of Moore's hatred of spies and informers breaks out in this curse, pronounced by the narrator, upon the traitor who betrays Hafed to the Moslems:

Oh for a tongue to curse the slave,
    Whose treason, like a deadly blight,
Comes o'er the councils of the brave,
    And blasts them in their hour of might!
May Life's unblessed cup for him
Be drugg'd with treacheries to the brim,—
With hopes, that but allure to fly,
    With joys, that vanish while he sips,
Like Dead-Sea fruits, that tempt the eye,
    But turn to ashes on the lips!
His country's curse, his children's shame,
Outcast of virtue, peace, and fame,
May he, at last, with lips of flame
On the parch'd desert thirsting die,—
While lakes, that shone in mockery nigh,
Are fading off, untouch'd, untasted,
Like the once glorious hopes he blasted!
And, when from earth his spirit flies,
    Just Prophet, let the damn'd-one dwell
Full in the sight of Paradise,
    Beholding heaven, and feeling hell!   (ll. 931–51)

The vicious oriental curse had become a staple in Eastern tales; it is prominently featured in *The Curse of Kehama* and in *The Giaour*, for instance. Moore's curse echoes the ferocity of the fisherman's damnation of the giaour, leading the *Lady's and Gentleman's Weekly Museum* to quote it and remark, "The following imprecation upon a Traitor to his Country's cause could never have been penned by any man who did not feel as a Patriot ought to feel. It is as energetic, as feeling and soul-touching as if warm from the pen of Lord Byron."[43]

The firmly anticolonial stance of *The Fire-worshippers* is striking in an era in which popular oriental poems often had the effect of reinforcing Britain's imperial ideology by reaffirming the legitimacy of received notions about the differences between East and West. Jeffrey's reaction to *Lalla Rookh* neatly demonstrates this set of assumptions about the fundamental moral difference between Western and "Asiatic" values. Europe is "rational, honourable, considerate, and humane," whereas Asia is childish, cruel, and profligate. Given this mind-set, the fact that Moore portrays Asian heroes and heroines who are every bit as heroic, honest, and vigorous as Western ones leads Jeffrey to conclude that the "characters and sentiments" of Moore's tales were not truly Asiatic, but were products of the "poetical imagination" of Europe. In much the same way that an intelligent woman was commonly said to have a "masculine" mind, here a courageous Asian is said to have a "European" heart. Moore's tale of principled Eastern rebellion against colonialism is acceptable to Jeffrey because he sees it as so fantastic, because these noble Ghebers can only be Europeans in disguise, engaged in a harmless pantomime. Jeffrey cannot accept what Moore's tale plainly tells him: that the Ghebers' heroic values come from nowhere else but their own, native, Eastern tradition.

By exposing the ways in which the European ideology of empire is upheld by defining the East as a corrupt and inferior "other," Edward Said's *Orientalism* (1978) helped lead the way toward a reassessment of such Romantic "orientalist" texts as Byron's "Turkish tales," which had previously been dismissed by most critics as insignificant and uninteresting "pot-boilers." Nigel Leask, in his book *Romantic Writers and the East* (1992), argues that Byron's Eastern tales are essentially an extended meditation upon the clash of European and "Asiatic" values involved in the exercise of colonial power, and use the erotic-horrific *frisson* of a European character "turning Turk" as the conceptual axis upon which this meditation revolves.[44] Like Butler, Leask sees Byron as deeply skeptical about the ideology of colonialism, yet Leask also notes that in Byron's tales the consequence of "turning Turk" or embracing the moral code of the east is to jettison civilized standards of behavior, to become capable (for instance), like Conrad or Lara, of employing assassination to achieve one's ends (as when Gulnare murders Seyd in his bed in order to save Conrad, or when the knight Ezzelin is assassinated). According to Leask, Byron's oriental poems reveal a dichotomy of light and darkness not between the modern West and the modern East, but between a vanishing honor ethic and the "barbaric," "Asiatic" values of the entirety of the modern world. In the case of *The Fire-worshippers,* Moore reveals less ambivalence about these issues than Byron. Not only does Moore's tale undermine the ideology of empire by implicitly condemning the English colonization of Ireland; it weakens the light-West/dark-East dichotomy so clearly articulated by Jeffrey by presenting an all-eastern cast of characters, some of whom are indeed capable of "childishness, cruelty, and profligacy" but some of whom are precisely as capable of reason, honor, consideration, and humanity as any European.

The influence of Byron's tales upon Moore's poem involves matters of style, versification, content, and ideology, but the influence does not stop there; the visual presentation of the many editions of *Lalla Rookh* generally mimicked that of Byron's tales. The illustrations of Moore's poems were firmly in the Byronic mode. William St. Clair has examined how Byron's heroes were always made to look like savage Eastern versions of Byron himself; in the most common illustrations of *Lalla Rookh,* Azim, Hafed, and the "man of crime" look like Byron's heroes. They are curly-haired, turbaned, baleful-eyed men with moustaches and long pistols or scimitars tucked into sashes. Similarly, Lalla Rookh, Zelica, Hinda, and the other women of Moore's poem are depicted as delicate, light-skinned Europeans in fancy dress, what St. Clair calls "the image of the submissive Byronic heroine."[45] In addition to this similarity of illustration, Moore's use of footnotes both visually and strategically resembles Byron's. All of the tales in *Lalla Rookh* borrow Byron's technique of balancing a fanciful Romantic story with notes that express a scientistic Enlightenment rationalism. As in Byron's tales, the footnotes seem to legitimize the poetry's spectacular exoticism by referring the skeptical reader to learned works of history, theology, and other disciplines, where he or she could find more detailed information on the scenes, costumes, and customs portrayed in the poem. Like Byron, Moore printed his notes directly beneath the text on the same page as the verses they referred to, thereby constructing a "frame" within which the wonders and horrors of his exotic tales could be better contained and circumscribed.

III

Byron, eager to read his friend's great work, was sincerely ready to be pleased. After hearing from Murray in early June that *Lalla Rookh* had become a sensation, Byron on 17 June replied, "It gives me great pleasure to hear of Moore's success—& the more so that I never doubted that it would be complete—whatever good you can tell me of him & his poem will be most acceptable;—I feel very anxious indeed to receive it; I hope that he is as happy in his fame & reward as I wish him to be—for I know no one who deserves both more—if any so much" (*BLJ* 5:239). By early July Byron had not yet received a copy of *Lalla Rookh,* but Murray (whom Byron began calling "the Mokanna of booksellers") sent Byron a review of it containing a synopsis and extracts from the first two poems. On 10 July 1817 Byron wrote cheerfully to Moore and explicitly associated himself with his friend as a poetical brother-in-arms:

> I am very much delighted with what is before me, and very thirsty for the rest. You have caught the colours as if you had been in the rainbow, and the tone of the East is perfectly preserved; so that [Ilderim?][46] and its author must be somewhat in the back-ground, and learn that it required something more than to have been upon the hump of a dromedary to compose a good oriental story. I am glad you have changed the title from "Persian Tale." * * * * * * *[47] I suspect you have written a devilish fine composition, and I rejoice in it from my heart; because "the Douglas and the Percy both together are confident against a world in arms." I hope you won't be affronted at my looking on us as "birds of a feather;" though, on whatever subject you had written, I should have been very happy in your success. (*BLJ* 5:249–50)

William St. Clair has published an alternate text of this letter in which the above extract is followed by the sentence, "I can better Judge of you in the one you have chosen—and still more so, because you have triumphed in this"; this sentence does not appear in the Marchand version, which is taken from Moore's biography of Byron.[48] Five days after this letter to Moore, Byron offered Murray a somewhat more candid reaction to the portions he had read:

> Of the extracts I can but judge as extracts & I prefer the "Peri" to the "Silver Veil"—he seems not so much at home in his versification of the "Silver Veil" & a little embarrassed with his horrors—but the Conception of the Character of

the Impostor is fine—& the plan of great scope for his Genius—& I doubt not that as a whole it will be very Arabesque and beautiful. (5:252)

The versification and the "horrors" of *The Veiled Prophet* were precisely the qualities that the reviewers found most like Byron's own style; perhaps the little he was able to read reminded him enough of what he considered his own bad qualities to make him uncomfortable.

By the beginning of September Byron had at last received a copy of Moore's poem. Whatever his opinions of the poetry of *Lalla Rookh*, reading it evidently provoked Byron to do some soul-searching, and seems to have confirmed him in his ever-increasing distaste for the modern poetry that he and Moore had come to represent. Byron's letter to Murray of 15 September has been quoted countless times by scholars as a defining moment in Byron's "development" as a poet, but his famous remarks on the "Lower Empire" of poetry are too often divorced from the specific comments on *Lalla Rookh* that precede them, and from which they naturally proceed.[49] Byron's whole train of thought deserves to be examined:

I have read "Lallah Rookh"—but not with sufficient attention yet—for I ride about—& lounge—& ponder &—two or three other things—so that my reading is very desultory & not so attentive as it used to be.—I am very glad to hear of its popularity—for Moore is a very noble fellow in all respects—& will enjoy it without any of the bad feelings which Success—good or evil—sometimes engenders in the men of rhyme.—Of the poem itself I will tell you my opinion when I have mastered it—I say of the *poem*—for I don't like the *prose* at all—at all—and in the mean time the "Fire-worshippers" is the best and the "Veiled Prophet" the worst, of the volume.——With regard to poetry in general I am convinced that he and *all* of us—Scott—Southey—Wordsworth—Moore—Campbell—I— are all in the wrong—one as much as another—that we are all upon a wrong revolutionary poetical system—or systems—not worth a damn in itself—& from which none but Rogers and Crabbe are free—and that the present & next generations will finally be of this opinion.—I am the more fully confirmed in this—by having lately gone over some of our Classics—particularly *Pope*—whom I tried in this way—I took Moore's poems & my own & some others—& went over them side by side with Pope's—and I was really astonished (I ought not to have been so) and mortified—at the ineffable distance in point of sense—harmony—effect—and even *Imagination* Passion—& *Invention*—between the little Queen Anne's Man—& us of the Lower Empire—depend upon it [it] is all Horace then, and Claudian now among us—and if I had to begin again—I would model myself accordingly. (*BLJ* 5:265)

It is striking that Byron's reading of a poem he had been urging Moore to write for five years should have been "desultory" and inattentive, and that after an initial reading he should feel that he had not yet "mastered" it. Byron's only specific critical remark about the volume was a negative one and regarded only its prose narrative, but from the subject of *Lalla Rookh* he shifted into his harsh criticisms of the entire "Lower Empire" to which "[Moore] and *all* of us" belonged. It is Moore's poems and his own that he seemed primarily interested in comparing to Pope; Moore's *Veiled Prophet* and Byron's *Corsair* and *Lara* were written in Popeian heroic couplets; were these the poems that he "went over . . . side by side with Pope's"? It seems from Moore's place in Byron's musings that *Lalla Rookh* was the catalyst for his critical reflections, and venting his displeasure at the whole modern poetical "system or systems" may have been a way for Byron to let out his frustration about *Lalla Rookh* without attacking Moore's poem directly, something that would have given pain to both authors (for Murray would surely have told Moore of at least the substance of Byron's comments). It seems very likely that Byron had such a hostile reaction to *The Veiled Prophet* because it closely approximated his "oriental" style, yet was of uneven quality; it is easy to imagine Byron becoming exasperated with this poem, becoming further exasperated with his own tales for inspiring it, and then muting the pain of his disappointment with Moore by damning the whole race of modern poets and blaming Moore's and his failures on the degraded modern era into which they were born.

Byron's distaste for Moore's prose narrative is puzzling, however. Moore's inclusion of Fadladeen's pedantic criticisms was daring, genuinely witty, and entirely original. Fadladeen's criticisms introduce a playful element of self-consciousness into the poem, creating a dynamic situation that is also an allegory for Moore's career: Feramorz (Moore) repeatedly tries to produce poetry that will overcome the sanctimonious criticisms of Fadladeen (Jeffrey, along with Moore's other legions of critics) and win the love of Lalla Rookh (the public—perhaps especially the upper-class female public). Stuart Curran calls this frame for Moore's tales "clever, light-hearted, and self-conscious . . . as enthusiastic a defense of the value of romance as any of those by the antiquarians."[50] Fadladeen's final summary of the qualities of Feramorz's poetry is a catalog of epithets that reads like a distillation of all the typical negative reviews of *Little's Poems, Epistles, Odes and Other Poems,* and the *Irish Melodies.* Perhaps Byron felt that following each poem with a severe critique spoiled the poem's effect, or perhaps he thought the criticisms were mainly an attempt at a peremptory defense against the reviewers, and that that was too much of a concession to their opinions. Perhaps, on the other hand, Byron, like Cunningham, interpreted Fadladeen's last-minute recantation to be a sly joke about the history of Byron's relations with the *Edinburgh Review.*

At one point in the frame tale, Moore actually seems to concede the superiority of Byron's poetry to his own. Some time after Fadladeen delivers his first contemptuous critique of Feramorz's poetry, Lalla Rookh approaches Fadladeen and pleads with him to moderate his criticisms:

> "It is true," she said, "few poets can imitate that sublime bird which flies always in the air and never touches the earth:—it is only once in many ages a Genius appears whose words, like those on the Written Mountain last for ever:—but still there are some as delightful perhaps, though not so wonderful, who if not stars over our head are at least flowers along our path and whose sweetness of the moment we ought gratefully to inhale without calling upon them for a durability beyond their nature." (*MCP* 6:418)

With a language that strangely anticipates Shelley's *Adonais,* Moore was surely thinking of Byron and himself. The comparison of the Genius-poet to a bird that never touches the earth recalls Moore's earlier comparison of Byron to the albatross who only sleeps "*high in the air* and *on the wing.*" Moore's letters and journals show that he consistently ranked Byron's poetry far more highly than he did his own, believing that the popularity of his own works would probably not outlive him. Byron always claimed to be exasperated by what he considered Moore's lack of faith in his own talent; perhaps the above passage struck Byron as defeatist or timid.

In any event, the surest sign that Byron was displeased with *Lalla Rookh* may be that his first letter to Moore after the one of 10 July 1817 already quoted (unless Moore did not supply an intervening letter or letters in his biography of Byron, which is unlikely) was not written until 2 February 1818, almost a full seven months later, and in that letter he wrote nothing about *Lalla Rookh* except a brief postscript: "I delight in the fame and fortune of Lalla, and again congratulate you on your well-merited success." For Byron to have effectively declined to give Moore his opinion of the poem must have spoken volumes to Moore. This letter also included an awkward and unconvincing qualification of Byron's remarks about the "Lower Empire," which shows that either Moore had asked to read or Murray had offered to share the portion of Byron's above-quoted letter dealing with *Lalla Rookh* and modern poetry. Byron explained to Moore:

> I don't know what Murray may have been saying or quoting. I called Crabbe and Sam [Rogers] the fathers of present Poesy; and said, that I thought—except them—*all* of "*us youth*" were on a wrong tack. But I never said we did not sail well. Our fame will be hurt by *admiration* and *imitation*. When I say *our,* I mean *all* (Lakers included), except the postscript of the Augustans. The next generation (from the quantity and facility of imitation) will tumble and break their necks off our Pegasus, who runs away with us; but we keep the *saddle,* because we broke the rascal and can ride. But though easy to mount, he is the devil to guide; and the next fellows must go back to the riding-school and the manège, and learn to ride the "great horse." (*BLJ* 6:10)

Although Byron tried to convince Moore that these remarks were merely clarifications of his earlier ones, they really present an entirely different argument. There was nothing in Byron's letter to Murray about the reputations of modern poets being damaged by "admiration" or "imitation"; Byron had said that their system was "not worth a damn" and their poetry was "ineffably" inferior to eighteenth-century neoclassicism in every possible way. Byron was nothing if not changeable, but his opinions on modern poetry did not alter over the space of the intervening seven months. A more likely explanation for the discrepancy is that Byron was simply trying to talk his way out of the inevitable inference that he thought badly of Moore's poem.

Byron reiterated his convictions about the "present deplorable state of English Poetry" in his 1820 essay "Some Observations upon an Article in *Blackwood's Edinburgh Magazine,*" in which he praised the superior poetic standards of Pope and the Augustans and asked of the modern era, "What have we got instead?" In answer to this repeated question, Byron offered a long list: the Lake School; "a deluge of flimsy and unintelligible romances imitated from Scott and myself"; Southey's oriental poems and epics ("gibberish"); Hunt, who had ruined his "Story of Rimini"; and lastly, Moore, about whom Byron wrote merely, "Moore has—but why continue?" Although Byron's essay does contain several flattering references to Moore, this particular half-finished thought is very suggestive. Byron had been pleased with all of Moore's major works up until 1820 except *Lalla Rookh;* this must be the work Byron had in mind when he wrote these five words. Byron apparently disapproved so strongly of *Lalla Rookh,* and associated it so firmly with the harmful poetic trend he was discussing, that he could not let his essay go by without at least suggesting his displeasure in this oblique way.

In the later stages of Byron's career, when he was forced to defend *Don Juan* against charges of indecency, he sometimes referred to *Lalla Rookh* as an example of a poem of somewhat loose morality that was nonetheless embraced by critics. In 1821 he joked to Moore, "I am not quite sure that I shall allow the Miss Byrons (legitimate or illegitimate) to read Lalla Rookh—in the first place, on account of this said *passion;* and, in the second, that they mayn't discover that there was a better poet than papa" (*BLJ* 8:140). This comment should almost certainly be understood as a casual compliment, rather than as any reflection of Byron's real feelings about the poem. In 1821 or 1822 Medwin brought up the subject of *Lalla Rookh* in conversation with Byron, and Byron mused, "Moore did not like my saying that I could never attempt to describe the manners or scenery of a country that I had not visited. Without this it is almost impossible to adhere closely to costume. Captain Ellis once asked him if he had ever been to Persia. If he had, he would not have made his Parsee guilty of such a profanity. It was an Irishism to make a Gheber die by fire."[51] As pedantic as such a comment might sound to a modern reader, it shows the great importance Byron placed upon accuracy of "costume." Nevertheless, Moore's poem raised far deeper questions for Byron. The real significance of *Lalla Rookh* with regard to Byron's and Moore's relationship was that for the first time, perhaps, Moore's poetry had deeply disappointed Byron, especially since this particular poem was meant to be Moore's masterpiece. Byron was too hard on the poem, but his reaction is understandable in the context of the personal and artistic changes that he was undergoing at the time. In any case, Byron's regret must have been all the worse, since from his point of view he had only himself to blame for having led his old teacher astray.

"Like Kean and Young, upon the stage together"

The Loves of the Angels and the Shadow of Byron

On 27 May 1822 Thomas Moore began writing the long narrative poem that was to become *The Loves of the Angels,* noting in his diary: "began a Poem called 'the Three Angels'—a subject upon which I long ago wrote a prose story & have ever since meditated a verse one—Lord B. has now anticipated me in his 'Deluge'—but n'importe—I'll try my hand" (*MJ* 2:564). The subject upon which Moore and Byron were both writing was the loves of angels for the women who lived before the Flood, a legend based on an ambiguous passage in the book of Enoch (Byron's "Deluge" would ultimately become his dramatic fragment *Heaven and Earth*). During the previous decade Moore had watched helplessly as the great success of Byron's "Turkish tales" spoiled the novelty of his *Lalla Rookh* (1817), and this time Moore was determined to avoid once again dwindling into what he called "an humble follower—a Byronian," if he could possibly help it (*ML* 1:275). In his preface to the first edition of *The Loves of the Angels* Moore explained the situation:

> This Poem, somewhat different in form, and much more limited in extent, was
> originally designed as an episode for a work, about which I have been, at inter-
> vals, employed during the last two years. Some months since, however, I found
> that my friend Lord Byron had, by an accidental coincidence, chosen the same
> subject for a Drama; and, as I could not but feel the disadvantage of coming
> after so formidable a rival, I thought it best to publish my humble sketch imme-

diately, with such alterations and additions as I had time to make, and thus, by
an earlier appearance in the literary horizon, give myself the chance of what
astronomers call an *Heliacal rising*, before the luminary, in whose light I was to
be lost, should appear. (vii–viii) [1]

When Moore recalled this period decades later, he chose a different metaphor and spoke of his anxiety about writing under Byron's "shadow":

Knowing how soon I should be lost in the shadow into which so gigantic a precursor would cast me, I had endeavored, by a speed of composition which must
have astonished my habitually slow pen, to get the start of my noble friend in
the time of publication, and thus give myself the sole chance I could perhaps
expect, under such unequal rivalry, of attracting to my work the attention of the
public. (*MCP* 8:xv–xvi)

Moore's poem was therefore both written and published under the shadow
of Byron, and in an even more immediate sense than *Lalla Rookh* had been.
In its final form *The Loves of the Angels* consisted of three verse tales connected
by a verse frame, and it was published on 23 December 1822, nine days before
Byron's *Heaven and Earth* appeared in the second number of the *Liberal*.

Moore had received a long letter from Byron on 21 June 1822, between
one and four days before he started writing the *Second Angel's Story*, the longest
and most accomplished of the three verse tales that comprise *The Loves of the
Angels*. This letter, which informed him of the death of Byron's daughter Allegra, touched Moore, who observed in his diary that "[Byron] seems to feel
[his loss] a good deal" and that despite Byron's previous affectations of indifference about Allegra, "he feels much more naturally than he will allow"
(*MJ* 568).[2] Moore's receipt of this letter, added to his consciousness of his race
against Byron, must have ensured that he had Byron much in mind during
the conception and composition of the *Second Angel's Story*, which might partly
explain why the poem ultimately took the form it did. The *Second Angel's Story*
not only recalls the plot and themes of Byron's tragedy *Manfred* but also reflects Moore's own thoughts and feelings about Byron's personal self-destruc-
tion through his incestuous relationship with his half-sister Augusta Leigh.
Moore announced in his preface that *The Loves of the Angels* had a "'veiled
meaning,'" and that he had used his story of fallen angels as an "allegorical
medium" through which to "shadow out" the "fall of the Soul from its original purity." However, Moore's *Second Angel's Story* also appears to "shadow out"

the fall of Byron from his position of eminence through the transgression of his love for Augusta. It is a veiled rumination upon a chapter of Byron's life about which Moore otherwise remained forever silent.

I

Before attempting to read *The Loves of the Angels* in this way, it will first be necessary to examine the evidence of Moore's knowledge in 1822 of Byron's incestuous relationship with Augusta Leigh. There can be little doubt that Byron told Moore of his incest with Augusta at some point before the publication of *Manfred* in 1817, and that Moore consequently read *Manfred* with a full awareness of the drama's autobiographical significance. The proof of this is provided by a postscript to a 10 July 1817 letter from Byron to Moore, in which Byron asked, "P.S.—What do you think of 'Manfred?' Considering *all things,* it must astonish *you.* But—always a but—I can't express myself, in writing—however you will understand me" (*MJ* 5:2230). It is not the fact of this postscript itself that proves Moore's knowledge of Byron's incest; rather it is the fact that Moore purposely censored it, printing only "P.S. What think you of Manfred? * * * *" at the end of the 10 July letter in his biography of Byron (*MLB* 2:134).[3] The decision to censor this postscript is explainable only if one infers both that the postscript refers to the incest and that Moore (whom Byron called his "father confessor") fully understood the meaning of "*all things.*" Fortunately Moore preserved the original postscript in his diary entry for the week of 3 March 1842, which contains a collection of sentences and passages that he had intentionally omitted from Byron's letters. He made the list when he was preparing to permanently expunge portions of the original manuscripts of Byron's letters, and wanted to "preserve whatever I think *may* be safely preserved—at least safely in *manuscript*" (*MJ* 5:2230).

Upon the publication of *Manfred,* many readers had of course made the connection between Manfred's apparent incest and Byron's, rumors of which had been rife during the separation scandal of 1816. A week after the poem's appearance, *The Day and New Times* had pointedly referred to the connection between its incest theme and Byron's own life, remarking, "*Manfred* has exiled himself from society. . . . He has comitted incest! Lord Byron has coloured *Manfred* into his own personal features."[4] Fourteen years later, when Moore published Byron's 10 July 1817 letter, Moore did not want his readers to conclude that Byron admitted his guilt or that Moore had been in on the secret. He barely mentioned Augusta in the 1,493 pages of his biography of Byron, and he was nervous about even those few instances in which he did.[5] That Moore definitely knew about Byron's incest is further revealed by remarks he made at other times: for instance, on 25 June 1827 Moore talked about Byron with Mary Shelley and noted in his journal: "[Byron] had told her all about his sister—her surprize & disgust at finding he had also told it to Medwin and (I believe) [Frederick Byng]" (*MJ* 3:1034). During the years that Moore spent writing the biography, Augusta often expressed to correspondents her absolute hatred of Moore. Perhaps she suspected that Moore knew about her relations with her brother and feared that he might somehow expose them in his biography.

If Moore knew about Byron and Augusta in 1817, then it follows that Byron most likely told him sometime between the summer of 1813, when the liaison began, and December 1814, the last time Byron saw Moore before leaving England. It seems extremely unlikely (although not impossible) that Byron would have fully revealed such a sensitive and emotional matter to Moore in a letter. Soon after the affair began Byron hinted to Moore about its nature in a letter of 22 August 1813; Leslie Marchand's text of this letter, taken from Moore's biography, reads: "I have said nothing, either, of the brilliant sex; but the fact is, I am, at this moment, in a far more serious, and entirely new, scrape than any of the last twelvemonths,—and that is saying a good deal. * * * It is unlucky we can neither live with nor without these women." Marchand speculates that Moore's asterisks indicate that Byron "told him more" about Augusta (*BLJ* 3:96). However, Byron probably had not told Moore anything very revealing by 10 January 1814, on which date he wrote to Lady Melbourne about his affair with Augusta and added that "Moore in a letter to me on a *different subject you may suppose*" was giving him advice about Lady Francis Wedderburn Webster (*BLJ* 4:21).

The most tantalizing hints about this matter occur in three letters that passed between the two poets in March 1814. Byron wrote to Moore on 3 March that lately he had had "'no lack of argument' to ponder upon of the most gloomy description, but this arises from *other* causes. Some day or other, when we are *veterans*, I may tell you a tale of present and past times; and it is not from want of confidence that I do not now,—but—but—always a *but* to the end of the chapter" (*BLJ* 4:76–77). Moore replied:

I was very proud of the little you gave me at the beginning of your last letter, because I am sure you thought *twice* before you honoured me with it, and I hope I may long deserve it. . . . I am sorry I must wait until "we are veterans" before you will open to me

> "The book, the story of your wandering life,
> "Wherein you find more hours, *due* to *repentance,*
> "Than time hath told you yet.—"

. . . . There is *one* circumstance of your late life which I am *sure* I have guessed rightly—tho I sincerely hope it is not so bad as sometimes horrible imaginings would make it—you need not recur to it till we meet, nor even *then*, if you don't like it—but at all events with me you are safe & the same *malgré tout*—I could love the Devil himself if he were but such a bon diable as you are—and after all this is the true kind of affection—Your love that *picks* its *steps* was never worth a rush— (*ML* 1:386–87)

Until now the proper context of these comments had been lost, because of an error in *The Letters of Thomas Moore*, where Dowden assumed that the "circumstance of [Byron's] late life" referred to Byron's marital difficulties and consequently misdated the letter "[January or February 1816]." Several details in Moore's letter, as well as in Byron's reply and in his letter of 3 March, prove that Moore's letter was in fact written sometime between 3 and 12 March 1814.[6] Byron's reply to Moore, written on 12 March, began: "Guess darkly, and you will seldom err. At present, I shall say no more, and, perhaps—but no matter. I hope we shall some day meet, and whatever years may precede or succeed it, I shall mark it with the 'white stone' in my calendar" (*BLJ* 4:79).

It seems almost certain that Moore's "horrible imaginings" concerned Byron and Augusta. Their liaison was at this point at least seven months old, and Byron was not involved in any other serious affair (certainly not one about which Moore would have to "guess darkly"). Byron and Moore next saw each other in London for about a month that May, during which time Moore recalled that they "were almost daily together" (*MLB* 1:551). It is therefore likely that it was during this month, May 1814, that Byron told Moore about his relationship with Augusta.

II

When Moore read *Manfred*, doubtless he was as "astonished" as Byron had predicted. Byron's tale of a powerful sorcerer whose love for his sister (whether she is understood to be his literal sister or some psychological equivalent or complement) destroys her and leads to his own downfall could not help but astonish anyone who knew or suspected that incest had played a part in Byron's own fall from grace. When Moore wrote his *Second Angel's Story* five years later, its plot paralleled that of *Manfred:* a Byronic angel's forbidden and unnatural sexual love for a mortal woman (who happens to be, in a figurative sense, the angel's "twin sister") destroys her and causes his own fall from heaven. A predominant theme of both poems is a superhuman character's Faustian thirst for forbidden knowledge, and the way in which the satisfaction of that thirst destroys his lover and leaves him a tormented shadow of his former self.

Moore's Second Angel, Rubi, first appears in the framing narrative of *The Loves of the Angels*. In the beginning of this story, three fallen angels gather on a hill on earth to mourn their fallen state. They proceed to tell each other the tales of how they fell through their different kinds of love for human women. After the First Angel tells his tale, Rubi is introduced. In heaven Rubi was a cherub, a spirit of knowledge, "who o'er Time / And Space and Thought an empire claim'd" (ll. 467–68). As cherubim are second in rank only to the seraphim, Rubi was something of an aristocrat among angels, and even among "the prime / And flower" of the cherubim. He is described in appropriately aristocratic language: he recalls being summoned "with his cherub peers," and is called an "angel-lord" (ll. 557; 1578). The *North American Review* noticed this, characterizing Rubi as "an angel of far higher rank and nobler attributes" than the first.[7] Rubi is described in terms of physical beauty, youth, intelligence, transgressive daring, eroticism, and most important, pride:

> Who was the Second Spirit?—he
> With the proud front and piercing glance—
> Who seem'd, when viewing heaven's expanse,
> As though his far-sent eye could see
> On, on into the' Immensity
> Behind the veils of that blue sky,
> Where God's sublimest secrets lie?—
> His wings, the while, though day was gone,
>   Flashing with many a various hue
> Of light they from themselves alone,
>   Instinct with Eden's brightness, drew—
> A breathing forth of beams at will,

> Of living beams, which, though no more
> They kept their early lustre, still
>   Were such, when glittering out all o'er,
>   As mortal eye-lids wink'd before.
>
> .   .   .   .
>
> 'Twas R U B I in whose mournful eye
> Slept the dim light of days gone by;
> Whose voice, though sweet, fell on the ear
>   Like echoes, in some silent place,
> When first awak'd for many a year;
>   And when he smil'd—if o'er his face
>   Smile ever shone—'twas like the grace
> Of moonlight rainbows, fair, but wan,
> The sunny life, the glory gone.
> Ev'n o'er his pride, though still the same,
> A softening shade from sorrow came;
> And though at times his spirit knew
>   The kindlings of disdain and ire,
> Short was the fitful glare they threw—
> Like the last flashes, fierce but few,
>   Seen through some noble pile on fire!   (ll. 362–72; 383–98)

Rubi is a celestial variant of the Byronic hero: proud, gloomy, disdainful, possessed of an erotically "piercing glance," fallen from grace, and doomed to brood forever over a terrible sin from his past. Rubi's particular sin links him more closely with Manfred than with any of Byron's other brooding protagonists.

Rubi relates the story of how his tragedy began. Upon witnessing the creation of Eve and of womankind, he became consumed with the desire to know Woman completely by finding "Some *one*, from out that shining throng, / Some abstract of the form and mind / Of the whole matchless sex" and descending into her "soul and sense. . . as doth the bee / Into the flower's deep heart, and thence / Rifle, in all its purity, / The prime, the quintessence, the whole / Of wondrous Woman's frame and soul!" (ll. 743–44; 750–55). He found Lilis, a woman whose mind and physical beauty were equally superior to those of the rest of her kind, and began to use his powers to seduce her, appearing in her dreams to beckon her toward vistas of exotic pleasure that would vanish as soon as she neared them. One night, maddened by curiosity and desire, Lilis prayed to Rubi to appear and spend one waking night with her. The now lovestruck Rubi appeared, not in his full glory but with his celestial nature partly concealed, and the angel and the human consummated their love.

Rubi stayed with Lilis, and months passed. To satisfy Lilis's curiosity the enamored angel took her to the ends of the universe, brought her wonderful gifts, and shared with her God's plans and secrets, all the while tortured by the knowledge that their sinful love would cause Lilis's damnation. Finally, at Lilis's request, Rubi appeared before her in his full angelic glory and embraced her. Because of the carnal nature of his love, Rubi's holy flames, harmless when he was innocent, had become scorching earthly fire, and Lilis burned to death in Rubi's arms, like Semele in Ovid's *Metamorphoses*. Her last act before her soul descended to hell was to kiss Rubi's forehead, leaving a mark of Cain, "A brand which ev'n the wreathed pride / Of these bright curls, still forc'd aside / By its foul contact, cannot hide!" (ll. 1489–91). While Rubi tells this story, he twice questions God's justice, first crying, "Great God! how *could* thy vengeance light / So bitterly on one so bright? / How could the hand, that gave such charms, / Blast them again, in love's own arms?" and then, "oh God, I still ask why / Such doom was hers" (ll. 1423–26; 1435–36). This daring willingness to question Providence further links Rubi with the boldness of Manfred as well as with that of Byron's other Promethean or Satanic heroes. After his fall Rubi refuses to pray to God, until he concludes his tale, at which point, overcome with remorse, he kneels down and implores God to transfer all of his vengeance to Rubi but to grant mercy to Lilis.

Like Manfred, Rubi is a tormented, superhuman being who, having taught himself almost all there was to know, yet still, "proud and restless, burn'd to know / The knowledge that brings guilt and woe!" (ll. 590–91). Rubi knew all the "deep-drawn mysteries" of the cosmos, but could not be content until he had known the physical love of a human woman, an unnatural desire forbidden by heaven. In Byron's drama, Manfred had essayed "Philosophy and science, and the springs / Of wonder, and the wisdom of the world. . . . But they avail[ed] not" (ll. 13–17); Manfred's desire to pursue knowledge to its uttermost ends leads him to black magic, incest, and the destruction of his lover Astarte. Rubi is driven by the same impulse: "The wish to know" urges him "onward, with desire / Insatiate, to explore, inquire—/ Whate'er the wondrous things might be, / That wak'd each new idolatry—/ Their cause, aim, source from whence they sprung, / Their inmost powers, as though for me / Existence on that knowledge hung" (ll. 572–78). His transgressive love for Lilis dooms her; like Manfred, he "loved her, and destroy'd her!" (II, 2, l. 117). When Lilis beholds Rubi's true form, she dies, "Withering in agony away" (l. 1458). The phrase recalls Manfred's depiction of Astarte's death: her heart "gazed on" Manfred's, and "wither'd."

The nature of the relationship is nearly the same in the case of Manfred and Astarte as in that of Rubi and Lilis. In Byron's drama, Manfred explains that his sister Astarte shared with him "the same lone thoughts and wanderings, / The quest of hidden knowledge, and a mind / To comprehend the universe" (II, 2, ll. 109–11). In Moore's poem, Rubi relates that Lilis was a woman of superior intelligence, who had a "passion, hourly growing / Stronger and stronger—to which even / Her love, at times, gave way—of knowing / Every thing strange in earth and heaven; / Not only what God loves to show, / But all that He hath seal'd below / In darkness, for man *not* to know" (ll. 1028–34). As is the case with Byron's brother and sister, the love of Moore's angel and human springs partly from what Rubi calls "The wish to know—that endless thirst, / Which ev'n by quenching is awak'd" (ll. 568–69). Lilis and Astarte are not innocent, and each is destroyed partly because of her own transgression. The deaths (and probable damnation) of their lovers make life unbearable for both Rubi and Manfred, leaving both wishing for death.

Even more suggestive than these similarities between the *Second Angel's Story* and *Manfred* is the way in which Moore hints that there is something incestuous in the character of Rubi's love for Lilis. Since Rubi and Lilis, as angel and human, belong to different species, they are not literally related as are Manfred and Astarte, but Rubi nonetheless describes his doomed lover as "my bright twin sister of the sky." She is a combination

> Of every thing most playful, bland,
> Voluptuous, spiritual, grand,
>   In angel-natures and her own—
> Oh this it was that drew me nigh
> One, who seem'd kin to heaven as I,
> My bright twin sister of the sky—
> One, in whose love, I felt, were given
>   The mix'd delights of either sphere,
> All that the spirit seeks in heaven,
>   And all the senses burn for here!   (ll. 808–17)

The most interesting aspect of this passage is that in the fifth edition of the poem Moore replaced "My bright twin sister" in line 813 with the less provocative "A bright twin sister," suggesting that Moore was fully conscious of and nervous about the hint of incest called up by the expression.

In the poem, Rubi seems to mean that Lilis was a woman who resembled him both in the celestial qualities of his mind and in the faults of his too-human desires. Like Manfred, who stands poised on a cliff of the Jungfrau, torn between heaven and earth, "Half dust, half deity, alike unfit / To sink or soar" (I, 2, ll. 40–41), Rubi's "half-lost soul" is "Like some high mount, whose head's in heaven, / While its whole shadow rests on earth!" (ll. 638–40). Lilis is the mirror image of Rubi; whereas he is an angel tainted by human desires, she is a human who has "The impress of divinity" (l. 805) and is, of all women, most fit

> To be a bright young angel's love,
>   Herself so bright, so exquisite!
> The pride, too, of her step, as light
>   Along the unconscious earth she went,
> Seem'd that of one, born with a right
>   To walk some heavenlier element,
> And tread in places where her feet
> A star at every step should meet.   (ll. 764–71)

Her thoughts are "Like summer clouds, 'twixt earth and skies, / Too pure to fall, too gross to rise" (ll. 899–900). She seems half-human and half-divine, just as Rubi does; the *London Magazine* observed that Rubi "gives us reason to believe that [Lilis] is a fallen angel also,"[8] and the *Examiner* noted that Lilis is as much an angel as her lover.[9] Rubi's and Lilis's mirroring of each other, though less literal than that of Manfred and Astarte, nevertheless recalls Manfred's statement that Astarte was "like me in lineaments" (II., 2., l. 105).

III

The full significance of these parallels with *Manfred* is exposed by a single sentence in an 1851 American edition of Moore's collected works. This edition featured an editorial preface to *The Loves of the Angels* in which the editor, "M. Balmanno," wrote: "It may, perhaps, interest the public to know that the Second Angel, Rubi, was intended to represent Lord Byron."[10] The editor does not elaborate on this remark, and the idea does not appear to have been mentioned in any of the contemporary reviews or notices of Moore's poem.

The editor who wrote this intriguing sentence was Mary Balmanno, an English-born poet, artist, and musical composer, author of *Poems* (1830) and *Pen and Pencil* (1858). At least seven versions of her edition of Moore's works appeared in New York and Philadelphia between 1850 and 1878, and she also edited an illustrated edition of Byron's works.[11] Mary Balmanno was the wife of Robert Balmanno (1780–1861), a Scottish-born bibliophile who lived in New York and contributed to the *Knickerbocker,* the *Evening Post,* and the Philadelphia *Graham's Magazine.*[12] Richard D. Altick writes that he had "lived in London literary and artistic circles in the 1820s" and "had known Tom Moore, Thomas Hood, [and] the Lambs."[13] He was a close friend of Hood, near whom he lived in the Strand[14] until 1830–31, when he and Mary left for the United States; while in London he had been secretary of the Artists' Benevolent Fund as well as one the original subscribers to Blake's plates for *Job.*[15] S. Austin Allibone, who was a friend of Robert Balmanno, wrote in his *Critical Dictionary of English Literature* that Balmanno "had contributed many articles to the London periodicals" and was,

> although now (1858) at an advanced stage of life . . . still distinguished for that literary enthusiasm and exquisite taste in literature and the fine arts that rendered him so great a favorite with Sir Thomas Lawrence, C. A. Stothard, Henry Fuseli, Thomas Moore, Sir Martin A. Shee, [Thomas] Crofton Croker, and a host of departed worthies, whose numerous unpublished letters to Mr. B. and now in his possession would form a rich entertainment to the present generation.[16]

Cassell's Biographical Dictionary (1867–69) also noted that Robert Balmanno "was the friend and correspondent of Lawrence, Fuseli, Moore, Shee, and many other celebrated men of his day."[17]

The most likely explanation for Mary Balmanno's revealing assertion that Moore "intended" Rubi "to represent Lord Byron" is that she was informed of this by her husband, who learned it either from his correspondence with Moore or from Moore's own lips when he knew him in London. Moore's connection with Robert Balmanno has been entirely forgotten since the nineteenth century, in that no part of their correspondence has ever been published and there does not appear to be a single reference to Balmanno in Moore's entire diary. Although Balmanno's absence from the diary is somewhat surprising, Moore probably knew, either personally or through correspondence, more prominent personalities than almost anyone of his era, and the sheer number of these acquaintances must have ensured that some of them would escape mention.

If Mary Balmanno's information about Rubi did not come from Moore, the only other probable explanation for her assertion is that she was merely repeating something she had heard elsewhere, a piece of literary gossip or a rumor. If this were the case, it would demonstrate that readers noted the parallels not merely between Manfred and Rubi, but between *Byron* and Rubi. Since readers commonly saw the character of Manfred as a self-portrait, there was perhaps only a short step from seeing Manfred in Rubi to seeing Byron in Rubi.

Such an interpretation might seem surprising to the modern reader, who could conceivably read the *Second Angel's Story* without thinking of Byron at all. However, comparisons of Byron to a fallen angel were common and all but inevitable after his fall from eminence and his exile from England, and the charges of Southey and others that Byron was a "Satanic" figure resonated all the more because the conservative and the pious liked to imagine that Byron had been righteously cast out of England in the same way that Satan had been cast out of heaven. Moore recorded in his diary on 2 June 1819 that he and Thomas Campbell had talked about Byron and that Campbell "said he was 'a fallen angel'" (*MJ* 1:181). Moore called Byron "a bright, ruined spirit" in his poem "Lord Byron's Memoirs, Written by Himself.—Reflections, When about to Read Them," written in 1819 (*MCP* 7:303; l. 38). Countless other writers of prose and poetry after 1816 also employed the simile when writing about Byron. Byron himself paved the way for such comparisons by so describing the heroes of his oriental tales, who were closely identified with Byron himself; for instance, he called Lara "a stranger in this breathing world, / An erring spirit from another hurl'd" (ll. 230–31). It would surely be no wonder if Moore's proud, noble angel, wrapped in gloom and fallen from heaven because of his sexual transgression with a "twin sister," even one "of the sky," could call forth, in some minds at least, thoughts of Byron. This circumstance seems even less surprising when one recalls that Byron's and Moore's romantic poetry was read by essentially the same audience, and that anyone who purchased *The Loves of the Angels* was almost sure to be very familiar with Byron's works (and the rumors about his life) as well.

If, as seems likely, Moore did tell Robert Balmanno that Rubi was meant to represent Byron, he certainly would not have revealed to him the full significance of the parallel. Like all of the friends and allies of Byron who were aware of the facts about Augusta, Moore scrupulously kept his silence about this matter. However, for Moore to retell the story of *Manfred* while thinking of his protagonist not as a version of Manfred but as a *figura* of Byron himself is a further indication that Moore read *Manfred* in an autobiographical light, with a full understanding of the significance of Manfred's incest with Astarte. If Moore thought of Rubi as Byron, the real-life equivalent of his sinful lover must have been Augusta; there is no other plausible candidate.

In his biography of Byron, Moore recounted the joyful five-day visit he paid to Byron at Venice between 7 and 11 October 1819. Byron told Murray that he and Moore reminisced about their London life and "did nothing but laugh," but the two friends also discussed more serious matters (*BLJ* 6:235). Moore recalled:

> The chief subject of our conversation, when alone, was his marriage, and the load of obloquy which it had brought upon him. He was most anxious to know the worst that had been alleged of his conduct, and as this was our first opportunity of speaking together on the subject, I did not hesitate to put his candour most searchingly to the proof, not only by enumerating the various charges I had heard brought against him by others, but by specifying such portions of these charges as I had been inclined to think not incredible myself. To all this he listened with patience, and answered with the most unhesitating frankness, laughing to scorn the tales of unmanly outrage related of him, but at the same time, acknowledging that there had been in his conduct but too much to blame and regret. (*MLB* 2:259–60)

Choosing his words carefully, Moore proceeded to imply that Byron admitted only to a few instances of rudeness and insensitivity toward his wife. Doubtless, however, Byron's account of his marriage and separation must have strayed into more obscure territory. Moore had not seen Byron in almost five years, and had never had a chance to speak to him about his marriage; Moore's journal records that within a few hours of his arrival the two "had much curious conversation about [Byron's] wife" in private (*MJ* 1:225). Knowing what he knew about Augusta, Moore must have wondered whether Byron's liaison with Augusta had helped to drive Lady Byron from him, as the rumors suggested it had. Whatever Byron told him, the whole episode of Byron's separation, exile, and fall from grace seems to have associated itself in Moore's mind with Byron's incest, and this association seems to lurk beneath the surface of the *Second Angel's Story*.

Moore wrote his best poetry when the subject before him was one that he cared about deeply. Just as the *Fire-worshippers* was the best of the four tales in *Lalla Rookh* because it was an allegorical treatment of the struggles of Catholic Ireland, the *Second Angel's Story* is the most vigorous and imaginative tale in *The Loves of the Angels* because of its veiled connection with Byron's life and the intense and natural interest this subject held for Moore. As the appointed biographer of Byron, Moore would spend years sifting through a greater mass of legends, mystifications, rumors, encomiums, and slanders than had been built up around almost any other man in English literary history, while always trying to protect the reputations of his friend and of those he had been involved with. In 1829 Moore told Mary Shelley how he intended to defend Byron: "[I must] blink nothing (that is, nothing but what is ineffable)—bring what I think shadows fairly forward, but in such close juxtaposition with the lights, that the latter will carry the day. This is the way to do such men real service" (*ML* 2:653). The "shadow" of Byron's life that seems to have haunted Moore's imagination the most is his love for Augusta, and that "ineffable" shadow seems to have fallen most starkly across *The Loves of the Angels*.

IV

The nearly simultaneous publication of *The Loves of the Angels* (23 December 1822) and *Heaven and Earth* (1 January 1823), as well as the reference to Byron's drama in Moore's preface, made numerous reviewers eager to compare the two poets' treatments of their subject. The *Times* presented extracts from both poems, noting that "the public curiosity has of course been a good deal excited" and that "two writers of such eminence must form a topic of conversation in every society that has the least pretensions to literature"[18] The *Gentleman's Magazine* was intrigued by "the singular circumstance of two of the most brilliant poetical luminaries of the present day . . . being engaged on the same subject."[19] Accordingly, several reviews of the two works not only compared the poetry but also the poets, who had come, as the *Scots Magazine* put it, "like Kean and Young, upon the stage together, in absolute opposition and rivalship."[20]

A joint review of the two poems appeared in the February 1823 *Edinburgh Review,* causing Moore to note in his journal entry for 1 April, "Received from the Longmans a copy of the new 'Edinburgh Review,' in which Lord Byron and I are reviewed together, and very favourably" (*MJ* 2:622). The authorship of this review has not been positively established, but P. P. Howe and Donald Reiman both speculate that it was written partly by Jeffrey and partly by William Hazlitt.[21] The *Edinburgh* article is an especially valuable document in that it is a perceptive comparative analysis of the two poets' careers, talents, and audiences, written at a time when both writers were well-established and mature artists. The review treats the two poets as equals in talent and popularity, but contends that each is the master of an entirely different kind of art. It begins by acknowledging the general apprehension caused by the news that the two leading poets of the "Satanic school" were writing upon the loves of angels:

> It is curious to see two writers, so very able, and so very different, both treating the same singular, and (as one might be tempted to suppose) almost intractable subject. . . . We may set the reader's mind at once easy by stating, that there is nothing (or next to nothing) of that speculative daring in Lord Byron's present production that gave such just offence in his MYSTERY of CAIN; and that Mr. Moore, in his new Poem, has kept his amatory vein within the strict bounds of decorum. The first of these very extraordinary performances may be read without incurring a frown from the brow of piety, and the last without calling up a blush in the cheek of modesty. Considering the nature of the subject, and the temper of the authors, this is a great and a rare merit.

Such a passage clearly illustrates one reason that Byron and Moore were so often linked in the public mind: "the temper of the authors" was thought to be similarly dangerous. Each poet's works were seen to represent a different kind of potential threat, but to conservatives, "speculative daring" and the "amatory vein" (or, less gently put, impiety and indecency) were closely related and equally political in nature, inasmuch as they were thought to be inevitable consequences of the Jacobinical or Radical position of hostility to the established order. Thomas Noon Talfourd, writing in the *Lady's Magazine,* acidly noted that neither poet "had before been exceedingly biblical."[22]

The review proceeded to quote Moore's self-effacing mention of Byron in the preface to his poem, and commented,

This is an amiable, but by no means a reasonable modesty. The light that plays round Mr. Moore's verses, tender, glancing, and brilliant, is in no danger of being extinguished even in the sullen glare of Lord Byron's genius. An aurora borealis might as well think of being put out by an eruption of Mount Vesuvius. They are both bright stars in the firmament of modern poetry, but as distant and unlike as Saturn and Mercury. Their rising may be at the same time, but they can never move in the same orb, nor meet and jostle in "the wide pathless way" of fancy and invention. Let Mr. Moore then shine on, and fear no envious eclipse, unless it be from an excess of his own light![23]

The metaphorical dichotomy of Byron as volcano (or nature in its "sublime" aspect) and Moore as aurora (or "beautiful" nature) is developed and transformed throughout the rest of the article. According to the review, Byron and Moore shared the same group of readers, but within that group, each half favored one or the other writer depending upon his or her own temperament:

We conceive, though these two celebrated writers in some measure divide the Poetical Public between them, that it is not the same Public whose favour they severally enjoy in the highest degree. They are both read and admired, no doubt, by the same extended circle of taste and fashion; but each is the favourite of a totally different set of readers. Thus a lover may pay the same outward attention to two different women; but he only means to flirt with the one, while the other is the mistress of his heart. The gay, the fair, the witty, the happy, idolize Mr. Moore's delightful Muse, on her pedestal of airy smiles or transient tears. Lord Byron's severer verse is enshrined in the breasts of those whose gaiety has turned to gall, whose fair exterior has a canker within, whose mirth has received a rebuke as if it were folly, from whom happiness has fled like a dream! If we compute the odds upon the known chances of human life, his Lordship will bid fair to have as numerous a class of votaries as his more agreeable rival!

Such generalizations are more facile than the critical remarks that follow, but this passage is interesting for the picture it seems to present of the roughly equal popularity of Byron and Moore in 1823.

The review next attempted to isolate the essential difference between the poetry of Byron and that of Moore:

We are not going to give a preference, but we beg leave to make a distinction on the present occasion. The poetry of Moore is essentially that of *Fancy;* the poetry of Byron that of *Passion.* If there is passion in the effusions of the one, the fancy by which it is expressed predominates over it: if fancy is called to the aid of the other, it is still subservient to the passion. Lord Byron's jests are down-right earnest; Mr. Moore, when he is most serious, seems half in jest. The latter plays and trifles with his subject, caresses and grows enamoured of it: the former grasps it eagerly to his bosom, breathes death upon it, and turns from it with loathing or dismay! The fine aroma, that is exhaled from the flowers of poesy, every where lends its perfume to the verse of the Bard of Erin. The noble bard (less fortunate in his Muse) tries to extract poison from them. If Lord Byron flings his own views or feelings upon outward objects (jaundicing the sun), Mr. Moore seems to exist in the delights, the virgin fancies of nature.

The review evidently does not use the word *fancy* in the Coleridgeian lesser sense, but in the way that Moore himself used it, as a synonym for *imagination* or *invention*. According to the review's formulation, Byron's personal emotions eclipsed his capacity for invention, whereas Moore's overactive imagination eclipsed his ability to communicate sincere feeling. The reviewer noted that in Moore's poetry the "sincere" expression of emotion is always in danger of being buried under images or conceits:

> Every page of [Moore's] works is a vignette, every line that he writes glows or sparkles. . . . The worst is, our author's mind is too vivid, too active, to suffer a moment's repose. We are cloyed with sweetness and dazzled with splendour. Every image must 'blush celestial rosy red, love's proper hue,'—every syllable must breathe a sigh. A sentiment is lost in a simile—the simile is overloaded with an epithet.

Moore was aware of this tendency in his writing, describing to Hunt in 1819 the "phantasmagoria that [my imagination] passes before me as I write": "You are quite right about the conceits that disfigure my poetry; but you (& others) are quite wrong in supposing that I *hunt* after them—my greatest difficulty is to *hunt them* away. . . . In short St. Anthony's temptations were nothing to what an Irish fancy has to undergo from all its own brood of will-o-th'-wisps and hobgoblins" (*ML* 2:471). We have also seen that Moore doubted poetry's ability to be "an interpreter of feeling," and preferred to depict "those emotions and passions, of which imagination forms a predominant ingredient,—such as love, in its first dreams, before reality has come to imbody or dispel them, or sorrow, in its wane, when beginning to pass away from the heart into the fancy" (*MLB* 1:664). Byron, on the other hand (according to the *Edinburgh* review), foregrounded the passions of his protagonists to the comparative exclusion of all else, losing in imaginative description what he gained in emotional intensity. Moore painted the "virgin fancies," or ideal aspect of nature, while natural objects and scenes in Byron's poetry were altered by the projections of his own psyche. The reference to "jaundicing the sun" must refer to Byron's 1816 poem "Darkness," which described the death of the sun and which most critics interpreted as a metaphor for Byron's own psychological state.

The reviewer's contrast between Byron's stark but passionate style and Moore's luxuriant imagery was developed through several other metaphorical images:

> We do not believe Mr. Moore ever writes a line, that in itself would not pass for poetry, that is not at least a vivid or harmonious commonplace. Lord Byron writes whole pages of sullen, crabbed prose, like a long dreary road that, however, leads to doleful shades or palaces of the blest. In short, Mr. Moore's Parnassus is a blooming Eden; Lord Byron's is a rugged wilderness of shame and sorrow. . . . Mr. Moore's poetry is the thornless rose—its touch is velvet, its hue vermilion, and its graceful form is cast in beauty's mould. Lord Byron's is a prickly bramble, or sometimes a deadly Upas, of form uncouth and uninviting, that has its root in the clefts of the rock, and its head mocking the skies, round which the loud cataracts roar, and that wars with the thunder-cloud and tempest.

This florid language is followed by some very acute critical remarks upon Moore's style. The review charged Moore's "serious poetry" with "two peculiarities": first, that it does not attempt to make common things beautiful, but confines itself to describing things that are already beautiful in themselves. Whereas Wordsworth, according to the review, "perversely reli[es] too much (or wholly) on [the] reaction of the imagination on subjects that are petty and repulsive in themselves," Moore "appeals too exclusively to the flattering support of sense and fancy." Second, Moore "hardly ever describes entire objects, but abstract qualities of objects," a tendency that produced in his poetry a "sort of sylph-like, spiritualized sensuality." The reviewer's comments comprise an excellent and perceptive identification of an important aspect of Moore's poetry: the persistent impulse to escape from the quotidian and the commonplace into a hazily beautiful, sensuous dreamworld. Moore preferred to portray powerful drives such as love and aggression only within a half-imaginary, mythologized world such as the Orient or the medieval past, a tactic that allowed Moore to indulge his talent for Spenserian or Keatsian lushness, but that for many readers has also made his characters and situations seem too distant or idealized.

Although the *Edinburgh* reviewer(s) did not express a preference for one or the other of the two poems, and other critics considered the *Liberal* to be beneath their notice, a few writers did explicitly prefer Byron's drama to Moore's tale. In a joint review that Moore called "a tolerably murderous discharge," John Wilson of *Blackwood's Edinburgh Magazine* mocked Moore and praised Byron: "Moore writes with a crow-quill, on hot-press wire-wove card-paper, adorned with Cupids sporting round Venus on a couch. Byron writes with an eagle's plume, as if upon a broad leaf taken from some great tree that afterwards perished in the flood."[24] The *Monthly Magazine* asserted, "Nothing which Lord Byron has yet written surpasses in sublimity, in force, and in pathos, this mystery of 'Heaven and Earth'. . . . That, in our opinion, he has far surpassed his competitor will be readily inferred."[25]

Despite these judgments, Moore's work was reviewed in at least thirty-five prominent English periodicals (Byron's drama was reviewed in about eight, some of which were the joint reviews with Moore), and for the most part *The Loves of the Angels* received favorable treatment and sold well (Moore wrote that the poem sold nearly five thousand copies in one week [*MJ* 2:512] and a thousand more within the month[26]). However, many critics chided or harshly attacked Moore for mixing religious and sexual themes, and some were outraged at what they claimed was a blasphemous reduction of God, heaven, and angels to mere trappings in an erotic love story. Upon publication of the first edition Moore was extremely apprehensive that the poem might revive his reputation for licentiousness, even though he himself considered it "the best, as well as the most moral thing I had ever written" (*MJ* 2:597–98). In his preface he tried to explain the poem's "moral" point of view, claiming that the subject of fallen angels afforded him

> an allegorical medium, through which might be shadowed out (as I have endeavored to do in the following stories,) the fall of the Soul from its original purity—the loss of light and happiness which it suffers, in the pursuit of this world's perishable pleasures—and the punishments, both from conscience and Divine justice, with which impurity, pride, and presumptuous inquiry into the awful secrets of God, are sure to be visited. The beautiful story of Cupid and Psyche owes its chief charm to this sort of "veiled meaning," and it has been my

wish (however I may have failed in the attempt) to communicate the same
moral interest to the following pages. (i)

Whatever Moore's moral intentions with regard to *The Loves of the Angels,* he
was too much of a skeptic to play the moralist convincingly. Moore's affection
and compassion for his characters, and the celebrations of "this world's per-
ishable pleasures" that appear in this poem and everywhere else in his poetry,
make his condemnations of the lovers' "sins" seem rather gratuitous.

Whereas many readers were disturbed by Moore's treatment of his religious subject, Byron's *Heaven and Earth* was generally lauded for its serene
and sublime rendering of the story of the Flood. Moore admired *Heaven
and Earth* as well; in 1841 he called the drama "one of the most sublime of
[Byron's] many poetical miracles" (*MCP* 8:xv). The *Gentleman's Magazine* observed of Byron's drama that "from its mitigated immorality, when compared
with former productions, we have no doubt, but the public censure [of Byron]
has produced a desirable effect."[27] "Former productions" was doubtless mainly
a reference to Byron's earlier Old Testament "Mystery," *Cain,* published in
1821, whose "impiety" provoked widespread outrage and brought threats of
prosecution against Murray. Moore must have noted that Byron was in some
measure redeeming his reputation, while Moore was imperiling his own once
again. Indeed, a month before the appearance of Moore's poem, the Longmans received an anonymous letter warning them not to publish it and concluding, "'Beware the fate of Murray and of Cain!'" (*MJ* 2:593).

Moore closely watched the public reaction to his poem during the first
weeks of 1823. One of the worst attacks, predictably, came from *John Bull,*
which regularly assailed both Byron and Moore. Moore noted on 9 January
1823 that in the newspaper "the 'Angels' are grossly abused, and strong efforts
made (which I rather fear may be but too successful in some quarters) to
brand it with a character of impiety and blasphemy. This is too hard. . . .
Should not wonder now if the tide were to set decidedly against it" (*MJ* 2:614).
Moore was particularly nervous about what the conservative *Quarterly Review*
would say about the poem, and so on 11 January he wrote to Murray:

> I am anxious to hear what you are doing *for* me, or *against* me, in the Quar-
> terly—Whatever may be said of the *talent* of the thing (which I give up, to be
> dealt with as you please) I only hope & trust that there will be no giving in to
> the cry of "impiety" "blasphemy" &c. which, I see, is endeavored to be raised in

> John Bull & other quarters, & which (if such a leading journal as yours should
> take it up) would leave me to be carried away down the current of Cant without
> redemption—This is all I deprecate—the charge is unjust, *certainly* with respect
> to the *intention,* and, as far as I can judge, with respect to the *execution,* also. . . .
> [B]ut all this is nothing if the d—d sturdy Saints of the middle class should take
> it into their heads not to buy me —for, *you* know well, how they can send one
> to Coventry. (*ML* 2:511)

Moore's unspoken appeal here was for Murray to treat him more fairly than
Murray was treated by the public over the *Cain* controversy. As it happened,
the *Quarterly* was one of the few major publications that did not review Moore's
poem.

By 18 January the Longmans told Moore that they believed the poem's
"connection with the Scriptures . . . [would], in the long run, be a drag on
the popularity of the poem," meaning that it might lessen the appeal of
future editions (*MJ* 2:617). Moore then hit upon the idea of "orientalising"
his poem for the fifth edition: changing all of its Christian references into
Muslim ones. The Longmans enthusiastically agreed, arguing, as Moore recorded, that the change "would materially serve me and my future works with
the public" (*MJ* 2:618). Moore told Archibald Douglas,

> I am revising for a fifth Edition, and in order to consult the scruples of future
> readers, mean to turn it into an Eastern Tale, which if I had had the luck to
> think of at first, I should never have heard a word of objection—The Koran sup-
> plies Angels, as poetical at least as the orthodox ones, and the name Allah
> offends nobody—as appears from Paradise & the Peri, where, because my spir-
> itual agents were Turks, no one ever thought of being shocked.[28]

Making such an alteration to a poem that Moore apparently felt was his best
work has seemed to some critics to be particularly cynical and perhaps even
cowardly. It is true that the outcry over the "immorality" of his poem seems
to have marked a turning point in Moore's career that has never been adequately examined. Already cynical about the English reading public, which
had branded him a libertine so many times before, Moore seems to have
become more so in response to its treatment of a poem that he believed to
be truly pious and moral. His "orientalising" of the poem, consisting as it
does of the mere alteration of certain words, such as "God" to "Allah," and
"Hell" to "Eblis," seems almost contemptuously cavalier, as if he were tacitly

making the point that his public cared more in the final analysis for proper words than proper sentiments.

Moore's previously unpublished comments to John Wilson Croker regarding the controversy are particularly sardonic and revealing. Croker was franking sheets of the corrected fifth edition to the Longmans for Moore in early February, and Moore told Croker in an accompanying letter: "My present inclosures contain the transmogrification of my angels into Mussulmans, which I rather think will amuse you, as showing what convenient things religions are sometimes, and how easily they slide one into another.—I have put in about four additional lines, and altered as many words, and the whole thing might now have been written by a Mufti."[29] Croker wrote back to Moore, and Moore replied on 17 February with a lengthy and indignant defense of his motives in writing the poem:

> You speak like a poet & a man of taste about angels—but where's your authority for their purity? not either Scripture or Milton, for both make them eat hearty dinners, and (unbecoming as their admiration of beauty may be,) a pretty woman is a more sentimental object than a veal-cutlet any day of the year—but you're quite right, though the very pious people are *not*—for they are the last that should express any fastidiousness with regard to spiritual natures. I am pious myself—warmly so—(however you may smile at the intelligence) and would not give up one of my *frequent* bursts of adoration & gratitude towards the Deity for all that those every-day religionists ever felt or imagined in their whole lives.—As to "making a light use of the Book of Enoch", that Book has never been promoted even to the Apocrypha—nobody knew any thing of its being still in existence till about [Bruce's?] time, and one might as well talk of "making a light use of the Arabian Nights" or of "the Book of Adam" which they profess to have also in the East.—but nothing can be truer than what you say— I have got into a scrape, and the world will not be willing to let me get out of it. <again>—but if ever they catch me at a moral and pious poem again <they> I'll give them leave to punish me for it as they do now.
>
> You shall have a copy in their Turkish Costume the moment it is ready, and I shall direct your attention to two or three changes which I think will amuse you.[30]

Moore was deeply interested in theology and the origins of Christianity; in 1833 he would publish an erudite two-volume defense of Roman Catholicism entitled *Travels of an Irish Gentleman in Search of a Religion*, even though he was himself little more than nominally Catholic. He took theology seriously, and his great familiarity with biblical scholarship made him all the more exasperated with "those every-day religionists" and their eagerness to accuse him of blasphemy.

On 20 February 1823 Byron wrote Moore, "And *you* are *really* recanting, or softening to the clergy! It will do little good for you—it is *you*, not the poem, they are at. They will say they frightened you—forbid it, Ireland!" (*BLJ* 10:105). On 2 April he continued,

> [The Blessingtons] give me a very good account of you, and of your nearly "Emprisoned Angels." But why did you change your title?[31]—you will regret this some day. The bigots are not to be conciliated; and, if they were—are they worth it? I suspect that I am a more orthodox Christian than you are; and whenever I see a real Christian, either in practice or in theory, (for I never yet found the man who could produce either, when put to the proof,) I am his disciple. But, till then, I cannot truckle to tithe-mongers,—nor can I imagine what has made *you* circumcise your Seraphs.
>
> I have been far more persecuted than you, as you may judge by my present decadence,—for I take it that I am as low in popularity and bookselling as any writer can be. (*BLJ* 10:137–38)

Surely one the factors inducing Moore to "conciliate" was the cautionary example of Byron himself; Byron's reckless disregard for public opinion was the main reason that he was (though still critically lauded) largely considered a debauched atheist. Byron's social status, financial reserves, and absence from England meant that he could afford to thumb his nose at his readers; by contrast, Moore had dependents and had to write to live. Dr. Henry Muir recorded a conversation with Byron on 10 October 1823 during which Byron discussed the controversy over Moore's poem:

> He said he had received a note from [Moore] when about to publish his *Angels*, telling him that he intended to castrate them; that he found the style would not do—it was too warm—too much of the Houri—the world was not yet ripe for such luscious fruit. Lord B. added, "I told him he was wrong, that he would get no credit by it: but, on the contrary, do what he would with them, he would not please; that mutilated angels could only make Mahometans at best, and never Christians, so that it was better to leave them angels as they were.[32]

Moore's response to Byron's advice is unknown; he printed the 20 February and 2 April letters from him in his biography of Byron without commenting on the matter.

Moore's disgust with the criticism of his "moral and pious poem" contributed to his growing disenchantment with the poetry-buying public in general. In a 17 July 1823 letter to Byron, Moore confided,

> This cursed Public tires of us all, good & bad, and I rather think (if I can find out some other more gentlemanly trade) I shall cut the connexion entirely. How *you*, who are not *obliged*, can go on writing for it, has long, you know, been my astonishment. To be sure, you have all Europe (and America too) at your back, which is a consolation we poor insular wits (whose fame, like Burgundy, suffers in crossing the ocean) have not to support us in our reverses. If England doesn't read us, who the devil will?—I have not yet seen your new Cantos, but Christian seems to have shone out most prosperously, and the truth is that *yours* are the only "few, fine flushes" of <our> the "departing day" of Poesy on which the Public can now be induced to fix their gaze. My "Angels" I consider as a failure—I mean in the impression <they> it made—for I agree with a "*select* few" that I never wrote any thing better.

(For the full text of this letter see Appendix B.) In part Moore was responding to a mid-1820s slump in the sales of poetry, but it appears that in any case Moore was tired of trying to please the "cursed Public." He had had high hopes for *The Loves of the Angels,* but although his poem *had* been a success, it was evidently not as great a success as Moore had expected. After 1823 Moore did "cut the connexion" with poetry in a sense: he published no more long, serious poems and concentrated instead upon prose works, such as his 1824 prose satire *Memoirs of Captain Rock,* his 1827 novel *The Epicurean,* his biographies of Sheridan (1825), Byron (1830–31), and Lord Edward Fitzgerald (1831), his *Travels of an Irish Gentleman* (1833), and his never-completed multivolume *History of Ireland* (1835–46). Also, as his letter to Byron clearly shows, Moore was still feeling overshadowed by his friend, and perhaps he no longer wanted to continue his unequal competition. Simultaneously inspired and intimidated by Byron the poet, Moore may have felt that it was finally time to surrender the field.

"What I myself know and think concerning my friend"

Moore's Representations of Byron

Since 1957 Leslie Marchand's biography of Byron has had no serious rival. However, for the century and a quarter preceding the publication of Marchand's standard work, that distinction belonged to Moore's two-volume *Letters and Journals of Lord Byron, with Notices of His Life*, published in 1830 and 1831. For generations of readers, their admiration of or hostility toward Byron was based in large part upon their reaction to Moore's characterization of him, making Moore's biography perhaps the most influential life of Byron ever written.[1] Moore's authority as one of Byron's closest friends and his privilege of reading hundreds of pages of Byron's letters, journals, and memoirs that have all since been lost or destroyed give his judgments about Byron's art and psychology an importance that should never be overlooked. Although its completeness was limited by Moore's very restricted access to materials and its candidness likewise hindered by the public morality of the day, Moore's biography presented the first trustworthy, detailed, and consistent analysis of Byron's character and career. Moore swept aside almost twenty years of wildly inaccurate and contradictory stories about Byron, and praised him when slander from many sources threatened to destroy Byron's already damaged reputation. Moore was the first to establish and stabilize the most basic orthodoxies regarding Byron's mind and art upon which almost all subsequent scholars of Byron have built their theories and interpretations. Given the extent to which the picture of Byron that prevails today is Moore's picture, the virtues of the biography, the strategy Moore used to defend Byron's genius and morals, and the impact of Moore's eloquence are all worthy of reexamination.[2]

I

In one sense, Moore's authorship of Byron's biography was the culmination of the literary and personal relationship between the two poets. Since the great majority of the letters Moore published in the book were addressed either to John Murray or to himself, Byron's relationship with Moore was foregrounded, however much Moore might try to avoid speaking of himself in his narrative. By interweaving Moore's precise prose commentary with Byron's exuberant letters, the book brought the contrast between the characteristic talents of the two writers into as sharp a focus as the reading public had ever experienced before. The *Literary Gazette* recognized this and remarked that "to the more philosophical inquirer [the biography] will present the curious phenomenon of exhibiting the minds and characters of two of the most distinguished Poets of the age;—for it is as much the life and opinions of Moore as it is of Byron."[3] The *Mirror* observed: "The very juxtaposition of two such illustrious names in one title-page is calculated to excite no ordinary expectations; the biographer's 'Notices,' as well as the 'Journals and Letters' of the noble deceased, are perhaps, of equal importance."[4] John Wilson of *Blackwood's* exclaimed, "Life of BYRON, by MOORE, dedicated to SCOTT, is a short sentence that sounds like a trumpet! 'Tis a spirit-stirring reveillé."[5]

Moore's literary eminence and the close friendship that was known to have existed between the two poets were both important reasons why Moore's life of Byron was such an eagerly anticipated work. By 4 July 1824 Moore had decided upon writing the biography,[6] and on 10 August the *Times* announced, "We hear with pleasure that Mr. Moore intends to write the life of his illustrious friend, Lord Byron. The world expects such a work from his hands . . . [and] the friendship and congeniality of pursuits which existed between him and the noble poet, point him out as the person eminently qualified to undertake such a task."[7] Notices and articles informed the public of Moore's progress and movements during his years of his research, and, when the first volume of the biography finally appeared in 1830, it was immediately reviewed by nearly every major newspaper and periodical in Great Britain.

Despite the public's intense interest in Byron's life, there were several discouraging factors that made Moore initially apprehensive about undertaking a life of Byron. Moore's first attempt at biography, his life of Richard Brinsley Sheridan, had appeared in 1825, and although it sold well, it had been criticized for a prose style that readers found overly florid and marred by fanciful similes. Moore had also offended adherents of both major political parties by criticizing the English aristocracy and lauding democratic principles. Far worse than the possibility of these sorts of problems, however, was the risk that writing about Byron's loves and infidelities would revive Moore's old reputation for licentiousness. Just as Byron was haunted throughout his career by the charge of impiety, Moore, despite all his efforts, had never been able to shake the idea that he had a particular relish for the salacious. When Moore's friend Lord John Russell learned of Moore's plan, he advised him, "Pray, if you are to write, write poetry; it will not do to undertake the life of a second reprobate. Or if you could find some good subject in prose, write prose; write anything, in short, but Byron's life."[8] Another potential difficulty was that biography was still a developing genre, and in the 1820s it was considered worse than bad taste to examine a public person's life too closely. Moore knew that any serious life of Byron would have to deal with matter far more risqué and embarrassing than might appear in a biography of nearly anyone else. Although Hobhouse had his own, uncharitable reasons for dissuading Moore from writing, he was correct when he told Moore in 1826 that "there was a very general feeling against life-writing as unfair and unprofitable."[9]

Despite such worries and despite resistance from Byron's family and the implacable opposition of Hobhouse to any life of Byron by anyone, there were still several reasons why Moore was determined to write some kind of account of his friend. First, and doubtlessly most important to Moore, was his desire to do his friend justice and to vindicate him both as a moral man and as an artist of genius. The newspapers had been full of eulogy when the shocking news of Byron's death had reached England on 14 July 1824, but scarcely had his grief-stricken countrymen begun to forget Byron's past sins when they were suddenly and vividly reminded of them. A mere four days after the *Times* obituary called Byron "a poet and a hero" of "stupendous intellect," whose "dominion was the sublime," the nation became aware that Byron's family and friends had burned his own memoirs.[10] The public was forced to conclude that the memoirs must have been obscene or vindictive and that, in the words of a reviewer for the *New Monthly Magazine,* "Mr. Moore and Lord Byron's other friends did not expurgate them only because they were incapable of expurgation."[11] The throne of Byron the noble poet had once again been usurped by Byron the moral reprobate.

The scandal over the memoirs could not have come at a more critical time for Byron's posthumous reputation. The nationwide sense of grief and loss was poisoned even before his body had reached England by this new and sinister "proof" of Byron's depravity. Moore could not help but feel that by failing to prevent the burning of the memoirs he had not only helped to cast a shadow over Byron's memory but had also ensured that Byron's version of the infamous separation from his wife would never be told. Byron had trusted Moore above all others to deliver his side of the story to the world, and, although after the burning Moore repeatedly tried to convince himself that Hobhouse and Murray had been right, he knew his debt to Byron remained unpaid.

Besides loyalty and guilt, feelings of outrage also motivated Moore to write his biography. Books and articles on Byron began to pour from the presses even before his burial, and many of these portraits of Byron were decidedly unflattering. Dubious anecdotes about Byron were borrowed, embellished, or simply invented by irresponsible writers until it quickly became difficult even for people who had known him personally to separate fact from fiction. Byron's friends looked on in horror as first R. C. Dallas, then Thomas Medwin, and then, worst of all, Leigh Hunt passed themselves off as impartial authorities on Byron in order to denigrate him and exalt themselves. Each new book seemed more malicious and inaccurate than the one before. Hunt's 1828 *Lord Byron and Some of His Contemporaries* provoked Moore to refer to his former friend as "this beast Hunt," to write and publish a slashing satire on Hunt called "The 'Living Dog' and 'the Dead Lion,'" and to retaliate against him very harshly in his own book.[12]

Lastly, Moore needed to write his biography because he was in financial straits that were desperate even for him. John Murray had originally given Moore an advance of two thousand guineas on the anticipated profits from the publication of the memoirs, but when the memoirs were burned Moore insisted on giving the money back, plus interest, even though technically the memoirs had become Murray's property. Not only did Moore's sense of honor demand that he return a fee for a service he could not now perform; he also wanted to avoid appearing as if he had wanted to publish the memoirs merely for financial gain, heedless of the damage such a publication would do to the reputation of his friend. While working on his biography, Moore indicated to Hobhouse that he was mainly writing it in order to repay his financial debts. Although this was evidently an attempt to mollify Hobhouse, who resented Moore's privileged position as Byron's "official" biographer and had always been jealous of the relationship between the two poets, it was true that Moore was in desperate need of the money to repay the Longmans firm, which had loaned him the money to compensate Murray.[13]

The idea of writing Byron's life was not new to Moore. As early as 1813, Byron had made half-jesting, half-serious remarks to Moore that he should someday become his biographer. In 1813, Byron wrote, "Remember you must edite my posthumous works, with a Life of the Author, for which I will send you Confessions, dated 'Lazaretto,' Smyrna, Malta, or Palermo—one can die any where" (*BLJ* 3:75). In a letter of 14 February a year later, Moore wrote to Byron, "Recollect you have appointed me your Editor and Historiographer (in case any enraged husband should be the death of you)" (*ML* 1:306). Although Lord Holland suggested to Moore in 1821 that Byron had written his memoirs mainly out of a desire for posthumous revenge on Lady Byron and others, it is clear that Byron had decided to furnish Moore with autobiographical materials as early as June 1814, when he sent Moore a journal for the period 14 November 1813 to 19 April 1814.

In 1821 Byron wrote to Murray that it was his "very sincere wish" that Moore, Hobhouse, and Murray all help to edit his letters and journals, for the task would "require delicacy" (*BLJ* 8:216). However, Byron continued to send all his materials to Moore, and in a letter to Douglas Kinnaird a year later, Byron wrote that Moore was under no obligation to him for the gift of the memoirs, "for he will have work enough to do for his legacy," a phrase indicating that Byron was primarily counting on Moore to write his life and/or edit his works (*BLJ* 9:85). The same year, Hobhouse wrote to Byron about Byron's tacit understanding with Moore, warning him that it looked as if he were "[buying] a biographer under pretext of doing a generous action."[14] Byron denied it and replied: "I suppose however that like most men who have been talked about—I might have had— . . . a biographer without purchase—since most other scribblers have two or three—gratis.—Besides—I thought I had written my own" (*BLJ* 9:88). Despite his evasions, Byron was shrewd enough to know that he needed an eloquent ally to defend him after he was gone and that Moore's friendship, integrity, and talent made him the best candidate for the job. After Byron's death, Moore told Colonel Doyle, "it was always [Byron's] own wish that I should, if I survived him, write something about him" (*MJ* 2:775).

The most immediate requirement for Moore's biography was that it should engender sympathy for those aspects of Byron's life that had made the British public turn against him so violently—"to clear away the mists which hung round my friend, and show him, in most respects, as worthy of love as he was in all, of admiration" (*MLB* 2:782). Moore was determined to "bring what I think shadows fairly forward, but in such close juxtaposition with the lights, that the latter will carry the day" (*ML* 2:653). For Moore and his readers, Byron's greatest "light" was his artistic genius, and his greatest "shadow" was his moral delinquency; accordingly, Moore decided to systematically juxtapose the two and try to prove that Byron's temperament was such that he could not have had the one without the other. Although Moore knew his biography could not entirely excuse Byron's bad behavior, he was daring enough to insist that it was "utterly unreasonable" to judge a man like Byron by "ordinary standards" (*MLB* 1:656). Moore's "Nietzschean, super-moral view" of Byron, as one twentieth-century critic has called it,[15] provoked angry protest in the conservative reviews, but the sensitivity and insight with which Moore presented Byron's case won over many others. Moore believed, as he wrote in the biography, that "knowledge is ever the parent of tolerance" (*MLB* 2:806), and accordingly trusted that the more his readers understood about nature of Byron's experiences and psychology, the less they would blame him for his defiant and unorthodox life.

II

According to Moore, Byron's genius was "connected with, and, as it were, springing out of his character" (*MLB* 1:175). Moore's theory, and the thesis of his biography, was that "the distinctive properties of Byron's character, as well moral as literary, arose mainly from those two great sources, the unexampled versatility of his powers and feelings, and the facility with which he gave way to the impulses of both" (*MLB* 2:795). In other words, Byron was, intellectually and emotionally, both more sensitive and more responsive to immediate stimuli than were ordinary people. Moore used Byron's own term, "mobility," to describe this quality of feeling and reacting intensely to the impressions of the moment. Artistically, Byron's mobility manifested itself as both his phenomenal versatility and his ability to convincingly render passionate feeling. Emotionally, however, his mobility made him moody, mercurial, reckless, and unpredictable. Thus Byron's psychological makeup doomed him to suffer more intensely and err more spectacularly, while also seeing further and writing better than other men.

Moore argued that the most profound effect of Byron's "extreme mobility" was that it left him without a center—without that simple set of basic attributes that in nearly all other people seems to constitute a recognizable self:

> There are few characters in which a near acquaintance does not enable us to discover some one leading principle or passion consistent enough in its operations to be taken confidently into account in any estimate of the disposition in which they are found. Like those points in the human face, or figure, to which all other proportions are referable, there is in most minds some one governing influence, from which chiefly . . . all its various impulses and tendencies will be found to radiate. In Lord Byron . . . this sort of pivot of character was almost wholly wanting. . . . So various, indeed, and contradictory were his attributes, both moral and intellectual, that he may be pronounced to have been not one, but many; nor would it be any great exaggeration of the truth to say, that out of the mere partition of the properties of his single mind a plurality of characters, all different and all vigorous, might have been furnished. (*MLB* 2:782–83)

Moore saw *Don Juan* as Byron's "most characteristic work" and "an epitome of all the marvellous contrarieties of his character" (*MLB* 2:789; 647–48); its nonlinear, digressive structure, its subversion of meaning and determinacy, its skeptical attitude toward fixed principles of morality, art, religion, or anything else, all had their origin for Moore in the uniquely "mobile" character of Byron's mind. Moore recognized that a personality so protean could find its natural expression only in a poem like *Don Juan*, "that diversified arena," as Moore called it, in which the different aspects of Byron's nature could "hold, with alternate triumph, their ever powerful combat" (*MLB*

2:393). Moore had been one of the friends of Byron who had originally urged him not to publish *Don Juan;* Moore objected mainly to the satire upon Lady Byron and feared the effect upon Byron's fame. Yet Moore considered the poem a work of genius, and his remarks upon it show his consciousness of both the poem's power and its close connection with Byron's changeable, skeptical, and passionate personality:

> Nothing less, indeed, than that singular combination of attributes, which existed and were in full activity in his mind at this moment, could have suggested, or been capable of, the execution of such a work. The cool shrewdness of age with the vivacity and glowing temperament of youth—the wit of a Voltaire, with the sensibility of a Rousseau,—the minute, practical knowledge of the man of society, with the abstract and self-contemplative spirit of the poet,—a susceptibility of all that is grandest and most affecting in human virtue, with a deep, withering experience of all that is most fatal to it . . . such was the strange assemblage of contrary elements, all meeting together in the same mind, and all brought to bear, in turn, upon the same task, from which alone could have sprung this extraordinary Poem,—the most powerful and, in many respects, painful display of the versatility of genius that has ever been left for succeeding ages to wonder at and deplore. (*MLB* 2:189)

Moore suggested that this unsettled poem was the work of an unsettled personality; had Byron's opinions and feelings been more fixed and determined, *Don Juan's* unique greatness would not have been possible to achieve.

When Moore wrote, it was a critical commonplace that Byron's poetry was the most confessional and personal of his era. The widespread willingness of Byron's readers to believe that his protagonists were accurate self-portraits and that his lyrics were sincere confessions led to serious speculation that he was, for instance, an ex-pirate or a murderer. Solely on the evidence of Byron's poetry, Goethe was persuaded in 1820 that Byron had been involved in a double murder in his youth in Florence. The idea that Byron's poetry is primarily concerned with earnest and narcissistic self-portraiture lingered on into the twentieth century, until modern critics such as McGann began to elucidate the elements of self-conscious role-playing and emotional masquerading in Byron's work. Yet Moore was in essence the first authoritative critic to controvert the over-literal identification of Byron with the Byronic hero. Moore attempted to show throughout his biography how Byron's mobility impelled him to assume a variety of disguises in his life as well as his poetry, none of which could be called the "genuine" Byron:

> With a genius taking upon itself all shapes, from Jove down to Scapin, and a dis-
> position veering with equal facility to all points of the moral compass,—not
> even the ancient fancy of the existence of two souls within one bosom, would
> seem at all adequately to account for the varieties, both of power and charac-
> ter, which the course of his conduct and writings . . . displayed. (*MLB* 2:647)

In Moore's plangent phrase, he was "not one, but many."

Moore conceded that Byron's poetry was almost always initially inspired by
his actual life and feelings, but carefully explained how "the embellishments
of [Byron's] fancy" (*MLB* 1:104) would transform such materials into entirely new shapes:

> As the mathematician of old required but a spot to stand upon, to be able, as
> he boasted, to move the world, so a certain degree of foundation in *fact* seemed
> necessary to Byron, before that lever which he knew how to apply to the world
> of the passions could be wielded by him. So small, however, was, in many in-
> stances, the connexion with reality which satisfied him, that to aim at tracing
> through his stories these links with his own fate and fortunes, which were, after
> all, perhaps, visible but to his own fancy, would be a task as uncertain as unsafe.
> (*MLB* 1:476)

Moore stressed that Childe Harold, the character that most readers considered to be virtually identical with Byron the man, was not Byron but was instead Byron's "poetical representative"—a fictionalized version of himself,
but ultimately as much of a mask as the many roles that Byron assumed and
experimented with in his actual life. Moore wrote of the instability of Byron's
moods and opinions—the "quick, cameleon-like changes" of his character
(*MLB* 2:648)—and the consequent danger of mistaking an emotional state
he expressed in a poem to be his actual and unchanging feelings about the
subject upon which he wrote. To illustrate this, Moore juxtaposed Byron's
statements about his affection for and interest in Mrs. Constance Spencer
Smith with the lines about the same woman in *Childe Harold's Pilgrimage*, in
which Harold lamented that his heart was wholly unmoved by her. Moore
observed: "In one so imaginative as Lord Byron, who, while he infused so
much of his life into his poetry, mingled also not a little of poetry with his
life, it is difficult in unravelling the texture of his feelings, to distinguish at
all times between the fanciful and the real" (*MLB* 1:200–201). Moore also
pointed out Byron's love of weapons and "every thing connected with a life

of warfare," which he always possessed, "in spite of his assumed philosophy on this subject, in Childe Harold" (*MLB* 1:256).

Moore associated Byron's role-assuming in his poetry with his role-playing in life, and he described Byron's romantic posturings and mystifications in London society, which Moore witnessed at first hand on many occasions, as stemming partly from shyness and partly from "that love of effect and impression to which the poetical character of his mind naturally led" (*MLB* 1:355). According to Moore, "There was indeed, in his misanthropy, as in his sorrows, at that period, to the full as much of fancy as of reality" (*MLB* 2:390). In order to illustrate the way in which Byron delighted in "taking upon himself all varieties of character" (*MLB* 2:795), Moore recalled the way in which at an early point in their acquaintance, Byron tried to assume a sinister persona:

> I have known him more than once, as we have sat together after dinner, and he was, at the time, perhaps a little under the influence of wine, to fall seriously into . . . [a] sort of dark and self-accusing mood, and throw out hints of his past life with an air of gloom and mystery designed evidently to awaken curiosity and interest. He was, however, too promptly alive to the least approaches of ridicule not to perceive, on these occasions, that the gravity of his hearer was only prevented from being disturbed by an effort of politeness, and he accordingly never again tried this romantic mystification upon me. (*MLB* 2:791)

Moore suggested that Byron possessed in a great degree a quality of impersonal, imaginative versatility. What Moore describes is very similar to the quality that Keats called "negative capability"—the very opposite of narcissistic confessionalism. Like Keats, Moore identified this attribute most strongly with Shakespeare and said of Byron's poetry that "in the works of no poet, with the exception of Shakspeare, can every various mood of the mind— whether solemn or gay, whether inclined to the ludicrous or the sublime, whether seeking to divert itself with the follies of society or panting after the grandeur of solitary nature—find so readily a strain of sentiment in accordance with its every passing tone" (*MLB* 1:592). In Byron's life, "this love and power of variety" manifested itself as "the pride of personating every description of character, evil as well as good, [which] influenced but too much . . . his ambition, and, not a little, his conduct" (*MLB* 2:790). In his poetry, such "mobility" meant that a reader could find him, for instance, "almost at the same moment, [writing in a comic voice and] personating, with a port worthy of such a presence, the mighty spirit of Dante, or following the dark footsteps of Scepticism over the ruins of past worlds, with Cain" (*MLB* 2:648).

Byron's "mobility" has been judged, in modern psychological terms, as a product of the insecurity arising from Byron's failure in his childhood and adolescence to construct a stable identity for himself. Byron lacked a father or siblings, had an unstable (or at least rather unlovable) mother, was sexually confused, and felt alienated from his peers both because of his intelligence and his ambiguous social position. Moore drew attention to Byron's constant but unsatisfactory attempts to find an appropriate role to inhabit— rake, dandy, poet, statesman, soldier, gothic villain, man of feeling, athlete, revolutionary—and suggested that the more Byron's feelings of loneliness and estrangement from his environment intensified, the more he turned to writing for a feeling of cathartic satisfaction, and the greater his poetry became. Although Moore claimed that Byron was born with superior talent, he also suggested that the disappointments and injustices of Byron's early life and later adulthood were the catalysts for the full flowering of his poetic power. Byron drew his greatest inspiration from his own pain, wrote Moore: "From the first to the last of his agitated career, every fresh recruitment of his faculties was imbibed from that bitter source" (*MLB* 2:2). Byron once wrote, "It is odd, but agitation or contest of any kind gives a rebound to my spirits, and sets me up for the time," and Moore uses this comment as evidence that Byron's power grew as his pain deepened (*MLB* 2:4). Elsewhere in the biography Moore also printed a letter to Murray in which Byron spoke of the "persecution" he suffered after the separation crisis and how it gave a "fillip to [his] Spirits" (*MLB* 2:531).

At the beginning of the second volume, Moore succinctly summarized Byron's sufferings up to his marriage, listing his abusive mother, his deformity, "the disappointment of his youthful passion,—the lassitude and remorse of premature excess,—the lone friendlessness of his entrance into life, and the ruthless assault upon his first literary efforts," and calling them "all links in that chain of trials, errors, and sufferings by which his great mind was gradually and painfully drawn out." Moore hypothesized that Byron could sense that his power derived from his pain, and that this caused him to spend his life "courting agitation and difficulties," even to the point of becoming obsessed with creating scenes of stress and violence in his poetry (*MLB* 2:3).

Moore frequently paused at critical points in his narrative to enumerate Byron's misfortunes, in the hope that knowledge would breed tolerance.

Moore dwelled to a greater extent than later biographers upon the loneliness of Byron's youth. He presented Byron's mother as a hot-tempered villain and endorsed the stories about various household items being launched at young Byron's head. He also treated Byron's entrance into Parliament as more of a crucial turning point than later biographers would; he wrote that Byron presented himself in the House of Lords "in a state more lone and unfriended, perhaps, than any youth of his high station had ever before been reduced to on such an occasion,—not having a single individual of his own class either to introduce him as friend or receive him as acquaintance" (*MLB* 1:163). Moore considered Byron's sudden ascension to the peerage to have been harmful to his emotional development: "Even under the most favorable circumstances, such an early elevation to rank would be but too likely to have a dangerous influence on the character; and the guidance under which young Byron entered upon his new station was, of all others, the least likely to lead him safely through its perils and temptations" (*MLB* 1:25). Moore presented Byron as a perpetual outsider, uncomfortable and insecure even in the midst of the whirlwind of adulation that greeted *Childe Harold's Pilgrimage.* Even among his fellow aristocrats, Moore wrote, "The inadequacy of his means to his station was early a source of embarrassment and humiliation to him; and those high, patrician notions of birth in which he indulged but made the disparity between his fortune and his rank the more galling" (*MLB* 1:181). Moore asserted that since Byron probably sensed that the source of his poetic inspiration was loneliness and pain, it became almost inevitable that Byron would seek out, however unconsciously, a disaster such as the one that would cause his self-imposed exile from England.

Moore pursued the theme of Byron's self-destructiveness throughout his book, proposing that Byron was haunted by a sort of imp of the perverse, "a propensity to self-misrepresentation" (*MLB* 1:346), a "perverse fancy . . . for falsifying his own character" (*MLB* 2:272). Not only did Byron court actual disaster as a means of liberating his powers, but he was also driven "to put, at all times, the worst face on his own character and conduct" (*MLB* 1:131). At the very end of his book Moore wrote that his intention as a biographer was always to do Byron "more justice than he would have done himself; there being no hands in which his character could have been less safe than his own, nor any greater wrong offered to his memory than the substitution of what he affected to be for what he was" (*MLB* 2:807). Psychologically, one may well conclude that playing the role of a villain was a way for Byron to aggrandize his own sense of alienation, to convert his basic shyness and fear into a perversely attractive or seductive quality. Moore observed that this was ultimately a dangerous and self-defeating practice that led people to believe any story about Byron, however sordid, especially after the separation. Implicitly referring to Lady Byron's well-known accusation of mental illness against her husband, Moore wrote that "to such a perverse length, indeed, did [Byron] carry this fancy for self-defamation, that if . . . there was any tendency to derangement in his mental conformation, on this point alone could it be pronounced to have manifested itself" (*MLB* 2:790). Given people's willingness to believe that Byron was a poseur, this was the most effective tactic Moore could have employed to discredit the worst of the gossip about Byron. The tactic met with some success; the *Athenæum* stated that Moore's book had "disposed us to think of [Lord Byron] more indulgently than before. We had long ceased to regard him as great; but we are now persuaded that he was not altogether bad."[16]

The two episodes of Byron's life that required the most tact of Moore were the separation from Lady Byron and his adulterous four-year relationship with the Countess Guiccioli. Moore told the story of Byron's marriage as quickly and as delicately as he could. It was a difficult task to try and vindicate, at least partially, Byron's behavior toward his wife without offending Lady Byron, Augusta Leigh, or their respective families. Moore's strategy, once more, was to insist that Byron's restlessness and temper were the price he had to pay for his genius. "The same qualities," Moore wrote, "which enable [geniuses] to command admiration, are also those that too often incapacitate them from conciliating love" (*MLB* 1:589). These qualities include, according to Moore, self-absorption, the need for solitude, and the inevitable and constant inferiority of the people and objects inhabiting the genius's actual life to those inhabiting his imagination. One of Moore's interesting conclusions regarded the mysterious cause of the separation. After alluding to Byron's early and abortive attempts to mystify him, Moore continued:

> From what I have known, however, of his experiments upon more impressible listeners, I have little doubt that, to produce effect at the moment, there is hardly

any crime so dark or desperate of which, in the excitement of thus acting upon the imaginations of others, he would not have hinted that he had been guilty; and it has sometimes occurred to me that the occult cause of his lady's separation from him . . . may have been nothing more, after all, that some imposture of this kind, some dimly-hinted confession of undefined horrors, which, though intended by the relater but to mystify and surprise, the hearer so little understood him as to take in sober seriousness. (*MLB* 2:791)

Of course, in one sense Moore was probably being disingenuous here, since he was actively trying to divert suspicion away from Augusta Leigh and to make it seem as if the rumors of Byron's incest were based on nothing more than a misunderstanding. But by drawing attention to the miscommunication between Byron, who was often facetious and "humbugging," and his wife, who was earnest and largely humorless, Moore led the way for later critics and biographers to expand upon this idea, and to develop the persuasive modern consensus that Byron may have said many things ironically that Lady Byron took to be insults or worse.

Although Moore shed no light on the reasons for the separation other than this, he was far less reticent in the matter of Countess Guiccioli. Many reviewers were offended enough by Moore's insistence that Italy's different standard of morality entitled him to speak more freely about Byron's amours there. They were outraged, however, when Moore contended that, given the extent of Byron's former debauchery, the affair with Teresa was "an event fortunate both for his reputation and happiness" (*MLB* 2:205). If Moore seems conservative now, he was bold by the standards of the day. Not only did Moore suggest that Byron was too great a genius to be married, that he transcended ordinary standards of morality, and that committing adultery made him happier than he had ever been, he even argued that Byron's sexual dissipations in Venice greatly intensified his intellectual powers. Those critics today who believe Moore to have been a model of propriety do not appreciate how subversive such positions were considered to be in 1830.

III

Most of the reviews regretted Moore's candor, and some were driven to furious condemnation of both the author and his subject. Andrew Elfenbein has recently written that Moore "enclos[ed] Byron within the bounds of respectability," but very few of Moore's contemporaries would have agreed with this assessment.[17] Charles Webb LeBas, in the *British Critic,* wrote that "after squeezing out from the mass of these volumes the cloying juices of Mr. Moore's confectionry, there remains a rank savour, such as comes up from the depths of an unsanctified and carnal mind."[18] The *Monthly Review* believed the second volume to be so obscene that copyright laws could not apply to it. The same reviewer was even offended by Moore's use of asterisks to conceal the identities of the people Byron referred to in his letters, asking, "Does [Mr. Moore], indeed, think that these asterisks are hieroglyphics, which cannot be decyphered? Does he flatter himself with the hope, that they will afford no occupation to prurient minds—no encouragement to depravity?" About the biography in general, "it is no justification of scandal, to say that it was promulgated for the sake of truth; truth itself is too expensive an acquisition, when purchased at so great a sacrifice."[19] This was the mind-set most reviewers shared in 1830, and it is a tribute to Moore's boldness that he revealed the things he did.

The first volume of *Letters and Journals of Lord Byron, with Notices of His Life* was published in a splendid quarto edition of 670 pages. Despite its high price of two guineas, the *Times* reported on 18 January 1830 that nearly two thousand copies had already been called for.[20] A month later, the *Literary Gazette* wrote that "this work is now in almost every body's hands."[21] John Gibson Lockhart, in a review for the *Quarterly,* observed that this was a work "than which none was ever more sure to be devoured by readers of all ages, and either sex, with equal eagerness."[22] John Murray was apparently well aware of the book's potentially wide audience of female readers; Hobhouse recorded in his journals that Murray told him, "'Well, let Lady Julia read the book and hear her opinion,'" a phrase that Hobhouse interpreted as "a clever mode of letting me know the book is written for the women."[23] The book's appeal proved universal enough; by 5 February Moore, being congratulated everywhere he went, could write in his journal, "My success in Byron . . . is far beyond my utmost expectation" (*MJ* 3:1287). The second volume of 823 pages came out a year after the first and was at least as anxiously awaited, since the new volume dealt with Byron's years of exile, the period of his life about which the public knew the least and expected the worst. Before the appearance of the second volume Moore wrote worriedly to Murray, "As of the *attraction* & *amusement* of this part of our 2nd Vol. there can be no doubt—and yet, having made so favourable an impression in the First, particularly with respect to Byron's character, one trembles at the idea of effacing or disturbing it" (*ML* 2:680). In any case Moore was right about its prospective popularity; by 1832, Moore could inform Murray, "I receive constant evidence by the Post of the circulation of the Byron—it has reached evidently quite a new class of readers" (*ML* 2:739). Nearly all the English reviews presented copious extracts from one or both volumes.

Although there was the widest possible range of critical reactions to the biography as a whole, Moore could take comfort from the fact that what objections there were were made on moral grounds, and that the overwhelming majority of the reviews enthusiastically praised Moore's writing as simple, clear, and "manly," the opposite of the florid style they had condemned in his life of Sheridan. A few critics called the book one of the best biographies ever written in English. In the most famous review of the book, Thomas Babington Macaulay classed it "among the best specimens of English prose which our age has produced."[24] The *Times* seemed to rate Moore's prose even more highly than Byron's letters, and concluded:

> That which confers on [the biography] . . . its greatest charm and power . . . is derived from the author. All that in common hands would have been common enough, acquires a new shape under the influence of genius such as his, and the kindred feeling which they possessed in some points has enabled the living poet to shed a lustre on the fame and character of the dead one which could have been produced by scarcely any other means.[25]

Besides praising the style, many reviewers also marveled at the extent to which Moore was willing to reveal Byron's faults. The *Monthly Review* called the amount of embarrassing material in volume one alone "a signal proof of the independent and historical spirit which the Biographer has brought to the execution of his task."[26] Perhaps the biography's greatest attraction, however, then as now, is that so much of it is told in Byron's own words.

It has often been observed that Moore allowed Byron, for the most part, to speak for himself. Byron's inimitable letters make up the bulk of both volumes, and the publication of the private correspondence of the most fascinating man of his time would have been exciting enough even without the added advantage of Moore's commentary. Even many of the reviewers who were hostile to the book often reveled in the letters. The *Athenæum* commented that the perusal of the letters "has impressed us with a higher idea of Lord Byron's genius than even his poetry gave us."[27] The *Quarterly Review* agreed, insisting, "These extracts cannot be perused without producing an enlarged estimation of the deceased poet's talents and accomplishments. They render it hardly doubtful that, had his life been prolonged, he would have taken his place in the very first rank of our prose literature also."[28] Hobhouse's prediction that Moore's biography would not raise Byron in the public's esteem had been proved wrong, at least as far as Byron's talent was concerned. Byron's character, on the other hand, was not so easily vindicated. It was almost universally condemned. The less conservative reviews looked upon the Byron of Moore's biography with sadness and regret, while others ferociously vilified him.

Probably the most valuable of all the contemporary remarks about the book are Mary Shelley's. After Moore's first volume appeared, she wrote to Murray on 19 January 1830, "I have done nothing but read since I got Lord Byron's life—I have no pretensions to being a critic—yet I know infinitely well what pleases me—Not to mention the judicious arrangement and happy *tact* displayed by Mr Moore, which distinguish this book." After praising Moore's "elegant and forcible" style, she assessed the truthfulness of his portrayal of Byron:

> The great charm of the work to me, and it will have the same for you, is that the Lord Byron I find there is our Lord Byron—the fascinating—faulty—childish—philosophical being—daring the world—docile to a private circle—impetuous and indolent—gloomy and yet more gay than any other—I live with him again in these pages—getting reconciled (as I used in his lifetime) to those waywardnesses which annoyed me when he was away, through the delightful & buoyant tone of his conversation and manners. . . . There is something cruelly kind in this single volume When will the next come?—impatient before how tenfold now I am so.
>
> Among its many other virtues this book is *accurate* to a miracle . . . I have not stumbled on one mistake with regard either to time place or feeling.[29]

Mary Shelley provided Moore with more valuable assistance than anyone else while he was writing the biography, and she had come to like Moore a great deal, so her reaction was not entirely unbiased. Yet such unqualified testimony as to the book's truth to life from someone who had known Byron as

intimately as Mary Shelley demonstrates the deep understanding of his subject that Moore brought to his task.

Although the biography has been generally praised by Byron scholars, it
has received little detailed critical analysis in the twentieth century. An exception is Joseph W. Reed Jr.'s *English Biography in the Early Nineteenth Century,* in
which Reed faults Moore for failing to produce a consistent, totalizing mas-
ter-theory to explain Byron's psychology and art. He claims that Moore draws
upon the conventional stereotype of the man of genius, but "now and again
seems to give up his organizing structure entirely. He clings to the germs
and catchwords of the theory but is not able to make them work in harmony
with the progress of genius. Contradiction is . . . beside the point. He uses
elements and terms of the theory impressionistically, painting away with
abandon."[30] In essence Reed criticizes Moore for being insufficiently theoretical, but it was never Moore's intention to explain Byron's character as
simply and neatly as Reed requires. The lack of an "organizing structure" of
the kind Reed expects in a biography is really a triumph of Moore's realism
and his respect for the disorderliness of human life, especially in the case of
Byron. Moore shared Byron's contempt for all things theoretical, totalizing,
and divorced from actual experience, and praised "those who do not suffer
themselves to be carried away by a theory" (*MLB* 2:730). One of the strengths
of Moore's biography is that it refuses to reduce, by means of a superimposed
and inappropriate novelistic unity, the complexity and self-contradicting
nature of Byron's own character. Moore reiterated near the end of his book
that Byron's "multiform aspect" rendered simple explanations reductive, and
admitted that "in trying to solve the strange variances of [Byron's] mind, I
[could] myself be found to have fallen into contradictions and inconsisten-
cies" (*MLB* 2:783), but such a rough-edged portrait is surely more true to
life than one with cleaner lines and fewer details. Moore's book is more
fairly treated by Clement Tyson Goode Jr., who calls it a "landmark" and "the
fullest, the most balanced, the best" of contemporary accounts, and praises
Moore's diligence, fairness, and skill.[31] John Clubbe calls Reed's remarks
"somewhat unfairly hostile," and observes that Moore's "personal knowledge
of Byron, his often acute psychological analysis of the poet's character, and
the primary documents he included or subsumed in his narrative make his
biography still well worth consulting."[32]

Richard D. Altick, in *Lives and Letters: A History of Literary Biography in England and America,* calls Moore's work "a masterly portrait of a complex personality" and particularly praises Moore's interest in the creative process and willingness to discuss embarrassing or scandalous matters.[33] When he was able, Moore presented early drafts and revisions of Byron's poems (notably the original conclusion of *Manfred*) in order to comment upon the processes of Byron's composition; as Altick observes, this was unusual in an age whose biographies were primarily concerned with "human—personal—values, not esthetic ones. . . . the psychology of artistic production rather than the anatomy of the finished product." Altick also argues that Moore "was, for the time, unusually conscious of the relation between the spirit of the age and poetic production," and that he consequently interpreted Byron's tumultuous life and art as symptomatic and emblematic of his era in a way that struck a chord with his nineteenth-century readers.[34]

As has been demonstrated earlier in this study, Moore differed from poets like Wordsworth or Shelley in that he did not necessarily believe that poetry was a medium amenable to perfect sincerity. For Moore, poetry adorned or decorated reality, placing real things under a light that made them appear better or more beautiful than they were. Poetry showed things in their ideal aspect, but did not transform them or reveal their essential nature. Therefore, although Moore wrote two "biographical" poems about Byron in which he idealized his friend, it was in the research and writing of his biography that Moore worked, tirelessly and meticulously, to tell what he understood to be the truth about Byron. Moore's two poems are illuminating, however, as public statements on his friend written in order to present a certain positive aspect of his character to a hostile public.

The first of these poems, which was included in Moore's *Rhymes on the Road* (1823), was probably written (or at least begun) at the time of his visit with Byron in Venice in October 1819. "Extract VII: Lord Byron's Memoirs, Written by Himself.—Reflections, When about to Read Them" contains the germs of several of the recurrent themes of Moore's later biography. Contradicting the many English critics who delighted in supposed signs that Byron's talent was dwindling, Moore asserted that since the first emergence of the "Aurora of his genius," Byron's "power . . . hath grown ampler, grander, every hour" (ll. 21–24); in his biography Moore would argue that the depth and versatility of Byron's artistic powers continued to grow throughout his career. Moore's poem, like his biography, claimed that Byron was not naturally melancholy or misanthropic, but that it was "desolating grief" and "wrongs" that had driven Byron's "noble nature into cold eclipse," even though his "spirit . . . From Nature's hands came kind, affectionate; / And which even now, struck as it is with blight, / Comes out at times in love's own native light." Byron was like a burned-out sun, which was "born not only to surprise but cheer / With warmth and lustre all within its sphere" (ll. 40–44).

Moore's poem concluded by listing what the Memoirs will contain, "If Truth with half so prompt a hand unlocks / His virtues as his failings." They would recount

> friendships, held like rocks,
> · And enmities, like sun-touch'd snow, resigned;
> Of fealty, cherish'd without change or chill,
> In those who serv'd him, young, and serve him still;
> Of generous aid, giv'n with that noiseless art
> Which wakes not pride, to many a wounded heart;
> Of acts—but, no—*not* from himself must aught
> Of the bright features of his life be sought.
> While they, who court the world, like MILTON's cloud,
> "Turn forth their silver lining" on the crowd,
> This gifted Being wraps himself in night;
>   And, keeping all that softens, and adorns,
> And gilds his social nature hid from sight,
> Turns but its darkness on a world he scorns.   (ll. 51–66)

On the last page of his biography Moore would present a similar enumeration of Byron's "bright features," listing such things as his generosity and the love and loyalty he inspired in friends and servants. Even more important, eleven years before Moore would make the argument that Byron had a "perverse fancy . . . for falsifying his own character" (*MLB* 2:272) driving him "to put, at all times, the worst face on his own character and conduct" (*MLB* 1:131), the concluding lines of Moore's poem contained the germ of that defense of Byron's reputation. The direct continuity between poem and biography suggests that Moore always held the same conviction regarding Byron's "misanthropy": that it was a defensive shell concealing an intense need to give and receive love. Moore's poem was, of course, a piece of public rhetoric and a deliberate defense of his friend, but Moore's private statements about Byron support and reinforce his public ones. Yet the poem did not reveal the whole of Moore's feelings about Byron; Moore would only embody his darker thoughts in his portrayal of Byron as the fallen angel Rubi in 1822.

Moore's other "biographical" poem appeared in the second number of his *Evenings in Greece* (1832), although it may have been written as early as September 1824.[35] Each number of this collection was a series of songs joined together by "a thread of poetical narrative," in which Moore's "chief object was to combine Recitation with Music, so as to enable a greater number of persons to join in the performance, by enlisting as readers those who may not feel willing or competent to take a part as singers." The setting of Greece enabled Moore to make poetic statements about liberty and to express the philhellenism that he shared with many liberals. Moore prefaced his song about Byron with a description of the dread that passed over a group of singing Greeks as a ship approached bearing the news of Byron's death. Although Byron is not named, it is clear that the passage refers to him:

> 'Twas from an isle of mournful name,
> From Missolonghi, last they came—
> Sad Missolonghi, sorrowing yet
> O'er him, the noblest Star of Fame
>   That e'er in life's young glory set!—
> And now were on their mournful way,
>   Wafting the news through Helle's isles;—
> News that would cloud ev'n Freedom's ray,
>   And sadden Victory 'mid her smiles.   (ll. 403–11)

The mariners speed off to continue their journey, and the grief of the mourners leads into Moore's poem, in which Byron is celebrated under the name of Harmodius, "the Athenian, who, to shed / A tyrant's blood, pour'd out his own" (ll. 419–20). Moore wrote to Power, "You will perceive that 'Thou art not dead' alludes (under the name of a celebrated antient Greek) to Lord Byron."[36] "Thou art not dead—thou art not dead! / No, dearest Harmodius, no," is the refrain of the song, and the lyrics celebrate Harmodius/Byron as an undying symbol of resistance to tyranny:

> The myrtle round that falchion spread
>   Which struck the immortal blow,
> Throughout all time with leaves unshed—
> The patriot's hope, the tyrant's dread—
>   Round Freedom's shrine shall grow.

Thou art not dead—thou art not dead!
 No, dearest Harmodius, no.

.   .   .   .

Thy name, by myriads sung and said,
 From age to age shall go,
Long as the oak and ivy wed,
As bees shall haunt Hymettus' head,
 Or Helle's waters flow.
Thou art not dead—thou art not dead!
 No, dearest Harmodius, no.

In this poem Moore presented a more mythic aspect of Byron the Greek lib-
erator than he had in his biography. In the biography he showed Byron as a
combination of pragmatist, cynic, and idealist, eager to aid the Greeks with
his money and influence but pulled almost helplessly between the conflicting demands of feuding factions and often fatalistic about the whole venture.
In the song to Harmodius, Moore canonized Byron as the latest in a centuries-
old line of martyrs to liberty, concentrating on the heroic and inspiring aspect
of Byron's sacrifice. With this song, which Moore knew would be performed
in many English and Irish households, Moore was helping to inaugurate the
myth of Byron the Romantic revolutionary that would sink its roots deep into
the imagination of Victorian liberalism. With all of his knowledge of Byron's
foibles and shortcomings, Moore doubtless still recognized the power of
Byron as a symbol of something much larger than himself. Moore must have
taken a wistful pleasure in the fact that the shy young friend whom he had
encouraged to speak out in the House of Lords so many years ago had in
death became the great hero of liberals throughout the world.

Moore's identification of Byron with Harmodius is significant for another
reason: in Moore's *Irish Melody* "Oh! blame not the bard" (1810), Moore had
written of his *own* desire to be a revolutionary patriot like Harmodius. The
song concerns the choice between a life of self-centered hedonism and a life
of self-sacrificing patriotism, a clash of impulses that is nearly always evident
in Moore's lyric poetry. The subject is obviously a very personal one, involving the conflict between Moore's anger over the mistreatment of Ireland and
his yearning for love, sensual pleasure, and escape. The song begins by im-
ploring, "Oh! blame not the bard, if he fly to the bowers, / Where pleasure is
carelessly smiling at fame; / He was born for much more, and in happier

hours, / His soul might have burned with a holier flame." Moore laments that Ireland cannot now be openly defended with either arms or words, "For 'tis treason to love her, and death to defend." The last stanza imagines a future time when Irish patriots will abandon love and poetry for war:

> Then blame not the bard, if in pleasure's soft dream,
>   He should try to forget what he never can heal;
> Oh! give but a hope: let a vista but gleam
>   Through the gloom of his country, and mark how he'll feel.
> That instant, his heart at her shrine would lay down
>   Every passion it nursed, every bliss it adored,
> While the myrtle now idly entwined with his crown,
>   Like the wreath of Harmodius should cover his sword.   (ll. 17–24)

This remarkable poem is in a sense Moore's *apologia pro vita sua,* and it is highly significant that in his song about Byron he imagines his friend wielding the myrtle-covered sword that he himself was unable to unsheathe.

The final, crucial point to consider in examining Moore's representations of Byron is the way in which Moore represented Byron in relation to himself as an artist. By becoming Byron's biographer, Moore ensured that he would be even more associated with Byron in the public mind than he had been in the past, but he also established once and forever his lesser status in relation to Byron. As is evident from their letters, both Byron and Moore were careful to prevent any hint of competitive feeling to enter into their personal relationship. However, despite the popular perception, during Byron's lifetime, of Moore as sharing with Byron (and Scott) the highest rank of literary achievement, Moore was nonetheless generally thought to be of a lower order of genius than Byron. Moore shared this view of the inferiority of his own powers to Byron's, for the most part accepting the fact with modest resignation. Moore's biography contains what must be the most revealing and remarkable comment Moore ever made upon his own comparative estimate of his and Byron's abilities. After observing that Byron, in his estrangement from other people, bore out Pope's dictum that to achieve greatness in poetry, "one must forget father and mother, and cleave to it alone," Moore continued:

On such terms alone are the high places of fame to be won;—nothing less than the sacrifice of the entire man can achieve them. However delightful, therefore, may be the spectacle of a man of genius tamed and domesticated in soci-

ety, taking docilely upon him the yoke of the social ties, and enlightening without disturbing the sphere in which he moves, we must nevertheless, in the
midst of our admiration, bear in mind that it is not thus smoothly or amiably
immortality has ever been struggled for, or won. The poet thus circumstanced
may be popular, may be loved; for the happiness of himself and those linked
with him he is on the right road,—but not for greatness. The marks by which
Fame has always separated her great martyrs from the rest of mankind are not
upon him, and the crown cannot be his. He may dazzle, may captivate the circle, and even the times in which he lives; but he is not for hereafter. (*MLB*
1:591–92)

Moore, with his famously happy marriage and devotion to his family, was almost certainly describing himself. Moore was popular and loved by his readers, his poetry was always characterized as "dazzling" (as opposed to "sublime"
or "profound," for instance), and he captivated the circle of aristocrats among
whom he spent his time as well as the era in which he lived. Moore's phrase
for his own poetic career—"enlightening without disturbing the sphere in
which he moves"—captures perfectly Moore's understanding of the difference between his own artistic pragmatism and Byron's daring, or recklessness.
Some readers were not as willing as Moore to accept that social ties hampered
the development of genius; in its review of the biography, the *Times* quoted
the above paragraph and concluded, "It is impossible not to understand the
allusion, but we think the writer proves the opposite side of the question."[37]

Our own post-Marchand Byron is much more complex than Moore's. We
now know immeasurably more about Augusta Leigh, about Byron's sexual
nature, about the Shelleys, Claire Clairmont, Lady Melbourne, and Caroline
Lamb. However, although Moore's biography has not remained definitive,
Moore performed a great service to later biographers by collecting as much
material as he could while the letters still existed and the anecdotes and
memories were still fresh in the minds of those he interviewed. Most important for posterity, Moore cleared away, while there was still time, the mass of
vengeful lies and gossip that had begun rapidly accumulating after Byron's
death. If Moore had allowed the opposition of Murray, Hobhouse, Augusta
Leigh, and Lady Byron to discourage him from writing his biography, we
might be considerably less sure today of what is truth and what is legend regarding Byron's life. Finally, Moore's firsthand observation of Byron, as well
as his status as a confidant and friend, gave his insights into Byron's psychology a degree of acuity sometimes startling to encounter. The *Quarterly Review*

was too sanguine in its prediction that no biographer after Moore would ever again attempt to savage the character of Lord Byron, but it may be said that the authority of Moore's book effectively prevented such attacks from being taken very seriously. Thomas Moore was probably the only person alive in 1830 who had the resources, the personal interest, the desire, and the talent to write a life of Byron that would not only satisfy his age but remain extremely valuable, readable, and insightful in ours as well. His many literary achievements are unfairly neglected today, but his crucial contribution to our modern understanding of Byron should not go unrecognized.

Conclusion

Thomas Moore was a larger presence in Byron's life and work than any other contemporary writer. Byron's writing, his sense of identity as a poet and a man, and the understanding of him left to posterity were all strongly influenced and affected by his association with Moore. Yet because of the current pervasive ignorance and even mischaracterization of Moore and his work, even among many of the best scholars of early-nineteenth-century writing, a large gap has been left in our total picture of Byron. The almost inexplicable critical neglect of Moore has also limited our understanding of the literary period as well as the cultures (both English and Irish) in which Moore's many and various writings played so prominent a role.

In her article "Repossessing the Past: The Case for an Open Literary History," Marilyn Butler argues for a reclamation of the Romantic writers that Victorian-era canon formation consigned to "minor" status. Proposing that "the relations between texts are always of crucial significance," she criticizes the willingness of twentieth-century critics to accept that "only major texts and major authors have meaningful relations." She insists that the ahistorical and hermetic milieu of "great" writers is misleadingly incomplete:

> Keats now communes too often with Shakespeare, Wordsworth with St. Augustine, everyone with the Bible. However much an artist is indebted to the mighty dead, he or she almost certainly borrows more from the living—that is, from writers no longer available for reading except in the better libraries. In the end, evaluation itself is threatened: how can you operate the techniques for telling who a major writer is, if you don't know what a minor one looks like?

Butler suggests that the wide division between "major" and "minor" writers has become a sort of self-fulfilling prophecy, since the lack of convenient modern editions of many marginalized writers makes it very difficult to study them in detail. Butler calls upon scholars to overcome such difficulties in order to recontextualize the "major" writers: "What kind of a critical difference would it make to study actual literary communities as they functioned within their larger communities in time and space? I propose that poets we have installed as canonical look more interesting individually, and far more understandable as groups, when we restore some of their lost peers."

Butler's example of a "lost" poet whose work rewards study is Robert Southey. She traces the ways in which his writings interact thematically, formally, and ideologically with the work of such "major" figures as Coleridge, Shelley, and Byron.[1] Other scholars besides Butler share her historicist point of view; in his anthology, *The New Oxford Book of Romantic Period Verse*,[2] Jerome McGann has attempted to restore some of the supposedly lesser poets of the early nineteenth century, and other scholars such as Anne Mellor have begun to treat the female poets of the period with the serious attention that they deserve. Donald H. Reiman helped make this trend possible, by publishing his 128-volume series *The Romantic Context: Poetry* (1976–79), which made available the works of sixty-seven Romantic-era authors, including such important figures as Joanna Baillie, Felicia Hemans, and Robert Bloomfield. Butler explains how in the case of Southey, the poet's conservative ideology and anti-Romantic practices excluded him from a canon that implicitly endorsed a particular and monolithic conception of poetry. Among Southey's many "non-canonical qualities" was the fact that "he was no solitary or recluse, amenable to study out of context, as the more favoured Wordsworth and Keats were; he engaged actively with his contemporaries, and they with him."

This quality of Southey's is one that Byron and Moore both shared, but Byron seemed to possess enough other "Romantic" attributes to overcome this disability and be included in the canon, whereas Moore did not. Moore was a liberal, but a moderate one; an emotional poet, but not a personal or confessional one; a man of the world, not a worshiper of nature; a commercial and public poet, not a lonely martyr to his art. Moore's reputation in the latter half of the nineteenth century also fell victim to other vicissitudes of history: the new breed of Irish radicals that his own songs and poems had inspired rejected his form of nationalism as too moderate; Lord John Russell's incompetent editing and publication of Moore's journal left an incomplete and misleading impression of his character;[3] and the politically based conservative animosities toward (as well as liberal jealousies of) Moore as a lower-class interloper in high society, manifesting itself as the accusation that he was nothing more than a superficial "social climber," took hold in the absence of any prominent defenders of Moore.[4] In a particularly bitter piece of historical irony, this last charge against Moore has been partially sustained by Byron's own alleged comment that "Tommy loved a lord." This remark, quoted (or invented), it must be remembered, by a vengeful Leigh Hunt at a point when he hated Moore intensely for humiliating him,[5] has been allowed to outweigh in significance the countless flattering remarks that Byron made in letters to many correspondents about Moore's honor, independence, and freedom from affectation.

The twin misconceptions of Moore's writings as inconsequential and his character as superficial have reinforced each other for over a century, during which time the stereotypes have persisted and serious studies of Moore have been slow to emerge. When Moore has not been misunderstood, he has often been ignored. Lately, however, the situation has been changing for the better. In 1975 Hoover H. Jordan published his definitive two-volume biography, *Bolt Upright: The Life of Thomas Moore,* a work of strenuous research devoted to providing the first accurate picture of Moore as poet and man, standing "bolt upright" in his political convictions and character. Since then, Wilfred Dowden has rediscovered, edited, and published Moore's *Journal* in six volumes, restoring the hundreds of deletions and suppressions made in the original edition by Lord John Russell, many of which were acute or harsh judgments upon the people and situations surrounding him. In recent years, other critics have finally begun to examine Moore's writings with an appropriate degree of seriousness and insight. Such essays include Thérèse Tessier's *The Bard of Erin* (1981), Norman Vance's excellent chapter on Moore and Drennan in his *Irish Literature: A Social History* (1990), Leith Davis's "Irish Bards and English Consumers: Thomas Moore's 'Irish Melodies' and the Colonized Nation" (1993), Mohammed Sharafuddin's chapter on *Lalla Rookh* in *Islam and Romantic Orientalism* (1994), Laura Sebastian-Coleman's "Music, Colonialism, and Moore's *Irish Melodies*" (1995), and Gary Dyer's outstanding analysis of Moore's satires in *British Satire and the Politics of Style, 1789–1832* (1997).

All of these recent works have treated Moore as an important writer and a talented artist, and have been admirably free from the condescension and apologies of earlier studies.

Even with the increasing attention paid to Moore's life and writings, misconceptions and gross errors regarding them still too often appear. As recently as 1990 Jonathan Wordsworth could write, "It was to Moore that [Byron] entrusted his *Memoirs,* and Moore who famously decided they must be burned," a statement directly contrary to the facts.[6] In 1991 Stanley Jones wrote that it "seems certain" that Moore wrote an insulting anonymous review of *Christabel,* even though the reverse had been all but proven decades before.[7] Richard Holmes called *The Fudge Family in Paris* "a popular children's series of stories."[8] As has been mentioned in chapter 2, McGann assumed that Byron had written Moore's "Lines on the Death of Mr. P[e]rc[e]v[a]l," even though the poem appears in Moore's *Collected Works.*[9] In 1993 the *Byron Journal* printed "A Newly-Discovered Poem by Thomas Moore," ten lines that were in fact merely a stanza of one of Moore's most famous and popular songs, "Oft in the stilly night."[10] Other writers still sometimes refer to the great wealth Moore gained from his writing, ignoring the fact that Moore was poor and in debt (sometimes disastrously so) for almost all of his professional life, and lived in perpetual fear that his latest work would fail to earn him enough to support his family. Still others accuse him of a lack of enthusiasm for the Irish cause, ignoring not only his *Melodies* and his satires, but also his 1824 *Memoirs of Captain Rock,* a vivid history of Ireland's mistreatment narrated by a terrorist; his 1831 *Life and Death of Lord Edward Fitzgerald,* a laudatory biography of the hero of the 1798 Irish rebellion, published in the wake of Catholic emancipation and against the express wishes of Moore's powerful Whig friends, and his 1833 *Travels of an Irish Gentleman in Search of a Religion,* a controversial two-volume defense of Catholicism dedicated to "the common people of Ireland." While toiling away at his multivolume *History of Ireland* in the 1830s and 1840s Moore turned down many lucrative offers from publishers to publish oriental poems and lyrics, ultimately sacrificing his health and his security in his fruitless mission to complete the work.

The latest manifestation of the lingering ignorance about Moore appears in Phyllis Grosskurth's 1997 *Byron: The Flawed Angel.* Grosskurth summarizes Moore's character and first acquaintance with Byron in two sentences: "Moore was a rather endearing little snob and his journals record his delight in mixing with the powerful and well connected. . . . It would be pleasant, Moore reflected, to add another lord to his repertoire."[11] Apart from the risible assumption that Moore simply wanted to meet every aristocrat in England, Grosskurth's statement is made more irresponsible by the fact that her book barely contains a single additional sentence of analysis regarding Byron's friendship with Moore, one of the two most important, enduring, and heart-felt friendships of Byron's life. The importance of their relationship as poets is wholly ignored.

In the context of such a general lack of knowledge about Moore, Marilyn Butler's call to widen the canon of Romantic-era poetry seems particularly apposite. Her demonstrations of Southey's interaction with Coleridge, Shelley, and Byron are persuasive, but the importance of Southey's work to any one of these writers is arguably still less crucial than the importance of Moore's work (and personal friendship) to Byron. Moore influenced other "major" poets as well. Jonathan Bate has concluded that Moore probably deserves "a considerable share of the credit for the making of [Keats's] 'Ode to Psyche.'"[12] Besides this example of direct influence, there are certainly stylistic similarities generally between the lush imagery and melodious prosody of Moore and those of Keats. Percy and Mary Shelley were ardent readers and admirers of Moore. On 13 October 1817 Shelley requested that the Longmans firm send the manuscript of his *Laon and Cythna* to Moore to obtain his opinion, and Leask has suggested that Shelley's epic was in part a response to the forms of Eastern revolution depicted in *Lalla Rookh*, published the year before.[13] Shelley's political satire *Peter Bell the Third* was dedicated to Moore's pseudonymous alter ego Thomas Brown the Younger, the "editor" of *The Twopenny Post-Bag* and *The Fudge Family in Paris*. Shelley also, of course, placed Byron with Moore, Ireland's "sweetest lyrist of her saddest wrong" (399), together at the grave of Keats in *Adonais*. In 1820 Shelley called Byron and Moore "much better and more successful poets than I am," and in 1822 Shelley referred to kind words from Moore by writing, "of course I cannot but feel flattered by the approbation of a man, my inferiority to whom I am proud to acknowledge." In the same letter Shelley went on to write, "My admiration of the character, no less than of the genius of Moore, makes me rather wish that he should not have an ill opinion of me."[14]

Moore's presence on the literary stage made itself felt in the work of other important contemporary writers as well. Hazlitt warmly praised Moore as a poet and patriot in his review of *The Fudge Family in Paris,* but later became harshly antagonistic to Moore for being insufficiently radical and (as Hazlitt saw it) helping to ruin Leigh Hunt's plans for *The Liberal.* Hunt began as an ally in Moore's "anti-Tory warfare" and included him in the various versions of his *Feast of the Poets,* but ended as a bitter enemy after Moore warned Byron away from him. Peacock satirized Moore in his *Crotchet Castle* and elsewhere.[15] Later writers responded to Moore as well: Poe considered him one of the greatest of poets, and Dickens's novels contain more allusions to Moore than to any other writer. The importance of Moore to nineteenth- and even twentieth-century Irish writers cannot be underestimated; he was the imposing literary precursor whom such writers often loved but from whose influence they struggled to free themselves. Joyce, for example, parodied Moore, but as Norman Vance points out, "the musician in him loved the songs: he incorporated snatches from virtually all the *Irish Melodies* into the rich ironic counterpoint of *Finnegan's Wake*" and partly based his story "The Dead" upon Moore's song, "O, ye dead!"[16]

For all of these writers, and doubtless for many others as well, Moore's writings were a vivid presence, whether those writings were Moore's satires, his lyrical poems, his prose works, or the songs that everyone knew and sang, the lyrics to many of which any of the above-mentioned writers could probably have repeated at will. His influence on his vast readership as well as on the currents of nineteenth-century Irish nationalism and culture was incalculably great; as Howard Mumford Jones observes, "Hundreds who turned a deaf ear to Wordsworth listened, enraptured, to Moore; thousands to whom Shelley was a filthy atheist learned of tyranny and nationalism from the persuasive Irishman."[17] The difference between our modern understanding of Moore and the contemporary understanding of him is enormous. For them, he was a formidable force, but for us, he is an almost invisible apparition. This study has attempted, in part, to demonstrate how much we may learn about Byron by restoring Moore to the total picture, not only of Byron's life, but of early-nineteenth-century writing and culture. It has also suggested how much a rediscovery of Moore's writings may increase our understanding of the literary period in which Byron and Moore "divided the poetical public between them."

Byron's Letters to Moore

In his article "The Temptations of a Biographer: Thomas Moore and Byron," William St. Clair presents an alternate text of Byron's 10 July 1817 letter to Moore taken from a transcription in a Regency scrapbook. St. Clair claims that this alternate text must have been copied "either from the original or from a copy of the original," although he is unable to offer any direct proof of this. However, the similarity of some elements of the alternate text to features of Byron's manuscript letters, such as idiosyncrasies of capitalization and punctuation, may indicate that St. Clair's supposition is correct, although the fact will probably never be known.

St. Clair's text of Byron's letter features several differences that seem to suggest that Moore's text contained some material lifted from a different letter from Byron, a common editorial practice of his time that Moore never denied following. However, on the basis of these differences, St. Clair develops a theory that Moore radically and systematically altered Byron's letters (even to the point of inventing sentences) in order to make them more flattering to himself and thereby improve his reputation. St. Clair also supposes that Moore might have deliberately destroyed the Byron letters in his possession in order to prevent the extent of this alteration from being found out. There are several problems with this theory, not the least of which is that, according to Moore's journal, in March 1842 Moore seriously considered selling all of the 160 Byron letters he possessed in order to help himself out of his financial difficulties (5:2230–32). A great part if not all of these must have been the letters to himself, as any letters loaned to him by others for the purposes of writing his biography of Byron would have been returned to their owners (there are 140 letters from Byron to Moore in the biography).

Moore knew that before selling them he needed to expunge those parts that he had replaced with asterisks in his biography, but he also considered leaving some of those passages alone "where the objects of [Byron's] satire have passed away from the scene" (5:2229). Moore would hardly have thought of selling his Byron letters if he had indeed engaged in as sinister and systematic a deception as St. Clair's article suggests. Certainly if Moore had regularly created whole sentences and passages out of whole cloth mere expurgation would not have concealed that fact.[1] St. Clair himself concedes that the only surviving *manuscript* of a letter from Byron to Moore (a long one from Missolonghi, of 4 March 1824) is word for word the same as Moore's printed version, with one exception: the word "truly" is replaced by "affectionately" in Moore's text. This altered signature, along with the altered signature in St. Clair's alternate text ("yours / Byron" appears in Moore's as "Yours ever, / B") is the only hard evidence St. Clair provides to support his theory that Moore altered the letters to enhance his stature. It is surely insufficient, as Moore printed many of Byron's letters with such laconic signatures as "Ever, &c."—lacking even Byron's name.

Furthermore, St. Clair's alternate text contains the same compliments to Moore as Moore's text does, and even features an additional one that Moore seems to have omitted, regarding Moore's having "triumphed" in his subject. Moore's reputation was in need of no assistance in the late 1820s when he was editing Byron's letters, and there is certainly no credible evidence at all that Byron's esteem for Moore was not exactly as high as Byron's letters say it was. In addition to all his other affectionate comments about Moore in letters to other correspondents, in 1822 Byron told Mary Shelley that the only two people in the world for whom he felt anything like friendship were Lord Clare and Moore (at least in this instance Byron ranked Moore even more highly than he did Hobhouse) (*BLJ* 10:34). Finally, Moore was under incredible time pressure and stress while he was assembling his biography of Byron; he had to locate and transcribe 561 letters, travel through England researching Byron's life, write the biography itself, cope with the long, lingering illness and death of his sixteen-year-old daughter Anastasia, and then work through the terrible depression that settled over both him and his wife afterwards. It is unlikely that under such conditions Moore would have wasted his time systematically inventing things to add to Byron's letters (and since nearly all of Byron's letters to Moore contain compliments, the invention would have to have been systematic and time-consuming indeed).

As for the reliability of St. Clair's scrapbook text, even if one accepts St. Clair's unproven assertion that it was copied from the original or a copy of the original, certainly there is no way to know how accurate or complete such a transcription might have been, though St. Clair seems to assume that it would have been nearly exact. This is an unwarranted assumption. For instance, because Byron's poem to Moore beginning "My boat is on the shore" appears in Moore's version but not in the scrapbook version, St. Clair assumes that Moore lifted it from a different letter and inserted it into the one of 10 July. But Moore quotes the 10 July letter in a letter to Joseph Strutt of 1 September 1817, and in this letter the poem follows the same pair of sentences that it does in the text of the letter that he later printed in his biography of Byron. This pair of sentences appears in the scrapbook text as well. To propose that Moore in his letter to Strutt would have taken the trouble to introduce Byron's poem with two sentences that came from a different letter entirely (and the two sentences were not so important that they would have any special significance to Moore), and then reproduce this arrangement in exactly the same way thirteen years later in his biography of Byron, is surely not credible. A more plausible explanation for the poem's absence from the scrapbook text is that whoever copied the letter into the scrapbook simply left out the poem.

Finally, St. Clair makes a mistake that seriously damages his assertion that Moore's alterations were "drastic." St. Clair prints this sentence from the scrapbook text, regarding Byron's affray with an impudent coachman: "He went sneaking to the Police, but a Soldier who had seen the matter & thought me right, went & counter-oathed him, so that he had to retire & cheap too— I wish I had hit him harder." St. Clair continues, "The meaning of the phrase 'and cheap too' which Moore did not print is not clear, but Byron may be boasting—perhaps ironically—that he did not have to pay a high price to bribe his witness." However, St. Clair missed the fact that this sentence *did* appear in the 1830–31 *American* edition of the biography;[2] evidently the sentence's omission in the London edition was an oversight on the part of John Murray's printer, and not a deliberate act on Moore's part.[3] Here is Moore's version of the sentence, taken from the American edition: "The fellow went sneakingly to the police; but a soldier, who had seen the matter, and thought me right, went and counter-oathed him; so that he had to retire—and cheap too—: I wish I had hit him harder." The only difference in Moore's version (besides the insertion of punctuation marks) is that Moore turned the word "sneaking" into an adverb. Most of St. Clair's logic therefore depends upon his own error, for the other alterations he cites are minor in comparison.

To suggest that Moore would have manufactured compliments to himself and inserted them into Byron's letters is to accuse Moore of a degree of insecurity, pettiness, and dishonesty that is (to say the least) extremely improbable, and to perpetuate a Victorian-era misunderstanding of Moore's character that twentieth-century Moore scholars have been laboring to correct. If Moore is to be accused of an irresponsible and wholesale rewriting of the letters Byron wrote to him, then the only evidence that ought to be admitted is the only surviving *manuscript* of such a letter—and that letter shows that a total of one word had been changed.

A New Text of a Letter from Moore to Byron, 17 July 1823

In his *Letters of Thomas Moore* Wilfred Dowden printed twenty-nine letters or excerpts of letters from Moore to Byron, of which sixteen were from the Murray archives, one from the Lovelace collection, one from the Maggs Brothers catalog, and eleven from Moore's biography of Byron. Eight of the letters, including seven from the Murray archives, are notes belonging to the correspondence regarding Byron's and Moore's projected duel. Of the remaining twenty-one letters, ten are edited and incomplete excerpts that Moore printed in the biography, and of the rest only two or three are letters of any real length or special interest. The relatively little that survives of Moore's side of the Byron-Moore correspondence should make any new discoveries of manuscripts of Moore's letters especially valuable to those interested in the dynamics of the two poets' relationship.

An excerpt from the following letter from Thomas Moore to Lord Byron was published by Dowden (2:518); Dowden's text was taken from the spring 1926 Maggs Brothers sale catalog. The entirety of the letter is now published for the first time, and several errors and omissions in the published text are corrected. The original manuscript is located in the Seymour Adelman collection of the Mariam Canaday Library at Bryn Mawr College. The note written on the back of the letter and signed "HM" may indicate that Byron gave the letter to Dr. Henry Muir, the health officer of Argostoli whom he befriended in Greece in 1823. In any event, the letter was evidently not among the letters of Moore to Byron that Hobhouse gathered and returned to Moore after Byron's death. All or nearly all of those letters are now missing.

This new text adds to Moore's commentary on his and Byron's relationship with the literary market, and the concluding paragraph is entirely new.
It is the latest surviving letter from Moore to Byron, and appears to show that
the warmth and self-deprecation that Moore always displayed in his letters
to his friend had not changed since the early years of their acquaintance. It
also shows the cynicism with which both poets regarded the poetry-buying
English public; one interesting difference between the manuscript and Dowden's version is the presence of the word *cursed* inserted before the word *public*.

MY DEAR BYRON —Why don't you answer my letter? It was written just
before the publication of my last catch-penny,[1] and gave you various particulars thereof, such as its being dedicated to you, the Longmans' alarm at its
contents,[2] Denmans[3] opinion &c. &c.—notwithstanding all which, nothing
could have gone off more quietly, and tamely, and I rather think my friends
in the Row (like Lydia Languish when she thought "she was coming to the
prettiest distress imaginable") were rather disappointed at the small quan-
tum of sensation we made—The fact is, the Public expected personality, as
·usual,[4] & were disappointed not to find it, and, though I touched five hundred pounds as my share of the first Edition, the thing is "gone dead"
\already,/ like Risk's dog, that snapped at the half-penny & died of it. This
\cursed/ Public tires of us all, good & bad, and I rather think (if I can find
out some other more gentlemanly trade) I shall cut the connexion entirely.
How *you*, who are not *obliged*, can go on writing for it, has long, you know,
been my astonishment. To be sure, you have all Europe \(and America too)/
at your back, which is a consolation we poor insular wits (whose fame, like
Burgundy, suffers in crossing the \ocean/) have not to support us in our
reverses. If England doesn't read us, who the devil will?—I have not yet seen
your new Cantos,[5] but Christian[6] seems to have shone out most prosperously,
and the truth is that *yours* are the only "few, fine flushes" of <our> \the/
"departing day" of Poesy on which the Public \can/ now be induced to fix
their gaze. My "Angels"[7] I consider as a failure—I mean in the impression
<they> \it/ made—for I agree with a "*select* few" that I never wrote any thing
better. Indeed, I found out from Lady Davy the other day that it was the first
thing <that> ever gave Ward (now Lord Dudley) any feeling of respect for my
powers of writing.[8]

I am just setting out on a five weeks tour to Ireland—to see, for the first time, "my own romantic" Lakes of Killarney. The Lansdownes, Countesses & Mrs are to be there at the same time. If I but *hear* that a letter has arrived from you, while I am away, I will write to you from the very scene of enchantment itself a whole account of what I feel \& think of it—/but if I find that you still "keep never minding me", why, I must only wait till I am again remembered, and in the mean time, spare you the never-ceasing cordiality with which I am,

my dear Byron, Faithfully yours
Thomas Moore.

Sloperton Cottage, Devizes
July 17th 1823.

Source: Mariam Canaday Library, Bryn Mawr College [ALS 1823 July 17, Seymour Adelman collection 10]

Address: Italia / Lord Byron / Genoa.

Notation: [on back—Dr. Henry Muir's hand?] Rec^d from L^d B / on expressing a wish to / see Mr Moore's hand / writing [signed:] HM.

Introduction

1. Although McGann identifies Inkel as Byron and Tracy as Moore (*BCP* 7:665), the evidence of the text clearly seems to point in the opposite direction. In *The Blues* Inkel is married and Tracy is pursuing the "blue" heiress and "mathematician" Miss Lilac, who is certainly meant to represent Annabella Milbanke. In addition, Inkel speaks of the initial failure of his own "grand romance" (l. 123); this must be an anachronistic reference to Moore's 1817 *Lalla Rookh, an Oriental Romance,* which was critically assailed upon its first appearance, but which quickly rallied to become an enormous popular and critical success. Tracy also asks Inkel to write him some songs with which to seduce Miss Lilac; as England's most popular songwriter, Moore would hardly ask someone else to write songs for him (86). Donald H. Reiman speculates that Byron incorporated aspects of himself in both characters, speaking through Tracy in "Eclogue the First" and through Inkel in the second. See Reiman, "The Oxford English Texts Byron Edition," *NCL* 50 (1995): 269. Although Inkel is essentially made to voice Byron's opinions in the second eclogue, for the most part they are opinions with which Moore would have agreed, and for this reason I find nothing to suggest that Byron did not intend Inkel to represent Moore in the second eclogue as well as the first.

2. All line references to Byron's poetry are taken from *BCP* unless otherwise indicated. Although there is no edition of Moore's complete poetry that features line numbering, all line references to Moore's poetry are taken from *MCP* unless otherwise indicated.

3. Marguerite, Countess of Blessington, *Conversations of Lord Byron,* ed. Ernest J. Lovell Jr. (Princeton: Princeton UP, 1969), p. 223.

4. For a detailed investigation of Moore's knowledge of Byron's incest, see chapter 5.

5. On 26 May 1826, while doing research for his life of Byron, Moore wrote in his journal that Thomas Barnes "mentioned to [him] B.'s strange conversation in Italy with a Mr. Gilly or Gallois (a Prebendary of Durham) about his practices at Harrow" (*MJ* 3:937). Bruce Lavalette told Moore in 1828 about his and Lord Sligo's "bad suspicions attached to the connexion" between Byron and Nicolo Giraud in Greece (*MJ* 3:1123). Lord John Russell deleted both of the above sentences in his edition of the

diary. In 1829, after having dinner with Moore, Charles Greville wrote in his diary: "Moore *said* he did not believe in the stories of [Byron's] fancy for Boys, but it looked as if he does believe it from his manner" (*The Greville Memoirs 1814–1860,* ed. Lytton Strachey and Roger Fulford [London: Macmillan, 1838], 1:326). Moore was anxious to protect Byron's image and of course would never have admitted his knowledge of Byron's bisexuality no matter what he knew. Finally, in a diary entry in 1840, Moore hinted that he knew that "Thyrza" was really John Edleston; mentioning a criticism of his biography of Byron, Moore wrote: "My critic then sets off upon a track which shows that neither he nor [Robert Charles] Dallas (whom he quotes) knew any thing more about Thyrza than they *suppose me* to have known" (*MJ* 5:2140). For more on Moore's knowledge of Byron's bisexuality, see also Louis Crompton, *Byron and Greek Love: Homophobia in nineteenth-Century England* (Berkeley: U of California P, 1985), pp. 81, 341–42 and passim.

6. Blessington, p. 292.

7. Thomas Medwin, *Conversations of Lord Byron,* ed. Ernest J. Lovell Jr. (Princeton: Princeton UP, 1966), p. 32.

8. Ibid, p. 148.

9. *His Very Self and Voice: Collected Conversations of Lord Byron,* ed. Ernest J. Lovell Jr. (New York: Macmillan, 1954), p. 387.

10. Leigh Hunt, *The Autobiography of Leigh Hunt,* ed. J. E. Morpurgo (London: Cresset Press, 1949), p. 315.

11. See *ML,* 1:350. Moore wrote Hunt on 18 December 1814 to express his regrets that he had to leave town without visiting Hunt: "[I] had set apart Thursday last for a visit to you with Lord Byron, who expressed strong & I am sure *sincere* eagerness upon the subject; but he failed me, and I have not had another moment since." Dowden dated the letter "[January 1815]," but Robert Brainard Pearsall supplied the correct date of 18 December 1814.

12. In his biography of William Hazlitt, Stanley Jones cites an unpublished 25 June 1816 letter from Jeffrey to John Allen in the archives of the British Museum: "It is rather provoking that I should have received the other day a very clever and severe review of [*Glenarvon*] from Tommy Moore (pray do not mention this however as he may not wish it to be known) which I should have been very much tempted to insert. It is full of contempt and ridicule rather than serious refutation. . . . You adhere however I suppose to the objection to any notice being taken of it . . . ?" See Stanley Jones, *Hazlitt: A Life* (Oxford: Oxford UP, 1989), p. 224. Jeffrey seems to have wanted to publish the review, but "the objection" probably came from Holland House and other important Whig allies of Jeffrey who might have been embarrassed by any further discussion of Lamb's roman à clef. After all, Lamb's husband was William Lamb, the future Whig prime minister. Francis Horner, the Whig politician, was one of those advising Jeffrey not to mention the novel at all in the *Edinbugh Review.*

13. *His Very Self and Voice,* ed. Lovell, p. 631.

14. Medwin, p. 239. The many compliments that Medwin records Byron as paying

to Moore are all the more significant because Medwin personally disliked Moore and one would expect that Medwin, if anything, might have played down or left out any kind words about him. Medwin even maintained that Moore's friendliness toward Byron was merely a sham, telling Mary Shelley that "there is a great deal of littleness in his character and no small degree of jealousy in his composition." Mary Shelley strongly disagreed, and indeed Moore consistently showed a great degree of self-deprecation and modesty in his relations with Byron. See Ernest J. Lovell Jr., *Captain Medwin: Friend of Byron and Shelley* (Austin: U of Texas P, 1962), p. 169.

15. Joint review of *The Loves of the Angels: A Poem* and *Heaven and Earth: A Mystery,* in *Edinburgh Review* 38 (1823): 27–48. The authorship of this review remains in dispute. Reiman believes that both Francis Jeffrey and William Hazlitt may have worked on the review. See, *The Romantics Reviewed*, ed. Donald H. Reiman (New York: Garland, 1972), Part B, vol. 2, p. 938.

16. "Portraits of Poets," *Weekly Entertainer* 56 (18 March 1816): 225–27.

17. Review of *Lalla Rookh, an Oriental Romance*, in *British Review* 10 (August 1817): 30–54.

18. "Critique on Modern Poets," *New Monthly Magazine* 12 (1 November 1819): 377–84; "Criticisms on the Modern Poets," *New Monthly Magazine* 13 (1 January 1820): 1–4. The first article primarily attacked Byron but also struck at Moore ("the loosest of modern poets"), while the second article dealt exclusively with Moore.

19. In a letter to John Rickman, 27 January 1821, written before his *Vision* had gone to press, Southey wrote: "Then in the preface I have a passage, by no means weakly worded, which my worthy friends Lord Byron and Moore will take to themselves, as a set-off in part, against some obligations due to them." See Robert Southey, *Selections from the Letters of Robert Southey,* ed. John Wood Warter (London: Longmans, 1856), 3:232. William Jerdan understood "Satanic School" to refer only to Byron and Moore; see Jerdan, *Autobiography of William Jerdan* (New York: AMS Press, 1977), 4:7. Much of Southey's indictment of Byron was actually recycled material from an attack Southey had made on Moore years earlier. Large portions of Southey's "Satanic School" remarks originally appeared in his review of Moore's *Epistles, Odes and Other Poems,* published in the *Annual Review* for 1806. See Emily Lorraine de Montluzin, "Southey's 'Satanic School' Remarks: An Old Charge for a New Offender," in *KSJ* 21–22 (1972–73): 29–33. Southey associated the two poets in much the same way in a letter to Caroline Bowles of 13 March 1834: "Byron and Moore and such men address themselves directly to the vicious part of human nature." See Southey, *The Correspondence of Robert Southey with Caroline Bowles,* ed. Edward Dowden (London: Longmans, 1881), p. 295.

20. George Darley, "The Characteristic of the Present Age of Poetry," *London Magazine* 9 (April 1824): 424–27.

21. Lady Louisa Stuart, *Letters of Lady Louisa Stuart to Miss Louisa Clinton,* ed. James A. Hone (Edinburgh: D. Douglas, 1901–3), 2:322.

22. Thomas Doubleday, "Shufflebotham's Dream," *Blackwood's Edinburgh Magazine* 8 (October 1820): 3–7.

23. Una Taylor, *Guests and Memories: Annals of a Seaside Villa* (London: Oxford UP, 1924), p. 223.

24. Henry Taylor, *Autobiography of Henry Taylor 1800–1875* (London: Longmans, 1885), 1:187–88.

25. D. M. Moir, *Sketches of the Poetical Literature of the Last Half-Century* (Edinburgh: W. Blackwood, 1851), p. 197.

26. "Preface," *The Byron and Moore Gallery. A Series of Characteristic Illustrations by Eminent Artists. With Descriptive Letter-Press in Prose in Verse, and Biographies of the Authors* (New York: Johnson, Wilson and Company, 1871), p. iii.

27. See, for instance, Thérèse Tessier, "Byron and Thomas Moore: A Great Literary Friendship," *Byron Journal* 20 (1992): 46–57; Terence De Vere White, "The Best of Friends," *Byron Journal* 8 (1980): 4–17.

28. Carl Woodring, *Politics in English Romantic Poetry* (Cambridge: Harvard UP, 1970), p. 71.

29. Hoover H. Jordan, "Byron and Moore," *MLQ* 9 (1948): 429–39.

30. Jerome J. McGann, *Fiery Dust: Byron's Poetic Development* (Chicago: U of Chicago P, 1968).

31. See Charles E. Robinson's *Shelley and Byron: The Snake and Eagle Wreathed in Fight* (Baltimore: Johns Hopkins UP, 1976), which examines this relationship in detail.

32. Review of *Irish Melodies,* nos. 6 and 7, *Monthly Review* 87 (1818): 419–33.

33. Ibid., 423.

34. My understanding of Byron's distinctive "lyrical dandyism" is greatly indebted to McGann's important article "Byron and the Anonymous Lyric," *Byron Journal* 20 (1992): 27–45.

35. Francis Jeffrey, review of *Beppo, a Venetian Story,* in *Edinburgh Review* 29 (1818): 302–10.

O N E   "In short a '*young Moore*'"

1. *Lord Byron: Selected Poems,* ed. Susan J. Wolfson and Peter J. Manning (London: Penguin, 1996), p. 782.

2. Hoover H. Jordan, *Bolt Upright: The Life of Thomas Moore* (Salzburg: Institut für Englische Sprache und Literatur, 1975), 1:54.

3. See for instance Jonathan Bate, "Tom Moore and the Making of the 'Ode to Psyche,'" *RES* 41 (1990): 325–33.

4. Review of *The Poetical Works of the Late Thomas Little, Esq.,* in *Poetical Register* (1801): 431.

5. Review of *The Poetical Works of the Late Thomas Little, Esq.,* in *Critical Review* 2d ser., 34 (1802): 205.

6. Samuel Taylor Coleridge, *Collected Letters,* ed. Earl Leslie Griggs (Oxford: Clarendon Press, 1956–71), 2:479.

7. Moore presumably chose the pseudonym "Little" because he himself was somewhere around five feet tall.

8. Jordan, *Bolt Upright,* 1:75.

9. "Table-Talk about Thomas Moore," *Bentley's Miscellany* 33 (1853): 655–56. The *Wellesley Index* does not identify the author of this article.

10. John Wilson Croker, *Familiar Epistles to Frederick J[one]s, Esq., on the Present State of the Irish Stage* (Dublin: John Barlow, 1804), p. xiv.

11. *Lord Byron: The Complete Miscellaneous Prose,* ed. Andrew Nicholson (Oxford: Clarendon Press, 1991), p. 220.

12. The "golden rule, all that is pleasurable is allowed" (my translation).

13. William Wordsworth, *The Poetical Works of Wordsworth* (London: Oxford UP, 1961), p. 735.

14. Moore always uses the terms *imagination* and *fancy* interchangeably in his writings, and by both words seems to designate a faculty similar to that which Coleridge calls the lesser "fancy" in chapter 13 of *Biographia Literaria.* Lines 1–19 of "Extract V" in Moore's 1823 *Rhymes on the Road* set forth Moore's basic understanding of "Fancy and Reality":

> The more I've view'd this world, the more I've found,
>> That, fill'd as 'tis with scenes and creatures rare,
> Fancy commands, within her own bright round,
>> A world of scenes and creatures far more fair.
> Nor is it that her power can call up there
>> A single charm, that's not from Nature won,
> No more than rainbows, in their pride, can wear
>> A single hue unborrow'd from the sun—
> But 'tis the mental medium it shines through,
>> That lends to Beauty all its charm and hue;
> As the same light, that o'er the level lake
>> One dull monotony of lustre flings,
> Will, entering in the rounded rain-drop, make
>> Colours as gay as those on Peris' wings!
>
> And such, I deem, the diff'rence between real,
> Existing Beauty and that form ideal,
> Which she assumes, when seen by poets' eyes,
> Like sunshine in the drop—with all those dyes,
> Which Fancy's variegating prism supplies.

According to this formulation, the "fancy" does not reveal "real, / Existing Beauty," or create, or transform, but merely colors and adorns. This idea is consistent with other remarks on imagination and reality that Moore made throughout his life.

15. Although for the most part Moore doubted, as I have described, the sincerity of poetic self-expression, he did look upon his political poetry (such as many of the *Irish Melodies* and *The Fire-worshippers*) as the honest and impassioned expression of his own patriotism. Hunt observed this in his *Autobiography,* when he wrote that Moore "had hardly faith enough in the sentiments of which he treated to give way to his impulses in writing, except when they were festive and witty; and artificial thoughts demand a similar expression. Both patriotism and personal experience, however, occasionally inspired him with lyric pathos" (p. 317).

16. In *The Fudges in England* (1835), Moore would satirize the excesses of Romanticism more explicitly, this time in the person of Fanny Fudge, young authoress of a "Romaint in twelve cantos" entitled "Woe, Woe."

17. In 1807 Byron wrote a short review of Wordsworth's *Poems* (1807), in which he praised Wordsworth for possessing some "native elegance" and quoted a sonnet about which he commented, "The force and expression is that of a genuine poet, feeling as he writes." Byron then proceeded to abuse Wordsworth for using "language not simple, but puerile" (*Complete Miscellaneous Prose,* pp. 8–9). Andrew Nicholson remarks that the review is "not without some covert irony" (p. 269). Byron's comment about a genuine poet "feeling as he writes" is made with specific reference to the quoted sonnet, which is political; although Byron approached his lyrical poetry with the self-consciousness I have described, like Moore he valued politics enough to expect that a political poem should be inspired by genuine conviction and "feeling."

18. Facsimile edition of *Fugitive Pieces* (New York: Columbia UP), p. ix. McGann's edition of Byron's poetry does not include the complete dedication.

19. In this chapter, the texts and line numbers of Byron's poems are taken from McGann's edition, but altered according to the appropriate edition. For instance, the text of "To the Sighing Strephon" in McGann's edition is a collation of the versions in *Fugitive Pieces* and *Poems on Various Occasions;* accordingly, I alter McGann's text to reflect the way it appeared in *Fugitive Pieces.*

20. Leslie Marchand, *Byron's Poetry: A Critical Introduction* (Boston: Houghton Mifflin, 1965), pp. 15–16.

21. In Moore's poem "To ——" (p. 119) and Byron's poem that begins, "When I hear you express an affection so warm," entitled "To Caroline" in the later collections.

22. Jerome J. McGann, "Byron and the Anonymous Lyric," *Byron Journal* 20 (1992): 27–45.

23. "Thomas Moore," *Bentley's Miscellany* 31 (1852): 423–37. The *Wellesley Index* does not identify the author of this article.

24. Francis Jeffrey, review of *Epistles, Odes and Other Poems,* in *Edinburgh Review* 8 (1806): 456–65.

25. Ibid.

26. Jordan, *Bolt Upright,* 1:161.

27. Stephen Gwynn, *Thomas Moore* (London: Macmillan, 1904), pp. 37–38.

28. McGann, *Fiery Dust,* p. 20.

29. Michael G. Cooke, *The Blind Man Traces the Circle: On the Patterns and Philosophy of Byron's Poetry* (Princeton: Princeton UP, 1969), pp. 17–25.

30. The *Antijacobin Review, Gentleman's Magazine, Monthly Review, Monthly Literary Recreations,* and the *Universal Magazine* all treated the volume as a collection of chiefly amatory poems.

31. Review of *Hours of Idleness,* in *Universal Magazine,* 2d ser., 8 (1807): 235–37.

32. Review of *Hours of Idleness,* in *Beau Monde* 2 (1807): 88–90.

33. Hewson Clarke, review of *Hours of Idleness,* in *Satirist* 1 (1807): 77–81.

34. Medwin, p. 147.

T W O   "Our political malice"

1. William Maginn, "Profligacy of the London Periodical Press," *Blackwood's Edinburgh Magazine* 16 (1824): 179–83.

2. James Chandler, *England in 1819: The Politics of Literary Culture and the Case of Romantic Historicism* (Chicago: U of Chicago P, 1998), p. 485.

3. *The Poetical Works of Thomas Moore. A New Collated Edition. To Which is Added, an Original Memoir, by M. Balmanno,* ed. Mary Balmanno (New York: Johnson, Fry and Company, 185–?), p. 219.

4. Review of "The Age of Bronze," in *Literary Gazette* (5 April 1823): 211–13.

5. In her unpublished dissertation *Moore and Moderation: A Study of Thomas Moore's Political and Social Satires,* Irene B. Lurkis writes that hostility to the Regent united "moderates" like Moore with "radicals" like Byron and Hunt (69) and elsewhere implies that political agreement between Byron and Moore was rare (124). This is a mistake; in his study *Byron's Politics* Malcolm Kelsall has demonstrated that Byron's political beliefs were in fact well within the mainstream of the Whig party during his time, just as Moore's were. As far as it is known, Byron's and Moore's disagreements over particular political issues were extremely rare. Howard O. Brogan, in "Thomas Moore, Irish Satirist and Keeper of the English Conscience," *PQ* 24 (1945), 255–76, associates Byron with Lady Oxford's "moderate radicals" and Moore with the more centrist Whigs of Holland House; however, neither poet was as firmly aligned with these factions as Brogan implies. Byron was influenced by Lady Oxford, but he certainly looked upon Lord Holland as a political mentor as well. Byron was also careful to draw distinctions between his own politics and Lady Oxford's (*BLJ* 2:263). He certainly would not have considered himself a Radical. As he told Hobhouse in 1820: "Upon reform you have long known my opinion—but *radical* is a new word since my time— it was not in the political vocabulary in 1816—when I left England—and I don't know what it means" (*BLJ* 7:81). However, as I have said, both poets were somewhat more liberal than the mainstream of their party: in 1826 Moore could be described as "a furious partisan of the ultra-whig school" (review of Moore's *Life of Sheridan,* in *United States Literary Gazette* 3 [15 February 1826]: 362). For more on Byron as a Whig, see Malcolm Kelsall, *Byron's Politics* (New York: Barnes and Noble, 1987).

6. Moore's phrase occurs in Medwin, p. 121.

7. See Byron's enthusiastic remarks on Lord Fitzgerald in Medwin's *Conversations,* pp. 220–22.

8. See David Erdman's articles: "Lord Byron and the Genteel Reformers," *PMLA* 56 (1941): 1065–94; "Lord Byron as Rinaldo," *PMLA* 57 (1942): 189–231; "Byron and Revolt in England," *Science and Society* 11 (1947): 234–48; and "Byron and the New Force of the People," *KSJ* 11 (1962): 47–64. See also Marchand's biography and Kelsall.

9. John Morley, *The Works of Lord Morley* (London: Macmillan, 1921), 6:107.

10. Byron avoided particular political allusions in the poem even to the point of replacing a reference to the dullness of G. L. Wardle's speeches with the neutral "patriot speeches" (l. 22).

11. Probably only lines 1–42 and 47–62 were composed in March; most of the rest of the poem was probably written around 17 November, with lines 149–56 added on 4 December. See *BCP* 1:445–46.

12. Stanzas 24–26 of canto I criticized the 1808 convention of Cintra, and stanzas 11–15 of canto II condemned Lord Elgin for despoiling the ruins of Greece and England for allowing Elgin's actions. Stanzas 41–44, about the battle of Albuera, contemptuously dismissed all the combatants, including the English soldiers, as the "broken tools" of "tyrants," as part of a sweeping condemnation of soldiery in general. The rest of the poem focused on the "fallen" states of Harold and on the European and Levantine countries through which he traveled, and not on Harold's own country.

13. George Croly, "Thomas Moore," *Blackwood's Edinburgh Magazine* 73 (1853): 109.

14. Claude M. Fuess, *Lord Byron as a Satirist in Verse* (New York: Russell and Russell, 1964), p. 42.

15. Decades later Moore could not recall "Corruption and Intolerance" achieving a second edition, but the *Morning Chronicle* for 13 October 1817 advertised a second edition of the volume in a listing of Moore's works available from Longmans.

16. Moore's best biographer, Hoover H. Jordan, claims that the Longman firm printed the "Parody" (1:208), but this appears to contradict Moore's own description of the transaction in the preface to volume 9 of Moore's collected poetry, in which he writes that it was Perry who "got some copies of it . . . printed off for me" (*MCP* 9:xii–xiii).

17. In his edition of Moore's letters, Dowden assigns the date of "Saturday [February] 1812" to Moore's letter to his mother describing the Holland House dinner of the previous evening (*ML* 1:177). However, Stanley Jones corrects this date in a note to his "Regency Newspaper Verse: An Anonymous Squib on Wordsworth," *KSJ* 27 (1978): 99, based on a reference in British Museum, Add. MS. 51951. According to Jones, the letter should be dated Saturday, 7 March 1812, which means that the Holland House dinner took place on 6 March 1812. Since Byron appears to have read the parody by 29 February, I believe that Moore wrote it in February and showed it to

Byron but waited until the day of Lord Holland's dinner to send out copies to the Whigs.

18. M. Dorothy George, *English Political Caricature, 1793–1832* (Oxford: Oxford UP, 1959), p. 133. Chapter 8 (pp. 129–57) provides a useful overview of Whig caricatures of the Regent between the years 1811 and 1815, including some discussion of satires by Byron, Moore, and others.

19. I have given these dates because the Regent composed his letter to the Duke of York on 13 February and Byron had apparently read the "Parody" by 29 February. The "Parody" was probably not composed before 20 February, when the Regent's letter was first printed in several newspapers including the *Morning Chronicle.* If Moore composed his poem before the twentieth, presumably he would have to have been shown a copy of the Regent's letter by one of the leaders of the Whig party, an unlikely circumstance despite his friendship with Lord Holland and other Whig politicians.

20. Gary Dyer, *British Satire and the Politics of Style, 1789–1832* (Cambridge: Cambridge UP, 1997), p. 78. Dyer's book is by far the best source of information on and analysis of the literary context and techniques of Moore's satire. Especially valuable is his insightful discussion of *The Fudge Family in Paris* (pp. 80–84).

21. See "Moore, Praed and the Modern Mockery in Rhyme," in C. W. Previté-Orton, *Political Satire in English Poetry* (New York: Russell and Russell, 1968), pp. 166–92.

22. Dyer, pp. 67–78.

23. Rogers's "epigrammatic example" has not been identified.

24. There are several reasons for this conclusion. First, Byron would have been more justified in his emphatic approval of "Parody" than in the other squibs Moore wrote around this time, as the "Parody" was more elaborate and more accomplished. Second, the poem's premier at Lord Holland's dinner occurred only six days later, on 6 March. Third, none of the other poems known to be Moore's and published during February or March was a parody in the strict sense, except perhaps "The Hare Who Abandoned His Friends" (published in the *Chronicle* on 9 March), an imitation of Gay's "The Hare with Many Friends," which Moore did not reprint in the *Post-Bag* or his collected works, probably because of its mediocrity. Finally, "Parody" was the poem that Moore was most excited about and most eager to show off, and therefore was the poem he would have been most likely to show Byron. Moore did tell Lord Holland in 1821 that "no one had seen [the "Parody"] before it was circulated but himself, Rogers, [James] Perry & [Henry] Luttrel," but Moore's memory for such details was sometimes faulty and it is likely that Moore forgot having shown it to Byron before the dinner (*MJ* 2:500–501).

25. The possible date of February is taken from Howard Mumford Jones's biography of Moore, *The Harp That Once—* (New York: Henry Holt, 1937), p. 139, but Jones does not indicate his authority for this date. The date cannot be confirmed because it is not known whether any of the satires printed during that month were in fact Moore's. Moore's authorship of the anti-Regent satire "Imitation of Anacreon" printed

on 27 February is possible, both because Moore had previously written a serious version of the same poem for his *Odes of Anacreon,* and because the satire is introduced by a humorous letter addressed "To the Editor of the Morning Chronicle"; several later squibs known to be Moore's were prefaced by similar humorous letters to the editor. Moore could also have written the anti-Regent "Epigram, Founded on Fact" (24 February), which is written in Moore's favored anapests. Stanley Jones speculates that a *Chronicle* poem entitled "The Outo'thewayisms of Paddy Delaney," published in three parts on 23 January, 8 February, and 19 February, might have been Moore's, but Jones offers no solid evidence to support this speculation (91–92). The first *Morning Chronicle* squib known to be Moore's is "The Hare Who Abandoned His Friends," published on 9 March.

26. See Howard Mumford Jones, pp. 139 and 341–42, on the "vexing problem" of identifying Moore's contributions to the *Chronicle* and, later in his career, to the *Times.*

27. This poem has only recently been identified as Byron's. See Jeffery Vail, "Byron's 'Impromptu on a Recent Incident': A New Text of a Regency Squib," *KSJ* 47 (1998).

28. Unpublished letter to Perry [June 1813], Bodleian Library, ms. eng. letters d. 275, f. 47.

29. R. C. Dallas, *Recollections of the Life of Lord Byron, from the Year 1808 to the End of 1814* (London: C. Knight, 1824), p. 235.

30. See Erdman, "Lord Byron as Rinaldo," 226–27.

31. *The Works of Lord Byron,* ed. Ernest Hartley Coleridge and Rowland Edmund Prothero (London: John Murray, 1898–1905), 7:135.

32. Mary Berry, *Extracts from the Journals and Correspondence of Miss Berry, from the Year 1783 to 1852* (London: Longmans, 1866), 2:495.

33. William Childers, "Byron's *Waltz:* The Germans and Their Georges," *KSJ* 18 (1969): 94.

34. McGann's Oxford edition of Byron's poetical works mistakenly attributed Moore's poem "Lines on the Death of Mr. P[e]rc[e]v[a]l" to Byron on the evidence of the existence of an undated copy of the poem in Lady Byron's hand. According to McGann's note, "The poem almost certainly dates from 1815, when Lady B was copying out the poems B was then writing." McGann also stated that the poem had never been published (*BCP* 3:475). However, the poem was first published (with minor variations) as "To ——" in the *Morning Chronicle* on 23 May 1812, reprinted in the 1818 *The Fudge Family in Paris,* and then included in the ten-volume edition of Moore's works published in 1840–41 and edited by Moore himself. In the "Corrections and Amplifications" section of McGann's edition, McGann added the note: "It is possible that Thomas Moore may have authored this work, or that Byron and Moore were the co-authors" (*BCP* 7:168). Although the idea of co-authorship is intriguing, it is wholly unsupported by available evidence; that Lady Byron copied down Moore's poem at some unknown point in time in no way supports the hypothesis that Byron wrote or co-wrote it. Additionally, it is very unlikely that Moore would have taken full credit for

a poem on which he had collaborated with Byron. Besides including the poem in his own collected works, in his diary Moore referred to the poem as "my verses on . . . Perceval's death" (*MJ* 2:449).

35. This poem was not reprinted in the 1840–41 edition of Moore's collected works.

36. The 10 November 1822 issue of *John Bull* advertised a seventeenth edition of the *Post-Bag,* "just published" by Carpenter (p. 793, col. 2).

37. Moore was generally known to have been the author of the *Post-Bag,* and some reviews of the volume identified his authorship. Other writers, including Samuel Rogers and George Colman the younger, were mistakenly rumored to have contributed to it. A letter written by Melesina Trench dated 31 July 1813 shows that Moore's authorship was common knowledge: "I suppose you know that Tommy Moore has lost all his prospects of advancement by publishing *The Twopenny Post Bag.* . . . He has gained in fame what he has lost in profit . . . all acknowledge the wit and humour of this last production." See Melesina Chenevix St. George Trench, *The Remains of the Late Mrs. Trench* (London: Parker and Bourne, 1862), p. 276.

38. Review of *Intercepted Letters; or, The Twopenny Post-Bag,* eleventh edition, in *Antijacobin Review* 46 (1814): 266–68.

39. Review of *Intercepted Letters; or, The Twopenny Post-Bag,* thirteenth edition, in *Satirist* 13 (1813): 553–57.

40. Hunt, *The Autobiography of Leigh Hunt* (London: Crescent Press, 1949), p. 314.

41. Dowden mistakenly dated this letter "[January or February 1816]," and the misdating is uncorrected by Pearsall. Moore's letter was actually written between 3 and 12 March 1814, as references in Byron's letters to Moore of those two dates clearly indicate. See *BLJ* 4:76–78; 79–81. For further information on this letter and its significance, see chapter 5, note 6.

42. Review of Edmund Lewis Lenthal Swifte's 1814 *Anacreon in Dublin,* in *Antijacobin Review* 46 (1814): 535. Swifte mentioned "Windsor Poetics" in his book's ironic dedication to Lord Byron.

43. Woodring, p. 169.

44. Peter J. Manning, "Tales and Politics: *The Corsair, Lara,* and *The White Doe of Rylstone,*" in *Reading Romantics: Text and Context* (Oxford: Oxford UP, 1990), pp. 195–215.

45. *Works,* ed. Coleridge and Prothero, 3:388–89.

46. George, p. 134.

47. *Works,* ed. Coleridge and Prothero, 3:481.

48. Ibid., 7:470–71.

49. Ibid., 7:475.

50. Ibid., 7:486–87.

51. Review of *The Corsair,* in *British Critic* 1 (1814): 279–93.

52. Edmund Lewis Lenthal Swifte, *Anacreon in Dublin* (London: J. J. Stockdale, 1814).

53. Ibid., pp. 42–43.

54. Ibid., pp. 137–38.

55. John Watkins, *Memoirs of the Life and Writings of the Right Honourable Lord Byron* (London: Henry Colburn, 1822), pp. 205–7.

56. Henry J. Palmerston, *The New Whig Guide* (London: W. Wright, 1819). "English Melodies" (pp. 108–41) included parodies of Byron's "The Destruction of Semnacherib," "Sun of the Sleepless," and "Fare Thee Well!," and of Moore's "Love's young dream" and "Believe me, if all those endearing young charms." These parodies first appeared in the *Courier* between 13 and 25 April 1816.

57. *John Bull* 5 (14 August 1825): 268, col. a.

58. This letter was incorrectly dated by Dowden. See note 41 above.

59. Byron did send an anti-Regent poem to Lady Jersey on 29 May 1814, but this poem was written in heroic couplets, devoted most its lines to Lady Jersey's beauty, and was not intended to be humorous. The conservative *Champion* got hold of the lines and printed them on 31 July, to Byron's professed displeasure (*BLJ* 4:152).

60. *Prose and Verse Humorous, Satirical, and Sentimental by Thomas Moore . . . ,* ed. Richard Hearne Shepard (New York: Scribner, Armstrong, 1878), p. 409.

61. "Extract VII.: Lord Byron's Memoirs, written by himself.—Reflections, when about to read them." This poem is discussed in chapter 6.

62. *Complete Miscellaneous Prose,* ed. Nicholson, pp. 103–4.

63. Erwin A. Stürzl, *A Love's Eye View: Teresa Guiccioli's "La Vie de Lord Byron en Italie"* (Salzburg: Institut für Anglistik und Amerikanistik, 1988), p. 104.

64. *Prose and Verse,* p. 410.

65. As publishers of books and of *Galignani's Messenger* (a daily newspaper), Jean Antoine and Guillaume Galignani appear to have arranged for the private printing of Moore's poem as an alternative to publishing it in their newspaper.

66. The poem appeared in the 15 April 1821 issue of the *Examiner,* and was also printed in the *Morning Chronicle.* The poem was signed "T. B." [Thomas Brown the Younger], and dated from "Champs Élysées, Paris." The *Examiner* noted, "The following verses are from the *Chronicle.* That fact and the date affixed to them might indicate the ardent patriot and elegant poet from whose pen they emanate, if the fine spirit and flowing stile did not preclude all doubts as to the author" (p. 234, col. a).

67. Medwin, p. 220.

68. *Works,* ed. Coleridge and Prothero, 4:551–61. An article entitled "The King's Voyage to Dublin" in the 26 August 1821 issue of the *Examiner* also defended Moore against the *John Bull* attack.

69. William Ruddick, "Don Juan in Search of Freedom: Byron's Emergence as a Satirist," in *Byron: A Symposium,* ed. John D. Jump (London: Macmillan, 1975), pp. 125–26.

70. "Posterity shall ne'er survey / a monument like this; / Here lie the bones of Castlereagh, / Stop, passenger, and p———!" (*MJ* 1:343). Moore's journal entry of 14 September 1820 mentions that he had only received the 2 January letter "the other day." My text of Byron's epigram is taken from Moore's journal entry rather than from

McGann, who collates the version of the poem in an 1831 issue of *The Republican* with that in Byron's 1832 *Collected Works*. McGann's text replaces the final two words with a dash and features other differences; Moore's is probably more accurate.

71. Medwin writes that the poem was sent to Byron from Paris. Medwin did not meet Byron until 1821, and Moore returned to England that same year.

72. Medwin, pp. 154–55. Apparently Moore eventually forgot that Medwin had printed his poem, since in a diary entry for 14–15 February 1842, Moore copied down the "Epitaph," writing, "Have just stumbled upon the following verses of mine which, I *rather think,* have never appeared in print. It is odd they should *not*—but, if it be true that they are not published any where, it must have been owing to my having made acquaintance with Southey that I suppressed them.—" There are several differences of word and phrase in the version Moore copied down in his diary, and there is an extra quatrain, but the manuscript of the diary was damaged such that each line of the extra stanza is incomplete, making it unintelligible (*MJ* 5:2225–26). Although Moore was hostile toward Medwin's book, it is almost certain that he read through it in its entirety, since he lifted some information from it for his own biography of Byron.

73. Ibid., p. 124.

74. Chandler, p. 350.

75. See Irene Lurkis-Clark, "Byron's *Don Juan* and Moore's 'The Two Penny Post-Bag,'" in *NQ* 226 (1981): 401–3.

76. Medwin, p. 240. However, Byron was apparently annoyed by one part of the book, in which he believed Moore was poking fun at his romantic protagonists. In one of Biddy Fudge's letters she describes a "fine sallow, sublime, sort of Werter-fac'd man, / With mustachios that gave (what we read of so oft) / The dear Corsair expression, half savage, half soft, / As Hyænas in love may be fancied to look, or / A something between ABELARD and old BLUCHER!" (98–102). When Moore was with Byron in Venice he learned of Byron's irritation: "On seeing this doggerel, my noble friend,— as I might, indeed, with a little more thought have anticipated,—conceived the notion that I meant to throw ridicule on his whole race of poetic heroes, and accordingly, as I learned from persons then in frequent intercourse with him [doubtless Mary Shelley], he flew into one of his fits of half humorous rage against me. This he now confessed himself, and, in laughing over the circumstance with me, owned that he had even gone so far as, in his first moments of wrath, to contemplate some little retaliation for this perfidious hit at his heroes. 'But when I recollected,' said he, 'what pleasure it would give the whole tribe of blockheads and Blues to see you and me turning out against each other, I gave up the idea'" (*MLB* 2:261–62).

77. Dyer, 91. The "Radical verse satires" that Dyer groups together for analysis are *The Fudge Family in Paris, The Vision of Judgment,* Percy Shelley's *Peter Bell the Third* (1819), Lady and Sir Thomas Morgan's *The Mohawks* (1822), and Hunt's *Ultra-Crepidarius* (1823). It should be noted that in *The Fudge Family in Paris* the epistles of Phelim Connor the radical Irish Catholic *are* written in a Juvenalian style and in the form of Augustan heroic couplets. Yet this is merely in keeping with Moore's plan of writing

in four different styles in order to represent four different kinds of political viewpoint. Those of the other three epistle writers are written in looser styles and Horatian tones. Connor's denunciations are so harsh and earnest, and so free from any irony, that Moore must have felt that the lighter verse form in which he normally wrote would not have been appropriate. The letters of Phillip Fudge (a spy for Castlereagh and the only truly venal and despicable of the characters) are not worthy of a stately verse form, as he is not a Tory ideologue, but rather a sycophant and an opportunist.

THREE   "That's my thunder, by G—d!"

1. Review of first four installments of *Irish Melodies,* in *Monthly Review* 71 (June 1813): 113–26.

2. Ibid.

3. Marchand, *Byron's Poetry,* pp. 15–16.

4. Medwin, p. 240.

5. Blessington, p. 151.

6. *Lord Byron: The Complete Miscellaneous Prose,* p. 107.

7. Mary Shelley, *The Journals of Mary Shelley,* ed. Paula R. Feldman and Diana Scott-Kilvert (Baltimore: Johns Hopkins UP, 1995), p. 478.

8. Jonathan David Gross, *Byron's "Corbeau Blanc": The Life and Letters of Lady Melbourne* (Houston: Rice UP, 1997), p. 280.

9. Nathaniel Parker Willis, *Pencillings by the Way,* 3 vols. (London: John Macrone, 1835), 3:108–9.

10. *Journals of Mary Shelley,* p. 502.

11. Leith Davis, "Irish Bards and English Consumers: Thomas Moore's 'Irish Melodies' and the Colonized Nation," *Ariel* 24 (1993): 7–25. Davis's article is an excellent and evenhanded consideration of the ways in which the *Irish Melodies* "both paved and blocked the way to the decolonization which is still in process in Ireland." Davis does, however, commit one or two factual errors, such as reading "Come send round the wine" as a dismissal of the importance of political differences, instead of as an articulation of the ideal of religious tolerance that Moore expressed throughout his life.

12. J. Cuthbert Hadden, *George Thomson, the Friend of Burns: His Life and Correspondence* (London: J. C. Nimmo, 1898), p. 189.

13. *Notes from the Letters of Thomas Moore to His Music Publisher, James Power,* ed. Thomas Crofton Croker (New York: Redfield, 1854), p. 35.

14. Ibid, p. 47.

15. Ibid, p. 44.

16. Ibid.

17. John Murray published his own version of the *Hebrew Melodies* around 23 May 1815, containing twenty-five poems printed without their accompanying music.

18. Joseph Slater, "Byron's Hebrew Melodies," *Studies in Philology* 49 (1952): 82.

19. *Memoirs, Journal, and Correspondence of Thomas Moore,* ed. Lord John Russell, 8 vols. (London: Longmans, 1853–56), 2:79.

20. Review of *Hebrew Melodies,* in *Theatrical Inquisitor* 6 (May 1815): 377–78.

21. Josiah Conder, review of *Hebrew Melodies,* in *Eclectic Review,* 2d ser., 4 (July 1815): 94–96.

22. Review of *Hebrew Melodies,* no. 2, in *Critical Review,* 5th ser., 3 (April 1816): 357–66.

23. "Essay on Song Writing," *Blackwood's Edinburgh Magazine* 7 (1820): 32–35. Alan Lang Strout does not identify the author of this article.

24. See chapter 2, section 2.

25. *Notes,* p. 46.

26. Ibid., pp. 42–43.

27. Marchand, *Byron's Poetry,* p. 133.

28. Thomas L. Ashton, *Byron's Hebrew Melodies* (Austin: U of Texas P, 1972), p. 68.

29. Marilyn Butler, "Orientalism," in *The Penguin History of Literature: The Romantic Period,* ed. David B. Pirie (London: Penguin, 1994), p. 425.

30. George Gordon, Lord Byron, and Isaac Nathan, *A Selection of Hebrew Melodies, Ancient and Modern,* ed. Frederick Burwick and Paul Douglass (Tuscaloosa: U of Alabama P, 1988), p. 17.

31. *Complete Miscellaneous Prose,* p. 39.

32. Isaac Nathan, *Fugitive Pieces and Reminiscences of Lord Byron* (London: Whittaker, Treacher and Company, 1829), p. 25.

33. See Norman Vance, *Irish Literature: A Social History* (Oxford: Basil Blackwell, 1990), pp. 116–17.

34. Ashton, p. 72.

35. Slater, pp. 86, 89.

36. Marchand, *Byron's Poetry,* p. 135.

37. Byron and Nathan, *Hebrew Melodies,* p. 15.

38. Ashton, p. 71.

39. Ibid.

40. Nathan (*Fugitive,* pp. 39–40) hinted that Byron might have been thinking of Napoleon when he composed this lyric.

41. Samuel Smiles, *A Publisher and His Friends: Memoir and Correspondence of the Late John Murray,* 2 vols. (London: John Murray, 1891), 1:351.

42. Slater, p. 86.

43. Hoover H. Jordan, "Thomas Moore: Artistry in the Song Lyric," *SEL* 2 (1962): 403–40.

44. For a complete study of Moore as "musical prosodist," see Thérèse Tessier's *The Bard of Erin: A Study of Thomas Moore's Irish Melodies (1808–1834)* (Salzburg: Institut für Anglistik und Amerikanistik, 1981), esp. pp. 59–81. See also her *La Poesie Lyrique de Thomas Moore, 1779–1852* (Paris: Didier, 1976), from which *The Bard of Erin* is excerpted and translated from the French.

45. *John Bull* 1 (17 June 1820): 213, col. c.

46. Ludwig Heinrich Hermann von Pückler-Muskau, *Tour in England, Ireland and France . . .* (Zurich: Massie, 1940), p. 279.

47. Review of *Irish Melodies*, nos. 6 and 7, in *Monthly Review* 87 (1818): 419–33.

48. Ashton, p. 72.

49. Moore, *Memoirs*, 8:213.

50. The poem appeared in the 9 January 1821 issue of the *Times* and the 21 January 1821 issue of the *Examiner*. The *Times* commented, "The following verses were addressed by Lord Byron to Mr. Thomas Moore, and are in circulation among a few of Mr. Moore's select friends. Their authenticity is undoubted" (p. 2, col. c). The *Examiner* wrote: "We have received a copy of the following verses, addressed by Lord Bryon [*sic*] to Mr. Thomas Moore, from Dublin, where they are in circulation among a few of Mr. Moore's more select friends. We are not informed of the particular occasion on which they were written, but for their authenticity we can vouch. The highly flattering compliment which they convey will not surprise those who recollect that the Noble Lord has publicly declared his brother bard to be 'the poet of all circles and ages, and the idol of his own.' Indeed it is Mr. Moore's rare fortune not to be more universally admired for his genius and patriotism, than enthusiastically beloved by all who are honoured with his friendship, and enjoy opportunities of knowing his manifold private virtues" (p. 42, col. a).

51. In his diary entry for 21 October 1827, Moore recorded a woman singing "with much spirit [Bishop's] setting of 'Here's a health to thee, Tom Moore!'" (*MJ* 3:1069). On 26 August 1835 Moore participated in a parade given for him in Ireland, during which a band played, "more than once, an Air that has been adapted to Byron's 'Here's a health to thee, Tom Moore'" (4:1713). The same year Moore was told by a friend returned from Germany that the Germans all referred to Moore as "Tom Moore" because of the popularity among them of Byron's song (4:1727). There are instances in the diary of people singing Bishop's setting to him at parties as late as the 1840s.

F O U R   "An humble follower—a Byronian"

1. Unpublished letter to Power, [16] September 1813, John J. Burns Library, Boston College.

2. *Notes*, p. 13.

3. Unpublished letter to Power, [23] December 1813, Boston Public Library.

4. *Notes*, p. 34.

5. The image of an albatross sleeping in midflight and high in the air, accompanied by an explanatory footnote, occurs in *The Fire-worshippers*, a fact that perhaps supports Moore's recollection that he had been working on that poem during these months (the quoted letter from Moore to Byron is dated by Dowden as "[February 1814]"). See *MCP* 6:240–41, lines 658–62 and n.

6. Dowden mistakenly dated this letter "[January or February 1816]"; it was actually written between 3 and 12 March 1814. See chapter 2, note 41, and chapter 5, note 6 for further information on the letter and its significance.

7. *Notes,* pp. 34–35.

8. *Works,* ed. Coleridge and Prothero, 3:394.

9. Moore's subtitle was actually "An Oriental Romance"; Byron was mistaken.

10. Butler, "Orientalism," p. 426.

11. John Cam Hobhouse, Baron Broughton, *Recollections of a Long Life* (New York: Scribner's, 1909), 1:77.

12. Review of *Lalla Rookh,* in *Literary Gazette* 1, no. 19 (31 May 1817): 292–95.

13. Review of *Lalla Rookh,* in *Sale-Room* no. 22 (31 May 1817): 173–75.

14. Review of *Lalla Rookh,* in *British Review* 10 (August 1817): 30–54.

15. Review of *Lalla Rookh,* in *New Monthly Magazine* 8 (August 1817): 52.

16. Review of *Lalla Rookh,* in *Critical Review* 5 (June 1817): 560–81.

17. John Wilson, review of *Lalla Rookh,* in *Blackwood's Edinburgh Magazine* 1 (June 1817): 279–285. The second part of Wilson's review appeared in the August issue, pp. 503–10.

18. Review of *Lalla Rookh,* in *Monthly Review* 83 (July 1817): 285–99. The first part of this two-part review appeared in the June issue, pp. 181–201.

19. Review of *Lalla Rookh,* in *British Critic* 7 (June 1817): 604–16. The quoted section describes Hinda's grief and is taken from *MCP* 6:315–16; ll. 2110–33.

20. George Brandes, *Main Currents in Nineteenth Century Literature* (New York: Macmillan, 1906), 4:94.

21. In 1910 W. J. Courthope expressed the prevailing nineteenth-century view when he wrote that Fadladeen's passages were "clearly intended as a good-natured satire on the philosophical disquisitions of Jeffrey in *The Edinburgh Review.*" This interpretation has been accepted by later twentieth-century critics as well; for example, Robert Birley writes that "Surely . . . Fadladeen is Jeffrey. Moore is laughing at his friend and also, in the most disarming way, having his revenge for the review which had first brought them together." Stuart Curran calls Fadladeen "transparently a caricature of Francis Jeffrey." See W. J. Courthope, *A History of English Poetry* (London: Macmillan, 1910), 6:119; "Thomas Moore: *Lalla Rookh,*" in Robert Birley, *Sunk without Trace: Some Forgotten Masterpieces Reconsidered* (New York: Harcourt Brace, 1962), p. 161; and Stuart Curran, *Poetic Form and British Romanticism* (Oxford: Oxford UP, 1986).

22. Allan Cunningham, "Moore," in *A Biographical and Critical History of the British Literature of the Last Fifty Years* (Paris: J. Smith, 1834), pp. 86–89. See also pp. 264–67 and 339–40.

23. C. Neale, review of *Lalla Rookh,* in *Eclectic Review* 8 (October 1817): 340–53.

24. Francis Jeffrey, review of *Lalla Rookh,* in *Edinburgh Review* 29 (November 1817): 1–35.

25. Mohammed Sharafuddin, "Thomas Moore's *Lalla Rookh* and the Politics of

Irony," in *Islam and Romantic Orientalism: Literary Encounters with the Orient* (New York: I. B. Tauris, 1994), p. 169.

26. Miriam Allen DeFord, *Thomas Moore* (New York: Twayne, 1967), p. 48.

27. For a useful description of Hunt's attempts to make the heroic couplet "do everything that Pope had avoided," see Walter Jackson Bate, *John Keats* (Cambridge: Harvard UP, 1963), pp. 79–82.

28. Wallace Cable Brown, *The Triumph of Form: A Study of the Later Masters of the Heroic Couplet* (Chapel Hill: U of North Carolina P, 1948), pp. 195–97.

29. *Lord Byron: Selected Poems,* p. 794.

30. The man was somewhat more wicked in an earlier draft of the poem, having been a poisoner. For this earlier version, which features many differences, see W. P. Trent, "Paradise and the Peri," *Ninth Year Book, Bibliophile Society of Boston* (1910): 109–27.

31. Gwynn, p. 87.

32. This parallel has more recently been noted by Nigel Leask and Hoover H. Jordan. See Leask, *British Romantic Writers and the East: Anxieties of Empire* (Cambridge: Cambridge UP, 1992), p. 113, and Jordan, "Byron and Moore," *MLQ* 9 (1948): 435.

33. "J. G. G.," "On the Genius and Writings of Moore," *Literary Speculum* 1 (Feb. 1822): 223.

34. "A. P." "Thomas Moore: An Essay on Moore's Life and Poetry," in *The Living Poets of England: Specimens of the Living British Poets, with Critical and Biographical Notices and an Essay on English Poetry* (Paris: L. Baudry, 1827), 2:279.

35. "Byron and Moore," *Lady's and Gentleman's Weekly Museum and Philadelphia Reporter* 3 (1818): 79–80.

36. Byron Porter Smith, *Islam in English Literature* (New York: Caravan Books, 1977), p. 196.

37. Howard Mumford Jones, p. 181. As Norman Vance points out, Moore's identification of Hafed with Emmet was a simplification, since Emmet was in fact not a Catholic but a Protestant. Vance notes that Moore was taking part in the "increasing tendency to identify Catholic and national causes" in Irish writing. See Vance, p. 112.

38. For Moore's denunciations of Reynolds as an arch traitor, see his *Life and Death of Lord Edward Fitzgerald* (London: Longmans, 1831).

39. *Prose and Verse Humorous, Satirical, and Sentimental by Thomas Moore,* p. 62.

40. Fehmida Sultana, *Romantic Orientalism and Islam: Southey, Shelley, Moore, and Byron* (Ph.D. diss., Tufts University, 1989), p. 133.

41. Birley, p. 159.

42. Marilyn Butler, "Byron and the Empire in the East," in *Byron: Augustan and Romantic,* ed. Andrew Rutherford (New York: St. Martin's, 1990), pp. 63–81.

43. "Byron and Moore," *Lady's,* p. 80.

44. Leask, pp. 13–67.

45. William St. Clair, "The Impact of Byron's Writings: An Evaluative Approach,"

in *Byron: Augustan and Romantic,* ed. Andrew Rutherford (New York: St. Martin's, 1990), pp. 20–21.

46. Marchand conjectures that the omitted title was *Ilderim,* the oriental poem by Henry Gally Knight published in 1816, and in an alternate text of this letter provided by William St. Clair (see chapter 5, note 3, and "Appendix A: Byron's Letters to Moore") the word is indeed *Ilderim.* In a letter dated 12 May 1817, ten days before the publication of *Lalla Rookh,* Byron assured Moore, "Your poetical alarms are groundless; go on and prosper" (*BLJ* 5:227). Moore's alarms were probably over the expected appearance of more Eastern tales by Knight; *Phrosyne* and *Alashtar* were both published in 1817.

47. It is difficult to imagine what Moore might have omitted here. The sentence preceding the asterisks may have been transferred by Moore from an earlier Byron letter, as it does not appear in St. Clair's alternate text (see chapter 5, note 3, and "Appendix A: Byron's Letters to Moore"). Perhaps the sentence was originally longer, and Moore cut it off after "Tale."

48. See William St. Clair, "The Temptations of a Biographer: Thomas Moore and Byron," *Byron Journal* 17 (1989); 50–56. But see also Appendix A: *Byron's Letters to Moore.*

49. For instance, in his article "Byron's 'Wrong Revolutionary Poetical System' and Romanticism," Hermann Fischer considers Byron's remarks in isolation from the references to Moore's poem that precede them, and prints those remarks (as many other scholars have done) only from the words "With regard to poetry in general" onwards. Fischer's article appears in *Byron: Augustan and Romantic,* ed. Andrew Rutherford (New York: St. Martin's, 1990), pp. 221–39.

50. Curran, p. 145.

51. Medwin, pp. 238–39.

F I V E   "Like Kean and Young, upon the stage together"

1. All quotations from *The Loves of the Angels* are taken from the first edition (London: Longmans, 1822). In the fifth edition Moore changed the Christian angels into Muslim ones and replaced references to God with "Alla." Moore's 1840–41 complete *Poetical Works* reprinted this later, "orientalized" edition.

2. This was Byron's letter of 17 May 1822, sent to Moore through Murray because Byron mistakenly thought Moore was in London (he was actually in Paris) (*BLJ* 9:160). When Moore printed this letter in his biography of Byron, he omitted a section following the word "squabble" that told the story of Byron's affray with the Italian dragoon. Moore explained that the omitted section merely contained "a repetition of the details given on this subject to Sir Walter Scott and others" (*MLB* 2:595). Marchand printed Moore's transcript of this letter in his *Byron's Letters and Journals* but neglected to note Moore's omission. Therefore, the "long letter" Moore refers to in his journal appears as a very short one in both Moore's and Marchand's texts. Because

the only surviving sentence on Allegra's death in this letter does not seem to justify Moore's journal observation on Byron's grief, it is likely that the section Moore omitted dealt not only with the dragoon but also with Allegra's death.

3. There is some confusion over Byron's 10 July 1817 letter because of the existence of an alternate text printed by William St. Clair. In St. Clair's text, the postscript does not appear at all. St. Clair theorizes that his text, taken from a Regency scrapbook, was copied from Moore's original manuscript or from a copy of that manuscript. If this is true, it is likely that Moore cut out the postscript before showing the letter; surely he would have considered the postscript far too sensitive to be shown about indiscriminately. In the 1842 journal entry mentioned above, Moore records the postscript as having been appended to "one of [Byron's] letters"; perhaps this inexactitude about the letter's date was due to the fact that he was transcribing from the undated scrap of paper he cut out of the original. On the other hand, perhaps the postscript did not actually belong to the letter of 10 July. Moore may have moved it from its proper place for some reason. If this is true, the postscript still must have been written at a time when Byron believed Moore had either recently read or heard about the contents of *Manfred,* which means that it must date from sometime in 1817. Whether or not the postscript actually comes from the 10 July 1817 letter, it nevertheless proves that Moore must have known about Byron and Augusta by 1822, when he wrote the *Second Angel's Story.*

4. Quoted in Leslie A. Marchand, *Byron: A Biography* (New York: Knopf, 1957), 2:699.

5. In a letter of 17 December 1829, Moore told Murray that he had had "great hesitation" in quoting two of Byron's poems to Augusta, and doubted whether he ought to have "given them the importance of concluding [volume one of the biography] with them" (*ML* 2:669). Another apparent reference to the Augusta Leigh controversy occurs in an earlier letter from Moore to Lord Holland, written on 5 November 1821, in which Moore discussed those parts of Byron's memoirs that seemed to him the most sensitive. Moore wrote that "what Lady Holland remarked yesterday about Mrs. L. is, I find upon recollection, founded entirely on her own suspicions as Lord B. merely mentions a nameless person whom he calls 'love of loves' & I never met with but one individual, besides Lady H. who supposed it to allude to the Lady in question" (*ML* 2:498). If "Mrs. L." was indeed Augusta, surely Moore was feigning ignorance in order to throw the Hollands off the scent.

6. The reasons for placing Moore's letter (no. 459, vol. 1, pp. 386–87 in Dowden's edition) between 3 and 12 March 1814 are as follows: (1) Byron's 3 March phrase "when we are *veterans*" is quoted in Moore's letter; (2) Moore's sentence "I am so very willing that the public not forget you" is quoted in Byron's 12 March letter; (3) Moore remarks that the fourteenth edition of his *Twopenny Post-Bag* is about to appear—it was published in 1814; (4) Moore asks Byron if he has any "*libels*" that Moore could include in this new edition, and Byron replies in his 12 March letter that he has "nothing of the sort you mention except ["Lines to a Lady Weeping"]"; (5) Moore con-

gratulates Byron on the wide circulation of his poem "Windsor Poetics"—on 12 March Byron facetiously replies that he "cannot conceive" how the poem has got about; (6) Moore mentions that he expects his wife Bessy to "lie in" around June—Olivia Byron Moore was born on 18 August 1814; (7) Moore informs Byron that he intends to set aside his *Lalla Rookh* for a while—on 12 March Byron replies, "*Think again* before you *shelf* your Poem," because he wishes Moore "to be out before Eastern subjects are again before the public." Byron's 12 March letter is essentially a direct and obvious reply to all the points Moore raises in his letter. Although Robert Brainard Pearsall corrects most of Dowden's dating errors in his article "Chronological Annotations to 250 Letters of Thomas Moore," *PBSA* 63 (1969): 105–17, he does not correct this one.

7. T. Parsons, *North American Review* 16 (Apr. 1823): 353–65.

8. J. Reynolds, *London Magazine* 7 (1823): 212–15.

9. Albany Fonblanque [?], *Examiner* 780 (5 Jan. 1823): 6–9.

10. *The Poetical Works of Thomas Moore. As Corrected by Himself in 1843* (New York: Martin and Johnson, 1851), p. 2.

11. The editions of Moore's works, in chronological order, are: (1) *The Poetical Works of Thomas Moore, as Corrected by Himself in 1843; to which is Added, an Original Memoir, by M. Balmanno* (New York: Martin and Johnson, 1851); (2) An edition with the same title published in New York by D. and J. Sadlier; (3) *The Poetical Works of Thomas Moore; a New Collated Edition* (Albany: Lyon, 1867); (4) *The Poetical Works of Thomas Moore. A New Collated Edition to Which Is Added an Original Memoir by M. Balmanno* (New York: Johnson, Fry, 1876); (5) *The Complete Poetical Works of Thomas Moore. America's Standard Edition* (New York: Johnson, 1878); (6) *The Poetical Works of Thomas Moore, to Which Is Added an Original Memoir by M. Balmanno* (Philadelphia: William T. Amies, 1878). Another edition, *The Poetical Works of Thomas Moore. A New Collated Edition to Which Is Added an Original Memoir by M. Balmanno* (New York: Johnson, Fry), dates from the 1850s.

12. S. Austin Allibone, *Allibone's Dictionary of English Literature and British and American Authors* (Philadelphia: J. Lippincott, 1891), 1:109.

13. Richard D. Altick, *The Cowden Clarkes* (London: Oxford UP, 1948), p. 169. Apparently on Allibone's authority, Altick claims that Mary Balmanno edited a book called *Gems of Moore's Poetry*. However, it is uncertain whether a book with that title exists.

14. Walter Jerrold, *Thomas Hood: His Life and Times* (New York: John Lane, 1909), p. 226.

15. Thomas Hood, *The Letters of Thomas Hood,* ed. Peter F. Morgan (Toronto: U of Toronto P, 1973), p. 78.

16. Allibone, p. 109. Evidence of Allibone's friendship with Balmanno is found in Mary Cowden Clarke, *Letters to an Enthusiast* (London: Kegan Paul, 1904), p. 154. Balmanno carried on a flirtatious eleven-year correspondence with Mary Cowden Clarke, the wife of Keats's friend Charles Cowden Clarke; *Letters to an Enthusiast* is a collection of her letters to Balmanno.

17. *Cassell's Biographical Dictionary* (London: Cassell, 1867–69), p. 98.

18. "Lord Byron and Thomas Moore," *Times,* 3 January 1823, p. 3, col. a.

19. Joint review of *The Loves of the Angels* and *Heaven and Earth,* in *Gentleman's Magazine* 93 (January 1823): 41–44.

20. "N. J. H. O," "Arot and Marot, and Mr. Moore's New Poem," *Scots Magazine,* n.s., 12 (1823): 78. During the 1822–23 season at Drury Lane, the actor Edmund Kean acted on the same stage with his great rival Charles Mayne Young. Kean and Young played Othello and Iago on alternate nights, among other roles. The two actors' styles were strongly contrasted; Kean was considered "natural" and passionate, Young studied and classical. The spectacle of the two rivals acting together created a sensation and their joint performances were reviewed by Hazlitt and others. For an account of the season, see F. W. Hawkins, *The Life of Edmund Kean* (London: Tinsley Brothers, 1869), 2:200–218.

21. See Reiman, *The Romantics Reviewed,* Part B, vol. 2, p. 938.

22. Thomas Noon Talfourd, joint review of *The Loves of the Angels* and *Heaven and Earth,* in *Lady's Magazine,* 2d ser., 4 (January 1823): 19–23.

23. Some other reviewers agreed that Moore's modesty was excessive. Regarding the preface, *The Literary Chronicle* wrote, "This is certainly a very elegant and a very high complement to pay Lord Byron; but we know no poet that has less to fear from coming in contact with his lordship than the bard of Erin" (review of Moore's *Loves of the Angels,* in *Literary Chronicle* 4 [28 December 1822]: 817). The Tory *British Critic* affected to believe that Moore was "covertly laughing at Lord Byron" (review of Moore's *Loves of the Angels,* in *British Critic* 19 [January–June 1823]: 645) and the Philadelphia *Port Folio* speculated that the preface was "a satire upon the noble lord" (review of Moore's *Loves of the Angels,* in *Port Folio* 15 [1823]: 327); these comments, however, obviously originated in the reviewers' hostility to Byron and the *Liberal,* rather than in admiration for Moore.

24. John Wilson, joint review of *The Loves of the Angels* and *Heaven and Earth,* in *Blackwood's* 13 (January 1823): 63–77.

25. Joint review of *The Loves of the Angels* and *Heaven and Earth,* in *Monthly Magazine* 55, no. 378 (1 February 1823): 35–39.

26. *Notes,* p. 100.

27. *Gentleman's Magazine,* p. 44.

28. Unpublished letter to Archibald Douglas [January or February 1823], Carl H. Pforzheimer Collection, NYPL.

29. Unpublished letter to John Wilson Croker [early February 1823], Pierpont Morgan Library.

30. Unpublished letter to John Wilson Croker, 17 February 1823, Pierpont Morgan Library.

31. Byron was misinformed; Moore did not change the poem's title.

32. *His Very Self and Voice,* ed. Lovell, p. 451.

s i x   "What I myself know and think concerning my friend"

1. In his *Byron and the Victorians* (Cambridge: Cambridge UP, 1995), Andrew Elfenbein observes of Moore's biography that "no book had a greater impact on Victorian perceptions of Byron" (78). Elfenbein refers to the book frequently in order to explain the ways in which Victorian writers responded to Byron.

2. For the best accounts of Moore's methodology, see Doris Langley Moore, *The Late Lord Byron* (Philadelphia: Lippincott, 1961), and Jordan, *Bolt Upright*. On the important subject of the involvement of Mary Shelley and the Countess Guiccioli in the development of the biography, see Paula R. Feldman's "Mary Shelley and the Genesis of Moore's *Life* of Byron," *SEL* 20 (1980): 611–20, and Doucet Devin Fischer, "Countess Guiccioli's Byron," in *Shelley and His Circle*, ed. Donald Reiman (Cambridge: Harvard UP, 1986), 7:373–487. For criticism of Moore's editorial practices see St. Clair's "The Temptations of a Biographer"; but see also "Appendix A: Moore's Letters to Byron," in which I question St. Clair's evidence and reasoning.

3. Review of *Letters and Journals of Lord Byron, with Notices of His Life*, in *Literary Gazette* no. 678 (16 January 1830): 33–38. (Hereafter the biography is referred to in the notes as *MLB*.)

4. Review of *MLB*, in *Mirror* 15, supplementary no. 161 (1830): 49–61.

5. John Wilson, review of *MLB*, in *Blackwood's Edinburgh Magazine* 27 (1830): 389–454.

6. Unpublished letter from Moore to Jean Antoine Galignani, 4 July 1824, Pforzheimer collection, NYPL.

7. *Times,* 10 August 1824, p. 2, col. c.

8. Lord John Russell, *Early Correspondence of Lord John Russell, 1805–1840*, ed. Rollo Russell (London: Unwin, 1913), 1:245.

9. Quoted in D. L. Moore, p. 264.

10. *Times,* 15 May 1824, p. 2, cols. c-d.

11. Quoted in D. L. Moore, p. 41.

12. "The 'Living Dog' and 'the Dead Lion'" was published in 1828, and Leigh Hunt promptly retaliated with his inferior "The Giant and the Dwarf." Moore's biography demolished whatever credibility Hunt might have had by presenting the extremely harsh comments on Hunt that Byron had confided to Moore during the controversy over *The Liberal.* Recounting his own and Byron's first visit to Hunt at Horsemonger Lane Gaol in 1813, Moore observed that "it is painful to think that, among the persons then assembled round the poet, there should have been *one* [John Scott] so soon to step forth the assailant of his living fame, while *another,* less manful, would reserve the cool venom for his grave" (*MLB* 1:402).

13. The most detailed accounts of the destruction of Byron's memoirs are to be found in Leslie A. Marchand, *Byron: A Biography* (New York: Knopf, 1957), 3:1244–53; Doris Langley Moore, *The Late Lord Byron* (New York: Lippincott, 1961), pp. 12–45; and

Thomas Moore, *The Journal of Thomas Moore* (Newark: U of Delaware P, 1983–1991), 6:2440–2445. The pages from Moore's journal that deal with this episode were not published by Lord John Russell in his *Memoirs, Journal, and Correspondence of Thomas Moore* (London: Longmans, 1853–56), and did not appear in print until 1991, when Dowden published them in volume six of his edition of Moore's journal. The basic facts regarding the affair of the memoirs are as follows. Byron gave the memoirs to Moore during Moore's visit to Venice in October 1819, intending that Moore should sell their publication rights to Murray. In 1821, Murray paid Moore two thousand guineas for them in a transaction that amounted to an outright purchase. However, Moore later asked Murray (as a precaution, as well as, he said, a favor to Byron and himself) to alter the terms of the transaction so that if Byron decided against publication at some point, the memoirs could be redeemed from Murray. Accordingly, on 6 May 1822, a second deed was executed that apparently stipulated that if Murray's two thousand guineas were repaid during Byron's lifetime, Byron, Moore, or any of their friends could redeem the memoirs and (presumably) prevent their publication. On 17 May 1824, three days after the news of Byron's death had arrived in London, Hobhouse, Moore, Murray, Henry Luttrell, Francis Hastings Doyle, and Robert Wilmot Horton met in Murray's drawing room at 50 Albemarle Street to settle the fate of the memoirs. Although neither Hobhouse nor Murray had read the memoirs (Moore and Luttrell were the only ones present who had, and they wanted to preserve them), they both vehemently insisted that the manuscript be destroyed, in order, so they maintained, to safeguard Byron's reputation; Augusta Leigh and Lady Byron were afraid of what the memoirs might contain and they both were in agreement with Hobhouse and Murray.

A heated argument ensued between Murray and Hobhouse on one side and Moore on the other, during which Moore responded to an insult from Murray by a threat to challenge him to a duel. Part of the disagreement was owing to confusion over who actually owned the rights to the memoirs: Moore believed that the altered 1822 agreement between himself and Murray had stipulated that Moore had the right to redeem the memoirs for up to three months after Byron's death. Nevertheless, prior to the meeting at Murray's, Moore had felt obliged to state that if the memoirs were indeed his own property, he would defer to the wishes of Byron's sister regarding their fate. Moore later insisted that he did not mean to imply that he would acquiesce to their total destruction. However, on the basis of Moore's statement regarding Augusta Leigh, Doyle (who was representing Lady Byron) announced that he would, according to the wishes of Mrs. Leigh, immediately destroy them, and he proceeded to tear up the memoirs and throw them onto the fire. Moore continued to strenuously object to this step even as they were being destroyed, declaring, according to Hobhouse's written account of the episode, "Remember I protest against the burning as contradictory to Lord Byron's wishes and unjust to me" (qtd. in D. L. Moore, *The Late Lord Byron*, p. 34).

Immediately after the memoirs were burnt, the agreement between Moore and

Murray was found and examined, and it was learned that the option to redeem the memoirs had indeed only existed while Byron was alive, and that therefore Moore had had no legal claim at all to ownership. Moore was stunned by this news, and Murray and Hobhouse reproached him for signing documents without making sure of what was in them. According to D. L. Moore (following Hobhouse's account), "Moore was forced to confess lamely that his memory had erred, and that he had never properly read the document" (p. 36). However, Moore's own characterization of the incident in his journal is quite different. According to Moore:

> The agreement was at length found and produced, where to my great surprise the clause which I had by Luttrell's suggestion desired to be inserted and which I thought I saw inserted in the rough draft of the agreement was not there at all. . . . This singular variation from the sort of clause I had intended together with the uselessness [of the] stipulation which it contained (and the manuscript, on becoming Mr. Murray's might be published next day, if he chose) seemed to strike everyone present with something worse than surprize. What my own opinion about it is I will not even here express because Mr. Turner (the solicitor of Murray) to whose son, in the presence of Murray, I dictated the clause, has the reputation of being a very honorable person & I have no reason to suspect his son of being otherwise. The circumstance is at least extraordinary. (*MJ* 6:2443)

It is evident from Moore's correspondence that he never fully trusted Murray after the burning of the memoirs, and when Moore was working on his biography of Byron he often complained of what he considered Murray's "shuffling" and deceitful ways. Moore distrusted Murray's motives so completely that he agreed with the Longmans when they maintained "that Murray's violent anxiety for the total destruction of the MS arose from his fears that any part of it should find its way into their [the Longmans'] hands" (6:2444). Moore's journal entries reveal that he was deeply angry and disturbed about the whole affair, and the evening of the confrontation, reflecting upon Hobhouse's "insulting looks and manners," he felt that he "would have given worlds at that moment to have been placed hostilely face to face with Hobhouse with pistols, not from any hostility to him but from feeling that nothing else could now set me right with myself" (6:2444). Moore actually sent a note to Hobhouse that evening challenging him to apologize for his conduct, and began preparations for a duel, but this new crisis was averted the next day by the intervention and calming words of Sir Francis Burdett. Although Moore was in no sense obligated to repay Murray's two thousand guineas, he did so out of considerations of honor, refusing offers from Lady Byron and Augusta Leigh to help offset what was to him a financially ruinous loss.

14. Hobhouse, *Byron's Bulldog*, p. 321.

15. G. Wilson Knight, *Lord Byron: Christian Virtues* (London: Routledge, 1952), p. 33.

16. Review of *MLB*, in *Athenæum*, 30 January 1830, p. 49.

17. Elfenbein, p. 79. Elfenbein also incorrectly writes that Moore's biography was commissioned by Murray in response to his outrage over Hunt's 1828 *Lord Byron and*

Some of His Contemporaries. The publication of Hunt's book did finally convince Murray to cooperate with Moore's efforts, but the book had been in preparation since 1824 and was not merely "written to refute Hunt's" (78). Elfenbein also makes the common mistake of claiming that both volumes of the biography were published in 1830.

18. Charles Webb LeBas, review of *MLB,* in *British Critic* 9 (1831): 257–324.

19. Review of *MLB,* in *Monthly Review* 1 n.s. (1831): 217–37.

20. Review of *MLB,* in *Times,* 18 January 1830, p. 2, col. e.

21. Review of *MLB,* in *Literary Gazette,* 13 February 1830, pp. 100–101.

22. John Gibson Lockhart, review of *MLB,* in *Quarterly Review* 44 (1831): 168–226.

23. Quoted in D. L. Moore, p. 291.

24. Thomas Babington Macaulay, review of *MLB,* in *Edinburgh Review* 53 (1831): 544–72.

25. Review of *MLB,* in *Times,* 30 January 1830, p. 3, col. b.

26. Review of *MLB,* in *Monthly Review* 13 (1830): 217–37.

27. Review of *MLB,* in *Athenæum,* 1 January 1831, pp. 1–6.

28. Lockhart, review of *MLB.*

29. Mary Shelley, *Selected Letters of Mary Wollstonecraft Shelley,* ed. Betty T. Bennett (Baltimore: Johns Hopkins UP, 1995), pp. 223–24.

30. Joseph W. Reed Jr., *English Biography in the Early Nineteenth Century: 1801–1838* (New Haven, Yale UP, 1966), pp. 102–26.

31. Clement Tyson Goode, Jr., "A Critical Review of Research," in *George Gordon, Lord Byron: A Comprehensive Bibliography of Secondary Materials in English,* ed. Oscar José Santucho (Metuchen: Scarecrow Press, 1977), pp. 20–21.

32. John Clubbe, "George Gordon, Lord Byron," in *The English Romantic Poets, A Review of Research and Criticism,* ed. Frank Jordan (New York: MLA, 1985), pp. 480–81. For further positive modern commentary upon the biography, see also Bernard Hickey, "'Quis Separabit?': Tom Moore's Loyalties: Lord Byron and Lord Edward Fitzgerald," in *Byron e la Cultura Venezia,* ed. Giulio Marra et al. (Venice: Universita à Degli Studi de Venezia, 1986), pp. 31–37, and *Lives of the Great Romantics by Their Contemporaries,* vol. 2, ed. Chris Hart (London: William Pickering, 1996), pp. 54–56.

33. Richard D. Altick, *Lives and Letters: A History of Literary Biography in England and America* (New York: Knopf, 1965), p. 231.

34. Ibid, pp. 107–109, 221.

35. The date of Moore's letter is given as 6 or 13 September 1824, but the dating of these excerpts is not reliable. If Moore did write the song in 1824, he would presumably have included it in the *first* number of *Evenings in Greece,* published in 1826. Hoover Jordan mistakenly writes that the song to Byron did appear in the 1826 number.

36. *Notes,* p. 114.

37. Review of *MLB,* in *Times,* 30 January 1830, p. 3, cols. b–d.

Conclusion

1. Marilyn Butler, "Repossessing the Past: The Case for an Open Literary History," in *Rethinking Historicism: Critical Readings in Romantic History*, ed. Marjorie Levinson (Oxford: Basil Blackwell, 1989), pp. 64–84.

2. Jerome J. McGann, ed., *The New Oxford Book of Romantic Period Verse* (Oxford: Oxford UP, 1993).

3. Often critics have used Moore's journal as evidence that he was excessively shallow, frivolous, or vain. Such critics never seem to realize that Moore never intended his journal to be published as it was written, nor do they seem to be aware that Moore knew his journal would not remain private. Moore kept the journal so that when he died, a friend such as Edward Raleigh Moran or Lord John Russell would use the information therein as the basis for a biography. This envisioned biography was Moore's way of ensuring that his wife and children would be provided for after he was gone. Lord John was roundly criticized for simply crossing out passages and then publishing the journal as it was. Moore did not keep the journal in order to record his most private thoughts, nor did he ever imagine that this rough document would be published and lead some readers to conclude that all he was interested in was recording the names of dinner-party guests and noting compliments to himself. The deleted passages sometimes expressed irritation and boredom with the circles in which he moved, and round out a portrait of a different kind of man than he who was presented by Russell's edition.

4. Probably the most unfairly hostile comments made by a major modern scholar regarding Moore's character occur throughout Doris Langley Moore's classic study *The Late Lord Byron*. The following is a typical remark: "Moore could never have cared as much for Byron as Byron for him, because the one was a deeply emotional temperament, the other primarily sentimental" (267). D. L. Moore also writes of the grief that Hobhouse felt in the weeks following the news of Byron's death, "a grief much deeper than the inveterately superficial Moore was capable of feeling" (34). Such facile comments must either originate in a naïve supposition that supposedly "superficial" sentimental poetry can only have been written by an unemotional person, or else in a reading of Moore's diary that is very selective indeed.

5. Byron's alleged remark, far too often recycled and far too infrequently contextualized, was quoted by Hunt in the 15 January 1831 issue of his newspaper *The Tatler*. The article in which it appeared was the last in a series of five lengthy front-page articles abusing and insulting both Moore and Byron that appeared daily between 11 and 15 January. Hunt was enraged by the appearance of the second volume of Moore's biography of Byron, which covered the period of Byron's association with *The Liberal* and contained the deadly abuse of Hunt featured in Byron's letters to Moore. Moore had no hesitation in presenting Byron's words in full, because he and all of Byron's other friends and relations were still furious over Hunt's 1828 *Lord Byron and Some of*

His Contemporaries, the most exaggeratedly hostile portrait of Byron ever produced. Hunt's first *Tatler* article began: "We do not pretend to give a notice of [Moore's biography] after the usual fashion. We shall comment on it, as it may happen; but our great object is to show that the author is an insincere man of the world, and that neither he nor his hero have a right to scatter charges of vulgarity and unworthiness. . . . We have suffered enough on all points; we have conceded enough in the case of Lord Byron. We shall concede no more. Our business will now be to give specimens of the blows we have withheld."

Hunt doubtless felt humiliated, and in the desperate and self-pitying tirade that followed and continued throughout the week Hunt accused Moore of opposing Byron's alliance with Hunt because Hunt was not an aristocrat. In actuality, Moore knew Hunt personally, and events proved that he (and Byron) had judged Hunt's character well; nothing justifies his warning to Byron more than Hunt's treacherous behavior after Byron's death. In his *Tatler* articles Hunt tried to hurt Moore by claiming that Byron only liked Moore insofar as Moore flattered him, that Byron maliciously mocked Moore's poetry, and that Byron had abused Moore as badly to him (Hunt) as Byron had abused Hunt to Moore. His depiction of Byron insulting Moore's poems and "retreat[ing] a little, doubling up in his peculiar manner, and uttering a kind of goblin laugh, breathing and grinning, as if, instead of his handsome mouth, he had one like an ogre, from ear to ear," is risible enough, but Hunt also wrote that Byron declared, "'Do but give Tom a good dinner, and a lord . . . and he is at the top of his happiness.—Oh!' added he, in the most emphatic manner, with a face full of glee as above described, doubling himself up as he walked, lifting up his arm, and bringing it down with a doubled fist upon the word in Italics, 'TOMMY *loves* a Lord!'" (457). Hunt had had an opportunity to present this anecdote in his 1828 book, but did not, although it included several other attacks on Moore for supposedly poisoning Byron's mind against Hunt. Hunt's anecdote supported his own self-serving narrative of the failure of the *Liberal,* namely, that Hunt was a selfless and embattled crusader for human rights undone by Byron's deceitful character and a group of aristocratic conspirators who disapproved of Hunt solely because of his class.

6. Jonathan Wordsworth, introduction to Thomas Moore, *The Poetical Works of the Late Thomas Little esq. 1801* (Oxford: Woodstock, 1990), p. ii.

7. Stanley Jones, *Hazlitt: A Life,* pp. 223–24. In 1962 Wilfred Dowden effectively ended the controversy over Moore's supposed authorship of the review by publishing two new letters of Moore's. In one of them Moore declared that he had given up his idea of reviewing *Christabel,* and in another he called the *Edinburgh Review* article that finally appeared "altogether disgraceful both from its dulness and illiberality." See Wilfred S. Dowden, "Thomas Moore and the Review of *Christabel,*" *Modern Philology* 60 (1962): 47–50.

8. Richard Holmes, *Shelley: The Pursuit* (London: Weidenfeld and Nicholson, 1974), p. 551.

9. See chapter 2, note 34.

10. William Cole, "A Newly-Discovered Poem by Thomas Moore," *Byron Journal* 21 (1993): 135.

11. Phyllis Grosskurth, *Byron: The Flawed Angel* (New York: Houghton Mifflin, 1997), pp. 141–42.

12. Jonathan Bate, p. 333.

13. See Leask, pp. 110–14, in which the two poems are explicitly compared. Leask writes that "on one level, Laon and Cythna's revolt against the Sultan Othman figures Shelley's reaction against the negativity of Tom Moore's 1817 account of oriental revolution, 'The Veiled Prophet of Khorassan' in *Lalla Rookh*" (110).

14. It might also be worthwhile to explore to what extent Shelley's enthusiasm for and writings upon the Irish cause might have been partially inspired by Moore's depiction of Ireland in his *Melodies* and in his 1810 prose *Letter to the Roman Catholics of Dublin*.

15. See Julia M. Wright, "Peacock's Early Parody of Thomas Moore in *Nightmare Abbey*," *ELN* 30 (1993): 31–38, for a sketch of Peacock's attitude toward Moore.

16. Vance, pp. 102–4.

17. Howard Mumford Jones, p. 110.

APPENDIX A   Byron's Letters to Moore

1. For more on Moore's plans to sell Byron's letters see Wilfred S. Dowden, "Byron's Letters and 'Journals': A Note," in *Lord Byron and His Contemporaries*, ed. Charles E. Robinson (Newark: U of Delaware P, 1982), pp. 237–42. It is not known what ultimately became of the Byron letters in Moore's possession; all that is known is that Moore still had them in 1842.

2. Thomas Moore, *Letters and Journals of Lord Byron, with Notices of His Life* (New York: J & J Harper, 1830–31), 2:93.

3. In his edition of Byron's letters, Marchand reproduced the version of the letter from the London edition of Moore's biography, thus inadvertently omitting the sentence that appeared in the American edition.

APPENDIX B   A New Text of a Letter from Moore to Byron,
17 July 1823

1. *Fables for the Holy Alliance*, by "Thomas Brown the Younger," published on 7 May 1823. The dedication was as follows: "TO LORD BYRON / Dear Lord Byron, — Though this Volume should possess no other merit in your eyes, than that of reminding you of the short time we passed together at Venice, when some of the trifles which it contains were written, you will, I am sure, receive the dedication with pleasure, and believe that I am, My dear Lord, Ever faithfully yours, T.B." Moore followed the above letter with another on 15 December 1823 that has not survived, although Moore transcribed a portion in his journal: "Wrote a letter to Lord Byron, on his long silence to

me; saying that I could not account for it unless it arose from 'one of those sudden whims against the absent which I have often dreaded from him; one of those meteor-stones which generate themselves so unaccountably in the high atmosphere of his fancy, and come down upon one, some fine day, when one least expects to be so lapidated; begging, however, if I am to be in the list of the *cut dead,* he will tell me so, that I may make my funeral arrangements accordingly" (*MJ* 2:692). In his final letter to Moore of 4 March 1824, Byron wrote: "Your reproach is unfounded. I have received two letters from you and answered both previous to leaving Cephalonia" (*BLJ* 11:125). Byron left Cephalonia on 26 December 1823. Moore received letters from Byron during the last week of February 1824 and on 3 May 1824.

2. On 17 April 1823 Moore noted in his journal: "Received, on my return home, a note from the Longmans, full of panic at an opinion they have just had from their legal adviser, Turner, that the 'Fables' are indictable, as 'tending to bring the monarchy into contempt'" (*MJ* 2:629). The next day Moore went to the Longmans to discuss the matter. "The Longmans expected that I should make alterations, but told them that was impossible. Asked Turner whether he thought the Constitutional Association (which is what he dreads) would be content with having the author delivered up to them. Said it was most probable they would. 'This then,' said I, 'might settle perhaps all alarms, as I was perfectly ready to meet the consequences myself in every way; though of there being any such consequences from the publication I had not the slightest apprehension.' Left them to consider the matter" (*MJ* 2:629–30).

3. Thomas Denman, first Baron Denman (1779–1854), solicitor-general for Queen Caroline (1820), lord chief justice (1832–50), and speaker of the House of Lords (1835).

4. Moore told Power in May or June 1823, "I never counted on a great sale of this book, as the want of personality makes it much less generally attractive than my former squibs" (*Notes,* p. 102). Moore's previous major satirical collections, *Intercepted Letters; or, The Twopenny Post-Bag* (1813), *The Fudge Family in Paris* (1818), and *Tom Cribb's Memorial to Congress* (1819), had all contained direct attacks on prominent politicians and heads of state, and had all been extremely popular and successful.

5. *Don Juan,* cantos VI–VIII, published 15 July 1823.

6. *The Island,* published 26 June 1823.

7. *The Loves of the Angels,* published 23 December 1822.

8. John William Ward, fourth Earl of Dudley, ninth Baron Ward. In Moore's diary entry for 19 June 1823 he notes that Lady Davy "told me that when my 'Angels' appeared, she had a letter from him, saying that he was happy at last to see something of mine exhibiting higher powers of writing than he had been in general inclined to allow me. This confirmation of a suspicion which I have always had, that Lord Dudley holds but a mean opinion of my talents, is, of course, not calculated to lessen much the distaste which I own I have (notwithstanding many efforts to the contrary) invariably felt towards him. I am not given to dislike people, and therefore tried hard to be pleased with him; but it would not do" (*MJ* 2:647–48).

Allibone, S. Austin. *Allibone's Dictionary of English Literature and British and American Authors*. 2 vols. Philadelphia: J. Lippincott, 1891.

Altick, Richard D. *The Cowden Clarkes*. London: Oxford UP, 1948.

———. *Lives and Letters: A History of Literary Biography in England and America*. New York: Knopf, 1965.

"A. P." "Thomas Moore: An Essay on Moore's Life and Poetry." In *The Living Poets of England: Specimens of the Living British Poets, with Critical and Biographical Notices and an Essay on English Poetry*. Vol. 2. Paris: L. Baudry, 1827.

Ashton, Thomas L. *Byron's Hebrew Melodies*. Austin: U of Texas P, 1972.

Bate, Jonathan. "Tom Moore and the Making of the 'Ode to Psyche.'" *RES* 41 (1990): 325–33.

Bate, Walter Jackson. *John Keats*. Cambridge: Harvard UP, 1963.

Beaty, Frederick L. *Byron the Satirist*. DeKalb: Northern Illinois UP, 1985.

Berry, Mary. *Extracts from the Journals and Correspondence of Miss Berry, from the Year 1783 to 1852*. 3 vols. London: Longmans, 1866.

Birley, Robert. *Sunk without Trace: Some Forgotten Masterpieces Reconsidered*. New York: Harcourt Brace, 1962.

Blessington, Marguerite, Countess. *Conversations of Lord Byron*. Ed. Ernest J. Lovell Jr. Princeton: Princeton UP, 1969.

Brandes, George. *Main Currents in Nineteenth Century Literature*. 6 vols. New York: Macmillan, 1906.

Brogan, Howard O. "Thomas Moore, Irish Satirist and Keeper of the English Conscience." *PQ* 24 (1945): 255–76.

Broughton, John Cam Hobhouse, Baron. *Byron's Bulldog: The Letters of John Cam Hobhouse to Lord Byron*. Ed. Peter W. Graham. Columbus: Ohio State UP, 1984.

———. *Recollections of a Long Life*. 2 vols. New York: Scribner's, 1909.

Brown, Wallace Cable. *The Triumph of Form: A Study of the Later Masters of the Heroic Couplet*. Chapel Hill: U of North Carolina P, 1948.

Butler, Marilyn. "Byron and the Empire in the East." In *Byron: Augustan and Romantic*, ed. Andrew Rutherford. New York: St. Martin's, 1990.

———. "Orientalism." In *The Penguin History of Literature: The Romantic Period*, ed. David B. Pirie. London: Penguin, 1994.

———. "Repossessing the Past: The Case for an Open Literary History." In *Rethinking*

Historicism: Critical Readings in Romantic History, ed. Marjorie Levinson. Oxford: Basil Blackwell, 1989.

Byron, George Gordon, Baron. *Byron's Letters and Journals.* Ed. Leslie A. Marchand. 12 vols. Cambridge: Harvard UP, 1973–82.

———. *His Very Self and Voice: Collected Conversations of Lord Byron.* Ed. Ernest J. Lovell Jr. New York: Macmillan, 1954.

———. *Lord Byron: The Complete Miscellaneous Prose.* Ed. Andrew Nicholson. Oxford: Clarendon Press, 1991.

———. *Lord Byron: The Complete Poetical Works.* Ed. Jerome J. McGann. 7 vols. Oxford: Clarendon Press, 1980–93.

———. *Lord Byron: Selected Poems.* Ed. Susan J. Wolfson and Peter J. Manning. London: Penguin, 1996.

———. *A Selection of Hebrew Melodies, Ancient and Modern.* Ed. Frederick Burwick and Paul Douglass. Tuscaloosa: U of Alabama P, 1988.

———. *The Works of Lord Byron.* Ed. Ernest Hartley Coleridge and Rowland Edmund Prothero. 13 vols. London: John Murray, 1898–1905.

"Byron and Moore." *Lady's and Gentleman's Weekly Museum and Philadelphia Reporter* 3 (1818): 79–80.

The Byron and Moore Gallery. A Series of Characteristic Illustrations by Eminent Artists. With Descriptive Letter-Press in Prose and Verse, and Biographies of the Authors. New York: Johnson, Wilson and Company, 1871.

Cassell's Biographical Dictionary. London: Cassell, 1867–69.

Chandler, James. *England in 1819: The Politics of Literary Culture and the Case of Romantic Historicism.* Chicago: U of Chicago P, 1998.

Childers, William. "Byron's *Waltz:* The Germans and Their Georges." *KSJ* 18 (1969): 81–95.

Clarke, Hewson. [Review of *Hours of Idleness.*] *Satirist* 1 (1807): 77–81.

Clarke, Mary Cowden. *Letters to an Enthusiast.* London: Kegan Paul, 1904.

Clubbe, John. "George Gordon, Lord Byron." In *The English Romantic Poets: A Review of Research and Criticism,* ed. Frank Jordan. New York: MLA, 1985.

Cole, William. "A Newly-Discovered Poem by Thomas Moore," *Byron Journal* 21 (1993): 135.

Coleridge, Samuel Taylor. *The Collected Letters of Samuel Taylor Coleridge.* Ed. Earl Leslie Griggs. 6 vols. Oxford: Clarendon Press, 1956–71.

Conder, Josiah. [Review of *Hebrew Melodies.*] *Eclectic Review* 2d ser., 4 (July 1815): 94–96.

Cooke, Michael G. *The Blind Man Traces the Circle: On the Patterns and Philosophy of Byron's Poetry.* Princeton: Princeton UP, 1969.

Courthope, W. J. *A History of English Poetry.* London: Macmillan, 1910.

"Criticisms on the Modern Poets." *New Monthly Magazine* 13 (1 January 1820): 1–4.

"Critique on Modern Poets." *New Monthly Magazine* 12 (1 November 1819): 377–84.

Croker, John Wilson. *Familiar Epistles to Frederick J[one]s, Esq., on the Present State of the Irish Stage.* Dublin: John Barlow, 1804.

Croly, George. "Thomas Moore." *Blackwood's Edinburgh Magazine* 73 (1853): 109.

Crompton, Louis. *Byron and Greek Love: Homophobia in Nineteenth-Century England*. Berkeley: U of California P, 1985.

Cunningham, Allan. *A Biographical and Critical History of the British Literature of the Last Fifty Years*. Paris: J. Smith, 1834.

Curran, Stuart. *Poetic Form and British Romanticism*. Oxford: Oxford UP, 1986.

Dallas, R. C. *Recollections of the Life of Lord Byron, from the Year 1808 to the End of 1814 . . .* London: C. Knight, 1824.

Darley, George. "The Characteristic of the Present Age of Poetry." *London Magazine* 9 (April 1824): 424–27.

Davis, Leith. "Irish Bards and English Consumers: Thomas Moore's 'Irish Melodies' and the Colonized Nation." *Ariel* 24 (1993): 7–25.

DeFord, Miriam Allen. *Thomas Moore*. New York: Twayne, 1967.

de Montluzin, Emily Lorraine. "Southey's 'Satanic School' Remarks: An Old Charge for a New Offender." *KSJ* 21–22 (1972–73): 29–33.

Doubleday, Thomas. "Shufflebotham's Dream." *Blackwood's Edinburgh Magazine* 8 (October 1820): 3–7.

Dowden, Wilfred S. "Thomas Moore and the Review of *Christabel*." *Modern Philology* 60 (1962): 47–50.

Dyer, Gary. *British Satire and the Politics of Style, 1789–1832*. Cambridge: Cambridge UP, 1997.

Elfenbein, Andrew. *Byron and the Victorians*. Cambridge: Cambridge UP, 1995.

Erdman, David V. "Byron and Revolt in England." *Science and Society* 11 (1947): 234–48.

———. "Byron and the New Force of the People." *KSJ* 11 (1962): 47–64.

———. "Lord Byron and the Genteel Reformers." *PMLA* 56 (1941): 1065–94.

———. "Lord Byron as Rinaldo." *PMLA* 57 (1942): 189–231.

"Essay on Song Writing." *Blackwood's Edinburgh Magazine* 7 (1820): 32–35.

Feldman, Paula R. "Mary Shelley and the Genesis of Moore's *Life* of Byron." *SEL* 20 (1980): 611–20.

Fischer, Doucet Devin. "Countess Guiccioli's Byron." In *Shelley and His Circle*, ed. Donald H. Reiman. Vol. 7. Cambridge: Harvard UP, 1961– .

Fischer, Hermann. "Byron's 'Wrong Revolutionary Poetical System' and Romanticism." In *Byron: Augustan and Romantic*, ed. Andrew Rutherford. New York: St. Martin's, 1990.

Fonblanque, Albany [?]. [Review of Moore, *The Loves of the Angels*.] *Examiner* 780 (5 Jan. 1823): 6–9

Fuess, Claude M. *Lord Byron as a Satirist in Verse*. New York: Russell and Russell, 1964.

Gaull, Marilyn. *English Romanticism: The Human Context*. New York: Norton, 1988.

George, M. Dorothy. *English Political Caricature 1793–1832*. Oxford: Oxford UP, 1959.

Greville, Charles. *The Greville Memoirs, 1814–1860*. Ed. Lytton Strachey and Roger Fulford. 8 vols. London: Macmillan, 1838.

Gross, Jonathan David. *Byron's "Corbeau Blanc": The Life and Letters of Lady Melbourne.* Houston: Rice UP, 1997.

Grosskurth, Phyllis. *Byron: The Flawed Angel.* New York: Houghton Mifflin, 1997.

Gwynn, Stephen. *Thomas Moore.* London: Macmillan, 1904.

Hadden, J. Cuthbert. *George Thomson, the Friend of Burns: His Life and Correspondence.* London: J. C. Nimmo, 1898.

Hawkins, F. W. *The Life of Edmund Kean.* 2 vols. London: Tinsley Brothers, 1869.

Hickey, Bernard. "'Quis Separabit?': Tom Moore's Loyalties: Lord Byron and Lord Edward Fitzgerald." In *Byron e la Cultura Venezia,* ed. Giulio Marra et al. Venice: Universita à Degli Studi de Venezia, 1986.

Holmes, Richard. *Shelley: The Pursuit.* London: Weidenfeld and Nicholson, 1974.

Hood, Thomas. *The Letters of Thomas Hood.* Ed. Peter F. Morgan. Toronto: U of Toronto P, 1973.

Hunt, Leigh. *The Autobiography of Leigh Hunt.* Ed. J. E. Morpurgo. London: Cresset Press, 1949.

———. *Lord Byron and Some of His Contemporaries, with Recollections of the Author's Life, and of His Visit to Italy.* London: Henry Colburn, 1828.

Jeffrey, Francis. [Review of Byron, *Beppo, a Venetian Story.*] *Edinburgh Review* 29 (1818): 302–10.

———. [Review of Moore, *Epistles, Odes and Other Poems.*] *Edinburgh Review* 8 (1806): 456–65.

———. [Review of Moore, *Lalla Rookh, an Oriental Romance.*] *Edinburgh Review* 29 (November 1817): 1–35.

Jerdan, William. *The Autobiography of William Jerdan.* 4 vols. New York: AMS Press, 1977.

Jerrold, Walter. *Thomas Hood: His Life and Times.* New York: John Lane, 1909.

"J. G. G." "On the Genius and Writings of Moore." *Literary Speculum* 1 (Feb. 1822): 217–26.

John Bull 1 (17 June 1820): 213, col. c.

John Bull 5 (14 August 1825): 268, col. a.

Jones, Howard Mumford. *The Harp That Once—: A Chronicle of the Life of Thomas Moore.* New York: Henry Holt, 1937.

Jones, Stanley. *Hazlitt: A Life.* Oxford: Oxford UP, 1989.

———. "Regency Newspaper Verse: An Anonymous Squib on Wordsworth." *KSJ* 27 (1978): 87–107.

Jordan, Hoover H. *Bolt Upright: The Life of Thomas Moore.* 2 vols. Salzburg: Institut für Englische Sprache und Literatur, 1975.

———. "Byron and Moore." *MLQ* 9 (1948): 429–39.

———. "Thomas Moore: Artistry in the Song Lyric." *SEL* 2 (1962): 403–40.

Kelsall, Malcolm. *Byron's Politics.* New York: Barnes and Noble, 1987.

"The King's Voyage to Dublin." *Examiner* no. 712 (26 August 1821): 529–31.

Knight, G. Wilson. *Lord Byron: Christian Virtues.* London: Routledge, 1952.

Leask, Nigel. *British Romantic Writers and the East: Anxieties of Empire.* Cambridge: Cambridge UP, 1992.

LeBas, Charles Webb. [Review of Moore, *Letters and Journals of Lord Byron, with Notices of His Life.*] *British Critic* 9 (1831): 257–324.

Lives of the Great Romantics by Their Contemporaries. Volume 2, Lord Byron. Ed. Chris Hart. London: William Pickering, 1996.

Lockhart, John Gibson. [Review of Moore, *Letters and Journals of Lord Byron, with Notices of His Life.*] *Quarterly Review* 44 (1831): 168–226.

"Lord Byron and Thomas Moore," *Times,* 3 January 1823, p. 3, col. a.

Lovell, Ernest J., Jr. *Captain Medwin: Friend of Byron and Shelley.* Austin: U of Texas P, 1962.

Lurkis-Clark, Irene B. "Byron's *Don Juan* and Moore's 'The Two Penny Post-Bag.'" *NQ* 226 (1981): 401–3.

———. *Moore and Moderation: A Study of Thomas Moore's Political and Social Satires.* Unpublished dissertation.

Macaulay, Thomas Babington. [Review of Moore, *Letters and Journals of Lord Byron, with Notices of His Life.*] *Edinburgh Review* 53 (1831): 544–72.

Maginn, William. "Profligacy of the London Periodical Press." *Blackwood's Edinburgh Magazine* 16 (1824): 179–83.

Manning, Peter J. "Tales and Politics: *The Corsair, Lara,* and *The White Doe of Rylstone.*" In *Reading Romantics: Text and Context.* Oxford: Oxford UP, 1990.

Marchand, Leslie A. *Byron: A Biography.* 3 vols. New York: Knopf, 1957.

———. *Byron's Poetry: A Critical Introduction.* Boston: Houghton Mifflin, 1965.

McGann, Jerome J. "Byron and the Anonymous Lyric." *Byron Journal* 20 (1992): 27–45.

———. *Fiery Dust: Byron's Poetic Development.* Chicago: U of Chicago P, 1968.

———, ed. *The New Oxford Book of Romantic Period Verse.* Oxford: Oxford UP, 1993.

Medwin, Thomas. *Conversations of Lord Byron.* Ed. Ernest J. Lovell Jr. Princeton: Princeton UP, 1966.

Moir, D. M. *Sketches of the Poetical Literature of the Last Half-Century.* Edinburgh: W. Blackwood, 1851.

Moore, Doris Langley. *The Late Lord Byron.* Philadelphia: Lippincott, 1961.

Moore, Thomas. *The Journal of Thomas Moore.* Ed. Wilfred S. Dowden. 6 vols. Newark: U of Delaware P, 1983–91.

———. *Letters and Journals of Lord Byron, with Notices of His Life.* 2 vols. New York: J & J Harper, 1830–31.

———. *The Letters of Thomas Moore.* Ed. Wilfred S. Dowden. 2 vols. Oxford: Oxford UP, 1964.

———. *The Life and Death of Lord Edward Fitzgerald.* London: Longmans, 1831.

———. *The Loves of the Angels. A Poem.* London: Longmans, 1822.

———. *Memoirs, Journal, and Correspondence of Thomas Moore.* Ed. Lord John Russell. 8 vols. London: Longmans, 1853–56.

————. *Notes from the Letters of Thomas Moore to His Music Publisher, James Power.* Ed. Thomas Crofton Croker. New York: Redfield, 1854.

————. *The Poetical Works of the Late Thomas Little Esq. 1801.* Oxford: Woodstock, 1990.

————. *The Poetical Works of Thomas Moore. Collected by Himself.* 10 vols. London: Longmans, 1840–41.

————. *The Poetical Works of Thomas Moore. A New Collated Edition. To Which Is Added, an Original Memoir, by M. Balmanno.* Ed. Mary Balmanno. New York: Johnson, Fry and Company, 1851. [Bibliographical information for several other versions of this edition is given in chapter 5.]

————. *Prose and Verse Humorous, Satirical, and Sentimental by Thomas Moore. . .* Ed. Richard Hearne Shepard. New York: Scribner, Armstrong, 1878.

Morley, John. *The Works of Lord Morley.* 15 vols. London: Macmillan, 1921.

Nathan, Isaac. *Fugitive Pieces and Reminiscences of Lord Byron.* London: Whittaker, Treacher and Company, 1829.

Neale, C. [?]. [Review of Moore, *Lalla Rookh, an Oriental Romance.*] *Eclectic Review* 8 (October 1817): 340–53.

"N. J. H. O." "Arot and Marot, and Mr. Moore's New Poem." *Scots Magazine* n.s., 12 (1823): 78.

Palmerston, Henry J. *The New Whig Guide.* London: W. Wright, 1819.

Parsons, T. [Review of Moore, *The Loves of the Angels.*] *North American Review* 16 (Apr. 1823): 353–65.

Pearsall, Robert Brainard. "Chronological Annotations to 250 Letters of Thomas Moore." *PBSA* 63 (1969): 105–17.

"Portraits of Poets." *Weekly Entertainer* 56 (18 March 1816): 225–27.

Previté-Orton, C. W. *Political Satire in English Poetry.* New York: Russell and Russell, 1968.

Reed, Joseph W., Jr. *English Biography in the Early Nineteenth Century: 1801–1838.* New Haven: Yale UP, 1966.

Reiman, Donald H. "The Oxford English Texts Byron Edition." *NCL* 50 (Sept. 1995): 259–71.

————, ed. *The Romantics Reviewed.* 9 vols. New York: Garland, 1972.

[Review of Byron, *The Age of Bronze.*] *Literary Gazette* (5 April 1823): 211–13.

[Review of Byron, *The Corsair.*] *British Critic* 1 (1814): 279–93.

[Review of Byron, *Hours of Idleness.*] *Beau Monde* 2 (1807): 88–90.

[Review of Byron, *Hours of Idleness.*] *Universal Magazine,* 2d ser., 8 (1807): 235–37.

[Review of Byron, *A Selection of Hebrew Melodies, Ancient and Modern,* no. 2.] *Critical Review,* 5th ser., 3 (April 1816): 357–66.

[Review of Byron, *A Selection of Hebrew Melodies, Ancient and Modern.*] *Theatrical Inquisitor* 6 (May 1815): 377–78.

[Review of Moore, *Intercepted Letters; or, The Twopenny Post-Bag,* 11th ed.] *Antijacobin Review* 46 (1814): 266–68.

[Review of Moore, *Intercepted Letters; or, The Twopenny Post-Bag*, 13th ed.] *Satirist* 13 (1813): 553–57.

[Review of Moore, *Irish Melodies*, nos. 1–4.] *Monthly Review* 71 (June 1813): 113–26.

[Review of Moore, *Irish Melodies*, nos. 6 and 7.] *Monthly Review* 87 (1818): 419–33.

[Review of Moore, *Lalla Rookh, an Oriental Romance.*] *British Critic* 7 (June 1817): 604–16.

[Review of Moore, *Lalla Rookh, an Oriental Romance.*] *British Review* 10 (August 1817): 30–54.

[Review of Moore, *Lalla Rookh, an Oriental Romance.*] *Critical Review* 5 (June 1817): 560–81.

[Review of Moore, *Lalla Rookh an Oriental Romance.*] *Literary Gazette* 1, no. 19 (31 May 1817): 292–95.

[Review of Moore, *Lalla Rookh, an Oriental Romance.*] *Monthly Review* 83 (June–July 1817): 181–201; 285–99.

[Review of Moore, *Lalla Rookh, an Oriental Romance.*] *New Monthly Magazine* 8 (August 1817): 52.

[Review of Moore, *Lalla Rookh, an Oriental Romance.*] *Sale-Room* 22 (31 May 1817): 173–75.

[Review of Moore, *Letters and Journals of Lord Byron, with Notices of His Life.*] *Athenæum* (30 January 1830): 49; *Athenæum* (1 January 1831): 1–6.

[Review of Moore, *Letters and Journals of Lord Byron, with Notices of His Life.*] *Literary Gazette* 678 (16 January 1830): 33–38; (13 February 1830): 100–101.

[Review of Moore, *Letters and Journals of Lord Byron, with Notices of His Life.*] *Mirror* 15, supplementary no. 161 (1830): 49–61.

[Review of Moore, *Letters and Journals of Lord Byron, with Notices of His Life.*] *Monthly Review* 13 (1830): 217–37; n.s., 1 (1831): 217–37.

[Review of Moore, *Letters and Journals of Lord Byron, with Notices of His Life.*] *Times*, 18 January 1830, p. 2, col. e; 30 January 1830, p. 3, cols. b–d.

[Review of Moore, *The Life of the Right Hon. Richard Brinsley Sheridan.*] *United States Literary Gazette* 3 (15 February 1826): 361–67.

[Review of Moore, *The Loves of the Angels: A Poem* and *Fables for the Holy Alliance.*] *British Critic* 19 (January–June 1823): 636–46.

[Review of Moore, *The Loves of the Angels: A Poem,* and Byron, *Heaven and Earth: A Mystery.*] *Edinburgh Review* 38 (1823): 27–48.

[Review of Moore, *The Loves of the Angels: A Poem,* and Byron, *Heaven and Earth: A Mystery.*] *Gentleman's Magazine* 93 (January 1823): 41–44.

[Review of Moore, *The Loves of the Angels: A Poem.*] *Literary Chronicle* 4 (28 Dec. 1822): 817–19.

[Review of Moore, *The Loves of the Angels: A Poem,* and Byron, *Heaven and Earth: A Mystery.*] *Monthly Magazine* 55, no. 378 (1 February 1823): 35–39.

[Review of Moore, *The Loves of the Angels: A Poem.*] *Port Folio* 15 (1823): 327–36.

[Review of Moore, *The Poetical Works of the Late Thomas Little, Esq.*] *Critical Review*, 2d ser., 34 (1802): 205.

[Review of Moore, *The Poetical Works of the Late Thomas Little, Esq.*] *Poetical Register* (1801): 431.

[Review of Swifte, *Anacreon in Dublin.*] *Antijacobin Review* 46 (1814): 533–46.

Reynolds, J. [Review of Moore, *The Loves of the Angels.*] *London Magazine* 7 (Feb. 1823): 212–15.

Robinson, Charles E. *Shelley and Byron: The Snake and Eagle Wreathed in Fight.* Baltimore: Johns Hopkins UP, 1976.

Ruddick, William. "Don Juan in Search of Freedom: Byron's Emergence as a Satirist." In *Byron: A Symposium*, ed. John D. Jump. London: Macmillan, 1975.

Russell, Lord John. *Early Correspondence of Lord John Russell, 1805–1840.* Ed. Rollo Russell. 2 vols. London: Unwin, 1913.

Santucho, Oscar José. *George Gordon, Lord Byron: A Comprehensive Bibliography of Secondary Materials in English.* Metuchen: Scarecrow Press, 1977.

Sharafuddin, Mohammed. *Islam and Romantic Orientalism: Literary Encounters with the Orient.* New York: I. B. Tauris, 1994.

Shelley, Mary. *The Journals of Mary Shelley.* Ed. Paula R. Feldman and Diana Scott-Kilvert. Baltimore: Johns Hopkins UP, 1995.

———. *Selected Letters of Mary Wollstonecraft Shelley.* Ed. Betty T. Bennett. Baltimore: Johns Hopkins UP, 1995.

Slater, Joseph. "Byron's Hebrew Melodies." *Studies in Philology* 49 (1952): 75–94.

Smiles, Samuel. *A Publisher and His Friends: Memoir and Correspondence of the Late John Murray.* 2 vols. London: John Murray, 1891.

Smith, Byron Porter. *Islam in English Literature.* New York: Caravan Books, 1977.

Southey, Robert. *The Correspondence of Robert Southey with Caroline Bowles.* Ed. Edward Dowden. London: Longmans, 1881.

———. *Selections from the Letters of Robert Southey.* Ed. John Wood Warter. 4 vols. London: Longmans, 1856.

St. Clair, William. "The Impact of Byron's Writings: An Evaluative Approach." In *Byron: Augustan and Romantic*, ed. Andrew Rutherford. New York: St. Martin's, 1990.

———. "The Temptations of a Biographer: Thomas Moore and Byron." *Byron Journal* 17 (1989): 50–56.

Stuart, Lady Louisa. *Letters of Lady Louisa Stuart to Miss Louisa Clinton.* Ed. James A. Hone. 2 vols. Edinburgh: D. Douglas, 1901–3.

Stürzl, Erwin A. *A Love's Eye View: Teresa Guiccioli's "La Vie de Lord Byron en Italie."* Salzburg: Institut für Anglistik und Amerikanistik, 1988.

Sultana, Fehmida. *Romantic Orientalism and Islam.* Ph.D. diss., Tufts University, 1989.

Swifte, Edmund Lewis Lenthal. *Anacreon in Dublin.* London: J. J. Stockdale, 1814.

"Table-Talk about Thomas Moore." *Bentley's Miscellany* 33 (1853): 655–56.

Talfourd, Thomas Noon. [Review of Moore, *The Loves of the Angels* and Byron, *Heaven and Earth.*] *Lady's Magazine*, 2d ser., 4 (January 1823): 19–23.

Taylor, Henry. *The Autobiography of Henry Taylor, 1800–1875.* 2 vols. London: Longmans, 1885.

Taylor, Una. *Guests and Memories: Annals of a Seaside Villa.* London: Oxford UP, 1924.

Tessier, Thérèse. *The Bard of Erin: A Study of Thomas Moore's Irish Melodies, 1808–1834.* Salzburg: Institut für Anglistik und Amerikanistik, 1981.

———. "Byron and Thomas Moore: A Great Literary Friendship." *Byron Journal* 20 (1992): 46–57.

———. *La Poesie Lyrique de Thomas Moore, 1779–1852.* Paris: Didier, 1976.

"Thomas Moore." *Bentley's Miscellany* 31 (1852): 423–37.

Times, 15 May 1824, p. 2, cols. c-d.

Times, 10 August 1824, p. 2, col. c.

Trench, Melesina Chenevix St. George. *The Remains of the Late Mrs. Trench.* London: Parker and Bourne, 1862.

Trent, W. P. "Paradise and the Peri." *Ninth Year Book, Bibliophile Society of Boston* (1910): 109–27.

Vail, Jeffery. "Byron's 'Impromptu on a Recent Incident': A New Text of a Regency Squib." *KSJ* 47 (1998): 29–31.

Vance, Norman. *Irish Literature: A Social History.* Oxford: Basil Blackwell, 1990.

von Pückler-Muskau, Ludwig Heinrich Hermann. *Tour in England, Ireland and France* . . . Zurich: Massie, 1940.

Watkins, John. *Memoirs of the Life and Writings of the Right Honourable Lord Byron.* London: Henry Colburn, 1822.

White, Terence De Vere. "The Best of Friends." *Byron Journal* 8 (1980): 4–17.

Willis, Nathaniel Parker. *Pencillings by the Way.* 3 vols. London: John Macrone, 1835.

Wilson, John. [Review of Moore, *Lalla Rookh, an Oriental Romance.*] *Blackwood's Edinburgh Magazine* 1 (June–August 1817): 279–85; 503–10.

———. [Joint review of Moore, *The Loves of the Angels: A Poem,* and Byron, *Heaven and Earth: A Mystery.*] *Blackwood's Edinburgh Magazine* 13 (Jan. 1823): 63–77.

———. [Review of Moore, *Letters and Journals of Lord Byron, with Notices of His Life.*] *Blackwood's Edinburgh Magazine* 27 (1830): 389–420.

Woodring, Carl. *Politics in English Romantic Poetry.* Cambridge: Harvard UP, 1970.

Wordsworth, William. *The Poetical Works of Wordsworth.* London: Oxford UP, 1961.

Wright, Julia M. "Peacock's Early Parody of Thomas Moore in *Nightmare Abbey.*" *ELN* 30 (1993): 31–38.